# Language Intervention
# and Academic Success

# Language Intervention and Academic Success

**Geraldine P. Wallach, Ph.D.**

Professor
Emerson College
Boston, Massachusetts

**Lynda Miller, Ph.D.**

Director
Language and Learning Institute
Chicago, Illinois

**A College-Hill Publication**
Little, Brown and Company
Boston/Toronto/San Diego

College-Hill Press
A Division of
Little, Brown and Company (Inc.)
34 Beacon Street
Boston, Massachusetts 02108
*Third Printing*

**Library of Congress Cataloging in Publication Data**
Main entry under title:

Wallach, Geraldine P.
    Language intervention and academic success/Geraldine P. Wallach, Lynda Miller.
        p.    cm.
    "A College-Hill publication."
    Bibliography.
    Includes index.
    1. Learning disabled children — Education — Language arts.
    2. Language disorders in children.    3. Speech therapy for children.
    4. Academic achievement.    I. Miller, Lynda.    II. Title.
    LC4704.5.W35 1988
    371.91'4 — dc19                                                    88-2684
                                                                          CIP

**ISBN 0-316-92049-5**


Printed in the United States of America

# CONTENTS

# ACKNOWLEDGMENTS

We wish to acknowledge and thank those who helped us in the preparation of this book. We shared many conversations with our friend and colleague, Barbara Hoskins, only to discover that the conversation hasn't ended; it looks to last a good long time. Kay Butler has provided generous support, particularly during one concentrated week of work when we techno-peasants met the Mac Plus. We exited the week stimulated on all fronts — and the book significantly furthered. Our thanks to Kay, too, for her timely forward. We would also like to thank Dr. Charles Klim, Chair of the Division of Communication Disorders and Dr. Jacqueline Liebergott, Vice President of Academic Affairs of Emerson College in Boston for their unwavering support and encouragement. The staff of College-Hill Press provided both sufficient leeway and professional support for us to design the book according to our own specifications. Thanks, too, to Rupert Sheldrake for copies of the drawings used in Figure 2-1 and Appendix A.

We talked with many people about this book. Being language people, they talked back. For talking back, we especially wish to thank: Diane German, Cathy Pidek, Alan Kamhi, Pat Launer, Tony Bashir, Arina Isaacson, Elaine Silliman, Marion Blank, Chris Marvin, Sylvia Richardson, and Donna Lee-Schachter. And to those language students and professionals who ask and continue to ask the best question of all: "But what do I *do?*" — thank you. Because that question surfaces in almost any conversation about children and school, it motivates this book.

# FOREWORD

Children with language disorders are thought to be at a distinct disadvantage when they enter the increasingly decontextualized ambience of the typical primary school classroom. While "going to school" may be a sought-after adventure by those whose linguistic, cognitive, and social skills permit them to benefit from the complex language of teachers and texts, even the best and the brightest may find themselves occasionally at a loss. Take, for example, the case of Alice, an adventuress deep in the heart of Wonderland. She encounters a Gryphon and a Mock Turtle. The latter recalls that they had the "best of educations" and implied that it was because they went to school every day. Alice, nonplussed, objects, indicating that she, too, attended school. Communication becomes increasingly strained and an argument ensues as to the quality of Alice's education. The Mock Turtle takes it upon himself to identify the components of "regular education:"

"Reeling and Writhing, of course, to begin with, . . . and then the different branches of Arithmetic — Ambition, Distraction, Uglification, and Derision."

"I have never heard of 'Uglification,' " Alice ventured to say. "What is it?"

The Gryphon lifted up both paws in surprise. "Never heard of uglifying!" it exclaimed. "You know what to beautify is, I suppose?"

"Yes," said Alice doubtfully. "It means — to — make — anything — prettier."

"Well, then," the Gryphon went on, "if you don't know what to uglify is, you *are* a simpleton."

Alice did not feel encouraged to ask any more questions about it: so she turned to the Mock Turtle, and said, "What else had you to learn."

"Well, there was Mystery," the Mock Turtle replied, counting off the subjects on his flappers — "Mystery, ancient and modern, with Seaography; then Drawling — the Drawling-master was an old congereel, that used to come once a week: *he* taught us Drawling, Stretching and Painting in Coils."

[Alice, eager for information about their individualized educational program, queried further:]

"And how many hours a day did you do lessons?" said Alice . . .

"Ten hours the first day," said the Mock Turtle, "nine the next and so on."

"What a curious plan!" exclaimed Alice.

"That's the reason they're called lessons," the Gryphon remarked, "because they lessen from day to day."

This was quite a new idea to Alice

(Carroll, 1936, pp. 103–104)

As can be seen, Alice — whose communicative competence was excellent before she fell down the rabbit hole, swam through a pool of tears, received advice from a caterpillar, attended a mad tea party, and met the King and Queen of Hearts on the croquet-ground — has come to realize that the language of Wonderland differs significantly from the language of her home. This change in context leaves Alice unsure of her ability to comprehend the meaning of what she hears. While much sounds similar to dialogues she has previously experienced with her family, there are mysterious differences that leave her unsure.

To be unsure is also the fate of language learning disordered children who encounter classroom instruction based upon patterns of dialogue with which they are unfamiliar, or whose comprehension constraints limit their performance. It is as if they, too, were studying Mystery, as well as Distraction and Derision. While Lewis Carroll (alias Charles Lutwidge Dodgson, 1832–1898) intuitively understood this problem in the mid-1800s, researcher–clinicians in the mid-1980s have come to similar conclusions, based upon new understanding of the school discourse problems (Blank, 1988; Butler, 1986; Nelson, 1984; Ripich and Spinelli, 1985; Silliman, 1986; Simon, 1985, 1986; Wilkinson, 1982). There is also a growing body of literature that attempts to address a multiplicity of intervention issues.

The authors of this text, two well-known and highly regarded researcher–clinicians, have not only addressed a number of the major issues, such as addressing the quadrangle of teacher talk, child talk, text talk, and clinician talk and their interaction during intervention, but they have also provided a tantalizing analysis of the current research and its implications for dealing with a significant number of language problems. Wallach and Miller have made explicit the linkages between research and practice across a number of disciplines. Drawing from language acquisition, speech-language pathology, reading, and learning disabilities research, they have melded the various strands of theoretical and experimental inquiry into a series of cohesive units that permit the discussion of relevant intervention guidelines and procedures. Much of this is placed with a multi-frame model of cognition (Gardner, 1983) that has been modified to express Wallach and Miller's approach to children's language and learning needs.

Readers who have been wondering what to do about intervention in the metalinguistic realm will find substantial information on the development of metalinguistic as well as metacognitive skills in children. In terms of intervention, Wallach and Miller avoid, to a large extent, the problematic aspects of the formal (or structural) approach and the in situ approach, as discussed by Kretschmer (1984). Much as

Kretschmer suggests, Wallach and Miller provide guidelines which permit the clinician–teacher to move among approaches, as dictated by the language-disordered child's acquisition of metaprocessing skills. The "meta's" are also viewed, as they must be, within the context of emerging literacy as children continue through the elementary school years — or, as the Mock Turtle puts it, learning to "reel and writhe." Recent research has made clear that there is an underlying oral language competence, which includes adequate phonological processing skills as evidenced by such metalinguistic skills as auditory segmentation, that occurs during the early stages of reading acquisition (Blachman and James, 1985; Liberman et al., 1980). Wallach and Miller go well beyond a discussion of phonemic segmentation and provide a number of intervention suggestions related to syntax, word order, and the literate language forms needed to move beyond decoding. Following these procedures would permit clinicians to assist Alice in understanding the beautification/uglification conundrum presented by the turtle.

This text is designed for practitioners and addresses their needs whether they be yet in swaddling clothes or sophisticated service providers. While a background in language acquisition and disorders is assumed, the clarity of style provides readers with the necessary knowledge to make use of both the theoretical constructs and the intervention guidelines. By selecting such topics as inference, cohesion, vocabulary, word naming, and metacognition among others, the authors provide a rich tapestry of research data, highlighting the most significant threads, and weaving a picture of clinical activities embedded in a coherent schema. It is an ambitious undertaking by two Renaissance women. The thoughtful reader will appreciate their contribution.

Katharine G. Butler, Ph.D.
Syracuse University

# PREFACE

This text began to form as part of an ongoing conversation between the authors about language, communication, children, learning, and schools. The conversation took place over several years, and it took a variety of forms. It originated in the communications surrounding our roles in the Wallach and Butler (1984) text. The conversation continued as we listened to each other in papers and presentations and as we talked about our experiences and thoughts. We began to see the complementarity of our ideas and beliefs. We found ourselves incorporating ideas from each other. After awhile, we realized the conversation was taking on a life of its own. Finally, with no little trepidation, we decided to put the conversation into writing.

In the writing of the text, we enjoyed examining, studying, and playing with language. We count ourselves fortunate because language provides each of us an important source of pleasure, humor, and thought. For many people, however, language is *not* a source of pleasure. For them, language is a difficult process, beset with vagaries and subtleties too obscure to apprehend. Many of these people are children in schools where they are confronted on a daily, perhaps hourly, basis with activities and curricula virtually loaded with language. A good number of these children have been already, or soon will be, diagnosed and labelled language disordered, learning disabled, reading impaired, or language learning disabled.

We have written this text for those who teach children experiencing difficulty acquiring and using language. Our hope in writing this book has been to reframe how we view language learning disorders. The reframing is twofold. One aspect of the reframing is to view children as more than language learners. To that end, we have presented a framework for conceptualizing learning across a variety of domains, including linguistic. Using the broader idea of learning domains, we have provided a set of principles that guide our language intervention decision making. We have emphasized the importance of what learners bring with them to school. Throughout the text we have argued that learning is a constant process of fitting incoming information into what one already knows. We have based our intervention program designs on the idea that language intervention is an ongoing process of discovering how best to facilitate the match-up between what the student already knows and the information we are trying to teach. In corollary fashion, we have argued that language intervention is also a process of designing theory-driven intervention programs. Consequently, though the intervention plans and programs we have described in the text rely on clinical experience, we have sought to base them solidly in theory.

A second major aspect of our reframing is to view children, not as disordered, but as beginniners. As we have traveled in schools, we have seen a common problem. Teachers and clinicians, burdened with paperwork, write student educational objectives that are unrealistic and stressful for all concerned. Somehow educators have concluded that if students are language disordered, they must be hurried along to competence. The result is that students are put into situations in which they are expected to work more often and harder at what they already find difficult. The students often spend a good portion of each day engaged in trying to achieve competence in areas of processing in which they are virtual beginners. The rationale is that students must move quickly in accomplishing each goal in order to catch up and get through the set curriculum. As a result, learning conditions are created for children in which there is tremendous pressure to be proficient. Children are given little room for mistakes or for learning to learn at their own rates. They are seldom allowed to be beginners in their learning. Because we have argued in the text that language intervention programs must take developmental evidence into consideration, we are implicitly arguing for building competence in a manner and at a pace suited to the learner rather than to curricular demands.

The actual content of the text is based on the reframing efforts just described. In the first two chapters, we set the scene for the chapters to follow. Chapter 1 contains the framework out of which we develop the intervention plans described in later chapters. Chapter 1 also contains the set of principles we use to guide the language intervention decisions and programs contained in the later chapters. Chapter 2 describes the larger organizing context within which language intervention takes place and provides a description of learning across multiple domains. Chapter 2 also includes a description of the layers of language and learning in a section on the meta's.

In Chapters 3 and 4 we turn to more specific teacher and learner considerations. As part of the process of designing intervention programs, we introduce methods for describing teacher and learner characteristics across domains, including linguistic. We present a set of questions designed to guide the building of the language intervention programs described in Chapters 5 through 8.

Chapters 5, 6, 7, and 8 contain sample language intervention plans and the theoretical considerations driving them. Each chapter centers on a particular area of language. Chapter 5 addresses three primary aspects of discourse: conversational, narrational, and instructional. Chapter 6 focuses on inference and cohesion as they fit into discourse processing. Chapter 7 centers on the structural aspects of sentences: the levels of syntax, words, and sounds. Chapter 8 describes how vocabulary, word naming, and word recognition can be taught at both the literal and figurative levels.

The Epilogue is both a summation and a set of reflections. We present a list of reminders about the main points made throughout the text. We conclude with an invitation to practitioners to examine their own intentions, motivations, and practices as part of their commitment to teaching children — and an invitation to continue in the ongoing conversation begun in this text.

# PART ONE

Chapters 1 and 2 outline a conceptual framework
for the intervention suggestions that follow.
Principles of language intervention are defined.
Communicative and linguistic proficiency is
discussed as it relates to information-processing
strategies and individual learning styles and
preferences.

# CHAPTER 1

## Language Intervention: An Overview

This text is about principles and possibilities. Its goals are to provide practitioners with a conceptual framework that combines higher level language sequences with information-processing principles and to offer suggestions that integrate activities across different aspects of language performance (communicative and metalinguistic) and language mediums (spoken and written). The intervention principles, procedures, and sequences outlined in this text are based on current developmental research in later language learning and problem solving. The management sequences, check lists, and model lesson plans are an outgrowth of the authors' research and practice with non-language- and language-disabled children and adolescents. The text is organized around a model of language performance, described in detail in Chapter 2, that incorporates metalinguistic and metacognitive theory as a map of human information processing through the school years.

Language intervention is approached as a problem-solving activity in this text. The school-age period is seen as a particular challenge for practitioners, by virtue of both the linguistic demands placed on students as they move through the grades and the nature of school curricula. The basic premise that language intervention recommendations cannot be separated from family, classroom, and curricular concerns underpins discussions throughout the text. Four concepts discussed next highlight the authors' orientation to language intervention in the school years and set the tone for the principles outlined at the end of this chapter.

3

## KEY CONCEPTS IN LANGUAGE INTERVENTION
## IN THE SCHOOL-AGE PERIOD

One of the themes addressed in this text is that becoming literate in today's world requires learning how to learn. Indeed, learning how to learn may be the single most important thing children acquire in school (Naisbitt & Aburdene, 1985). Learning involves many things, including the ability to manage large amounts of information in efficient and effective ways, the ability to express what is known, and the ability to record information for future use. Clearly, both verbal and written communicative ability underpins much of what is learned and influences further learning.

Efforts to help children and adolescents with language, learning, and reading disabilities are reflected in the conceptual framework for language intervention that is developed in this chapter and Chapter 2. A strong theoretical base, coupled with a tremendous amount of experience, judgment, and knowledge about development, may provide the best foundation for designing longer lasting intervention programs. Four concepts, related to language and school learning, should be part of the working knowledge of teachers and clinicians who are making intervention and remediation decisions. The concepts include: (1) understanding the pervasive nature of language disorders; (2) recognizing school as a culture; (3) appreciating communication style differences as a bridge to literacy; and (4) incorporating metalinguistic and metacognitive strategies into language and academic programs.

### Recognizing the Pervasive Nature
### of Language Disorders

To a great extent, understanding language disorders means understanding the way in which language disorders change over time. This area of research is important for many reasons. First, language disorders persist through the school years and through adulthood (Bashir, 1986; Maxwell & Wallach, 1984; Snyder, 1982). Language-delayed preschoolers do not outgrow their early language disorders. They need long-term, varied intervention throughout their school careers. Second, early language problems become more covert as children get older. Some symptoms of language disability wash away over time, whereas others change their form (Bashir, et al., 1983; Fowler, 1986; Spreen & Haaf, 1986). Bashir (1986) reminds us that "the problems of the language disordered preschooler may go underground, even seem to disappear for awhile, only to resurface in a different form, perhaps as a reading problem, perhaps as a problem with classroom discourse." Third, language-disabled children are often relabeled *learning-disabled, reading-disabled, dyslexic,* or a variety of other terms as they move through school (*American Speech-Language and Hearing,* 1982; Wallach & Liebergott, 1984). Bashir and his colleagues (1983) question the changing-labels phenomenon in language learning reading disabilities by asking, "Are we speaking about a group of children, who, by virtue of time and learning context, are called by different names, but who in reality evidence a continuum of deficits in language learning?" (Bashir et al., 1983, p. 99).

Ongoing language problems in both learning-disabled and reading-disabled populations remain a current concern when reviewing school curricula, Individualized Education Program (IEP) goals, and pre-packaged kits and assessment batteries. We need to reevaluate IEPs written for language learning disabled (LLD) students that would be unrealistic even for non-disabled children. An IEP recently reviewed for a ten-year-old LLD student indicated that the goal for the student was to learn 15 metaphors within two and a half months. This goal would be unrealistic for a *non*language learning disabled ten-year-old, who might take four years to learn fifteen metaphors (Nippold, 1985; see Chapter 8).

Teachers make assumptions about the spoken language abilities that children bring with them to school (Nelson, 1984; Weade and Green, 1985). Many children in learning disability (LD) and reading classes have ongoing problems with language. The challenge to us in schools is to learn more about the interactions among children's learning styles, their inherent language abilities, the curricula they are exposed to, and their classroom environments.

Part of this challenge lies in examining carefully the implicit and explicit assumptions we hold for schoolchildren. For instance, a stated goal of public schools in the United States is to engender literacy, with a primary emphasis in the early grades on the so-called basics — reading, writing, and arithmetic. Implicit in the emphasis on the three Rs is an assumption that every child learns oral and printed language in the same way and at the same rate; school curricula are heavily weighted with assumptions about linguistic proficiency that severely handicap the language-disordered child. The heavy reliance on purely linguistic methods for teaching literacy is reflected in the programs frequently eliminated from school programs: art, physical education, music, dramatics. Such cuts reflect another implicit assumption, namely that linguistic proficiency is the only means by which children can achieve literacy.

## Recognizing School as a Culture

Part of recognizing school as a culture means recognizing the difference between home and school language (Ripich & Spinelli, 1985; Silliman, 1984, 1985). Home language (and that of more casual conversation) tends to be informal. That is, meaning is largely extrinsic to the language itself (Olson, 1977). Speakers and listeners use many cues (facial and physical, etc.) while giving and receiving messages. The words and specific sentence structures are frequently less important than what surrounds them. Classroom language, on the other hand, is more formal than home language. It tends to be colored with fewer contextual cues. Meaning is largely intrinsic to the language (Olson, 1977). The words and sentences, i.e., the language itself, are the major focus of attention. The need for students to master the content of the curriculum, the bulk of which is presented in printed form, is part of the decontextualized nature of school language (Wallach, 1985). Nelson (1984) describes the contextualized-decontextualized distinction in this way: "As children advance in school, more meaning is encoded linguistically and less of the meaning is available in the surrounding context" (p. 157).

Public education assumes that children come to school with intact language systems (*American Speech-Language and Hearing,* 1982). Indeed. it is generally believed that children have enough home language to begin to handle the more decontextualized language of school. Early school curricula are structured with this assumption (Bashir, 1987). Some children come from homes where the language is quite sophisticated; other children come from homes where the language is less sophisticated (see Chapter 5). Still others come from homes where the language and the culture are different from those of their school environment. These children may have a harder time than others making the transition to school because of the linguistic demands placed on them and because of the mismatch between their home experiences and the curriculum. Bloome and Theodorou (1985) remind us that "classrooms and schools have a culture and classroom reading and writing reflects that culture" (p. 29). They say that some children adapt to school more quickly than others because their home and school cultures (as well as their home and school language) are more closely matched.

We are frequently reminded to evaluate our language service delivery models in schools by considering the language and the culture of classrooms. Silliman (1985) points out that when children enter school, the rules of the game change for how social interaction takes place. She goes on to say that "disability" may reside in the interaction rather than in the child's head. Practitioners who are more comfortable with one-to-one therapy sessions are challenged to consider the dynamics of the instructional context (Weade & Green, 1985). One-to-one language exchanges are quite different from group interactions, yet teachers instruct in a group situation. "Whether students will or will not participate in a lesson is influenced by the peer group, especially after grade 4" (Weade & Green, 1985, p. 12). We might ask ourselves how individual language sessions and resource room sessions help students with classroom language problems (Wallach, 1985). We might also ask whether pullout programs can provide students with the communicative compentence needed to participate in reading and classroom activities (Bloome & Theodorou, 1985).

## Appreciating Communication Style Differences as a Bridge to Literacy

Olson (1977) says that the primary task of children entering school is making the transition from oral language ("utterance") to written language ("text"). This shift from orality to literacy marks children's introduction to the thoughts and conventions typical in a literate culture. This achievement marks the beginning of the ability to exist in a linguistically specified hypothetical world. The ablity to handle written text also enables children to extract the logical implications of what is written in text and to live in the multifaceted worlds opened up by texts.

Westby (1984) discusses oral and written communication in great detail, and her work can be consulted for more information. She says that oral styles of communication are participant and situation oriented (as per the earlier discussion of contextualized language). Literate styles of communication are somewhat removed from situations. Oral and literate styles of communication also have different structural properties. Chafe (1982), Collins and Michaels (1980), and Westby (1984) point out that oral styles (most commonly reflected in talking) are acompanied by gestures, facial expressions, etc. Although speakers can choose any number of conjunctions, *and* or *and then*, accompanied by gesture and situation, usually work well to join thoughts and describe event sequences in oral exchanges. On the other hand, overuse of *and* and *and then* in written reports and clinical summaries might be considered too informal (Chafe, 1982; Wallach, 1985).

Literate styles of communication (most commonly reflected in writing) are devoid of facial expressions and other cues that frequently accompany spoken words and sentences, and that highlight important points or transitions. The writer's meaning is made explicit by the language itself. Through careful use of conjunctions, transitional words, pronoun-noun referents, embeddedness and subordination, and other linguistic devices, writers connect their thoughts. Westby (1984, p. 108) provides examples of oral-literate variations from Collins and Michaels (1980). Some adapted examples are presented below:

*Oral style:* And then he had a wreck on his bike.

*Literate style:* The boy who was on his bike had a wreck.

*Oral style:* The man was sitting over there. And then he decided to pick some pears.

*Literate style:* There was a man who decided to pick some pears after he had been sitting down for a while.

Additional information about oral and literate language is provided in Chapters 5 through 7. For the moment, it is important to recognize that these stylistic differences exist. Choice of styles frequently depends on the situation, which is an example of operating on the level of pragmatics. For instance, a casual note written to one's best friend is closer to spoken language; it is almost speech written down. A classroom lecture, on the other hand, is closer to the written word; it is like an oral rendition of a textbook. As observers of language, we need to become more aware of the communication styles of our students, their teachers, and their textbooks. Are students capable of altering their communicative styles to match situations? For example, discussing a baseball game with one's friends over lunch requires a different communicative style than reporting a baseball game on television or for the sports page (see Chapter 5; Miller, 1978; Wallach, 1985). As researchers, we have moved far beyond viewing spoken-to-written language connections as simply auditory-to-visual transfers. As practitioners, we are just beginning to understand the implications of oral and literate style differences for assessment and intervention.

## Incorporating Metastrategies into Language and Academic Programs

It is difficult to open up a current journal or book without seeing the terms *metalinguistic* and *metacognitive*. In the early days of language research, we studied children's mastery of the implicit rules of language. By mastery of implicit language rules, we meant internal and covert knowledge of phonological, syntactic, semantic, and pragmatic systems. Today, we also focus on children's mastery of explicit language. Explicit language knowledge, sometimes defined under the general term *metalinguistics*, involves the ability to make conscious judgments about one's language. Adult language users are capable of making many metalinguistic judgments. They can decide whether sentences are grammatical, they can correct written language, and they can decide whether words have equivalent meanings. Children demonstrate metalinguistic ability when they tell us the first sound in *dog*, when they circle all the pictures that begin with the /K/ sound, and when they tell us whether a sentence looks all right (van Kleeck, 1984b; Wallach, 1985).

The three-year-old boy who says, "The zebra looks like a horse but he has funny stripes," demonstrates implicit language knowledge. He communicates an idea in a grammatical sentence that is spoken in an appropriate context. The same three-year-old would be unable to tell us how many words are in the sentence or how many sounds are in the word *zebra*, because the word and sound judgments require metalinguistic ability, which is a later acquisition. This shows how one can be quite capable of talking (as reflected in the zebra sentence) without being able to talk about talking.

There are many aspects of metalinguistic development that have their roots very early in the preschool years (Clark, 1978; Kamhi, 1987; van Kleeck, 1984a). Preschoolers possess some metalinguistic awareness, which seems to set the stage for more advanced metalinguistic judgments in the later years (Smith & Tager-Flushberg, 1982; see Chapter 2 and 7). It has even been suggested that metalinguistic awareness can facilitate overall language development. Indeed, many researchers believe that there is more interaction between primary linguistic competence and metalinguistic development than was previously thought (Smith & Tager-Flushberg, 1982). The notion that metalinguistic awareness influences linguistic competence is a fascinating topic for further research.

Olson (1977) believes that metalinguistic development is distinct from primary language acquisition. According to Olson, true metalinguistic awareness does not emerge until most children reach school age (see Chapters 2 and 7). Speech-language practitioners and others who are engaged in implementing assessment and intervention programs should not obscure the linguistic-metalinguistic distinction. Many meta-acquisitions appear quite late developmentally. School activities, as mentioned earlier, also require a great deal of metalinguistic ability. Even in the early grades, children are asked to compare sentences, to count the number of words in a sentence, to listen for the first sound in a word, to identify a rhyming word, and to decide which sentence is the "proper" way to say something. The discovery that the alphabet corresponds with particular sounds requires rudimentary metalinguistic ability. In addition, standardized tests and intervention materials have a metalinguistic focus. Van Kleeck (1984b) reminds us about the metalinguistic nature of tests. She also reiterates the differences between social and instructional language. Using examples from IQ tests, van Kleeck (1984b) writes, "It appears that verbal intelligence measures require that the child focus on and consciously manipulate language. Such tests often contain subtests in which children are asked to give definitions, rhyme, solve anagrams, check secret codes, complete verbal analogies, etc. Such an assessment tells us far more about a child's metalinguistic skill than how he or she functions using language in social interactions" (p. 187). The challenge to us is to understand that there is a distinction between a practical skill and conscious knowledge of the skill, between knowing how to do something and knowing that we know. Metalinguistic orientations also encourage us to reevaluate many practices and procedures currently in use in schools and clinics.

Metacognition, perhaps an even broader concept, refers to a collection of means by which individuals assess the successes and failures of their problem-solving strategies (Flavell, 1976, 1977). Metacognition involves knowing what one knows and — maybe even more importantly for LLD children — knowing what one needs to know in order to achieve a goal (Miller, 1986; see Chapter 2). The concept of metacognitive awareness lies at the heart of our argument about the importance of self-responsible learning and learning how to learn. To develop strategies for learning how to learn and for directing one's own learning requres a modicum of awareness of oneself as a learner. The challenge for particioners working with school-aged children is to begin developing awareness on two planes: (1) of themselves as learners as a metaphor for understanding children's cognitive and metacognitive abilities; and (2) of children's inherent cognitive and metacognitive abilities and the environments that will provide the best opportunities for new learning (see Chapter 2).

## MANAGEMENT PRINCIPLES FOR STUDENTS WITH LANGUAGE LEARNING DISABILITIES

The following principles set the big picture for this text. They describe the general concepts upon which the text's intervention suggestions are based. The principles and suggestions remain tentative. They represent a beginning and are contingent upon thorough assessments of students' language and learning abilities across a variety of contexts. Whereas the first three principles are student oriented, the fourth principle is teacher and clinician oriented.

**PRINCIPLE 1.** The first goal in providing intervention for LLD students is to assist them in becoming self-responsible, active learners. We want to help children learn how to learn. We want to help them recognize and use linguistic and non-linguistic strategies, including metalinguistic and metacognitive strategies, that may be generalizable across learning contexts.

**PRINCIPLE 2.** The second goal is to help students develop profiles of themselves across language and learning domains and to understand their own learning styles and preferences. We want to help them discover their intrapersonal strengths and weaknesses in a variety of areas including linguistic, logical-mathematical, musical, and spatial domains, to name only a few. We want to help students become aware of their own successes in non-linguistic as well as linguistic areas.

**PRINCIPLE 3.** The third goal is to help students make smoother transitions to literacy. We want to help them master aspects of decontextualized and literate communication that may facilitate classroom success. We want to help students understand the differences between the social and academic uses of language and help them understand and use various types of discourse.

**PRINCIPLE 4.** The fourth goal is to keep sight of the meaningfulness and relevance of the language and academic goals we write for students with language learning disabilities. We should frequently ask ourselves how the lessons, procedures, and materials being used relate to more effective and efficient communication and learning (see Chapter 3 and 4).

---

## CLOSING REMARKS

The past two decades of research and clinical and educational practice have provided an enormous amount of information about the role that verbal proficiency plays in academic success (Ripich & Spinelli, 1985; Wallach, 1985; Wallach & Butler, 1984; Wiig & Semel, 1980b). Proficient language users have a variety of language and problem-solving strategies available to them (Miller, 1984). They learn how to modify and change strategies when necessary. Average students deal with the changing demands of the curriculum, and they shift from learning-to-read to reading-to-learn strategies as they progress through the grades (Bashir, Kuban et al., 1983). Students with language learning disabilities frequently have difficulty making the transition from grade to grade. The intervention programs developed for them should include suggestions for classroom and curricular modifications as well as suggestions for modifications of students' language and learning styles.

In the following chapters, ideas are presented for intervention that reflect the overlap and interaction among the four principles presented in this chapter. Chapter 2 outlines some of the current views held about intelligence and provides a conceptual framework for the information-processing principles that complement our focus on language and communication. Chapters 3 and 4 provide ideas about where to begin when making decisions about language intervention. Chapters 5 through 7 present intervention sequences and lesson plans in a number of areas including narrative and instructional discourse, cohesion and inference, and sentence, word, and sound awareness. Chapter 8 integrates the intervention information presented in Chapters 5 through 7, highlighting semantic mapping, visual imagery, and other creative approaches that are available today. The Epilogue summarizes the concepts covered in the text and addresses some of the lingering dilemmas that clinicians and educators face.

# CHAPTER 2

## Strategies for Organizing Information

This chapter presents a perspective on language and learning that is broader than that customarily taken by language practitioners. Tremendous power is provided by this broader view in that it affords a context within which to view language acquisition and performance. From this context, intervention strategies can be designed that match the principles described at the end of Chapter 1 and that take into account the individual learning styles and preferences of each student.

Humans are pattern seekers. We look for relatedness, for connections. Because we are equipped with neurological systems limited in processing capacity, we search for ways to clump what we know into manageable chunks. These polymorphous chunks constitute what we know and how we know. They organize the knowledge structures that form the basis for the strategies we develop to incorporate new information. How we arrange what we know exerts a strong influence over how we learn and how we utilize language. Knowing how children arrange and systematize what they know, both linguistically and in general, provides the scaffolding upon which are based the intervention principles and strategies in this text. As outlined in the principles stated at the end of Chapter 1, three areas critical for LLD children in particular are learning to be self-responsible learners, understanding their own learning styles and preferences, and learning about themselves across information-processing domains.

## THE ORGANIZING CONTEXT

### What Does Organizing Mean?

Organizing involves arranging. It reflects a pulling together of experiences and information into an orderly, functional, structural whole (Morris, 1969). Organizing involves the search for patterns. In the broadest sense, knowledge can be described as an ongoing search for regularities or patterns. What we know is a summary or abstraction of our actual experiences. The way we organize our experiences serves as the basis of our knowledge; knowledge structures, sometimes referred to as schema, provide regularities for what we know and for what we learn (see Chapter 5 and 6). Language is one example of information that is organized in an orderly, systematic whole; however, there are many ways to organize what and how we know.

One concept that is interesting to consider is the notion of goodness-of-fit analysis. Goodness-of-fit entails finding in our existing model of experiences the best niche within which to fit incoming information. Attending to incoming information, whether feelings, pictures, sounds, tastes, or other sensory impressions, involves goodness-of-fit analysis. Auditory perceptual errors made by young children demonstrate the goodness-of-fit principle. The child who says, "Give us this day our jelly bread," for "Give us this day our daily bread," is involved in a goodness-of-fit analysis. The child who in reciting the pledge of allegiance says, "I pledge a legion to the flag," or "And to the Republic for Richard stands," does the same thing. He or she tries to fit something new into something already known. Children who interpret "The baby feeds the mother" as "Mother is feeding the baby" are involved in yet another type of goodness-of-fit, which we examine further in Chapters 4 and 7.

Our goodness-of-fit analyzer is always at work. When it finds a fast fit, we are confident and assured. When it is faced with information that is extremely dissimilar, we become frightened, frustrated, angry, or confused; we withdraw. There seems to be a comfort zone between the too familiar (boring) and the too new (frightening) within which we do our goodness-of-fit analyzing. It is precisely within this comfort zone that the best learning takes place. Learning is the discovery of a good fit between relatively new incoming information and what one already knows. As shown in Chapter 6, this notion has particular importance for how we design intervention programs for children with language learning disabilities. Practitioners need to pay attention to the nature of information, language and otherwise, that they present to LLD children in terms of a goodness-of-fit orientation.

## How Do Children Develop
## Organized Knowledge Systems?

Children's organizational systems stem from very early attending patterns. Understanding how infants attend forms the basis for understanding the development of organizational strategies and preferences. Attending in infants is how they organize, select, and clump. Obviously, infants possess some biological and individual proclivities that provide structure for their clumping of sensory experiences. However, it is in relation to surrounding humans that infants develop the attending patterns that allow them to survive and to become autonomous people able to function effectively as informed participants in their society.

Bruner (1975) has described the relational attending between an adult and infant as joint attending. He argues that the rituals and patterns that quickly develop between parent and child serve as the foundation for the infant's cognitive and communicative development. Joint or mutual attending serves to focus the infant's attention and self-energy in specific ways. Chief among these are emotional and communicative patterns, which the infant quickly discovers. The majority of infants can engage in joint attending within a communicative turn-taking frame within the early weeks of life (Snow, 1977). The turn-taking is characterized by vocalizing, gesturing, touching, and watching. As the parent-infant dyad continues its communicative relating over time, each participant gradually shifts joint attention away from the other and onto an object or event. This is called mutual attending. Both parent and infant continue taking turns vocalizing and gesturing about the object/event to each other. As adults take their turn, they segment the ongoing experience into discrete elements through the use of both gesture and language. This segmenting is what Bruner (1975) calls joint referencing. He believes it is the basis for further language development and describes early development as the beginning of the communication game.

Blank (1986) takes Bruner's idea a step further. She argues that the social and intellectual foundations of language take two different, yet related, streams of development. The social uses of language, usually described as part of pragmatics, may grow partly out of the early turn-taking games described by Bruner, but they are extremely complex acquisitions. Blank (1986) suggests that it may be quite difficult to teach the social uses of language because there are so many behaviors involved in one interaction. According to Blank, there may be a real innateness factor that also makes the social aspects of cogni-

cognition and language more difficult to teach than the intellectual aspects of cognition. The intellectual aspects of cognition, reflected in the classic Piagetian tasks and traditional language intervention tasks, are the ones we have tended to focus on in the past. We are much more sensitive to the social and interactional aspects of language today, but we must be cautious about the claims we make regarding teaching pragmatics in view of the elusive nature of social awareness and the complex interactions among people's innate abilities, their environments, and the developmental changes that occur across time and tasks (Blank, 1986).

Bates (1979) and Bruner (1975) take a somewhat different position from Blank regarding the acquisition of early organizational strategies. Bates (1979) believes that infants' organizational schemes are influenced directly by the adults with whom they relate and communicate. She states that many organizational structures emerge from infants' early communication experiences. Blank (1986) agrees with this position but adds that there may be different organizational structures for the social and the intellectual aspects of language. Both Bates and Bruner argue that children's linguistic coding emerges out of their early inter-actions with parents who structure attention and reference. These authors say that infants focus on the features of ongoing experience that are important to those around them. Spoken language, and ulti-mately written language, may develop from the organizational frames of the adult with whom the child relates regualrly. Whereas these early experiences may set some of the foundations for future learning, we now know that there are numerous spurts and plateaus throughout development that require careful scrutiny (Maxwell & Wallach, 1984). In view of Blank's notion and in view of the multifaceted nature of development, we remain cautious about connections made between early and later language learning. Adult influences on children's oral and literate language are discussed further in Chapter 3 and 5.

## Play and School Learning

By the time children enter school, they have developed a rich reper-toire of pretend and social play, replete with aspects of the literal and nonliteral, the communicative and metacommunicative. Play reper-toires represent how children organize themselves. Play also tells us what children know about their experiences and about the people around them. Children with play repertoires enter school with consider-able experience in communication in a variety of play contexts and roles. They have practiced with metacommunicative interactions by creating dialogue for play characters and by telling their peers who will say what to whom. They have made use of metacognitive strategies by planning play sequences and reflecting on what to do next in their play.

Children develop knowledge structures and self-organizing strategies through play. We are not arguing that children *must* play in order to develop organizational abilities. We are suggesting that play constitutes an important, perhaps even critical, aspect of children's development of organizational ability. Garvey (1982) reminds us of the importance of play by writing, "At the basic level of childish attempts to enact adult behavior, pretend role play may be as important to children's survival as are the physiological characteristics of immaturity that Lorenz viewed as innate releasing mechanisms of affectional and nurturant behavior by adults" (p. 81).

As children organize their own actions and immediate plans into play sequences, and as the sequences are recognized by others as intelligible and clear, they are forming the basic structure of interpersonal communication upon which they will build for the rest of their lives. At higher levels of development, role-playing can provide a basis for helping children make transitions from oral to literate and contextualized to decontextualized communication.

### Pretend Play

Infants' play consists mainly of the development of knowledge about the relationship between self and not-self during the first year of life. The complexity of their play changes dramatically toward the end of the first year. No longer infants, these children begin to represent in their play what they know and want to know. They begin to abstract the "real" world to the extent that they can use a spoon to represent a telephone receiver. A wooden block becomes a truck; a stick stands for a snake. The appearance of symbolic, representational play signals the emergence of a powerful organizational process in children. Pretend play is a nonliteral re-presenting of adult behaviors in safe (nonsurvival) contexts. Well before children began to engage in cooperative peer play (somewhere before the fourth birthday), those who have been encouraged in pretend play have acquired a significant repertoire of "conventional behavior for role enactments, as well as some of the communicative techniques by which such play can be shared with others" (Garvey, 1982, p. 81). As shown in Chapter 5, play repertoires, along with the communicative techniques that accompany those repertoires, are of primary importance in children's development of literacy. Knowing how to use one doll to represent a mommy and another to represent a doctor enables the child to begin taking another perspective. The child manipulates and transforms that perspective and uses language outside of literal contexts. Again, we see that understanding how young children develop organizational patterns affords us rich information from which to draw in our attempts to design intervention strategies for LLD children. Garvey (1982) further describes some of the important characteristics of pretend play as follows.

• *Decontextualization* is the "decreasing dependence on perceptible context of setting" (Garvey, 1982, p. 82). As children represent experience, they begin to displace actions and events from their immediate contexts. This ability to decontextualize becomes a critical factor in being successful in most academic settings, as we showed in Chapter 1 and as reflected in the language intervention lesson plans presented in Chapters 4 through 7.

• *Object substitution* is a decreasing dependence on the actual characteristics of object properties and functions so that they can be used to represent something else. Piaget called this function *symbolic representation* (Piaget, 1926). Learning that words, phrases, paragraphs, and units of discourse can be taken as symbolic re-presentations of real and imagined experience is another factor critical to academic success. Indeed, we argue that the ability to entertain not just one but a variety of re-presentational possibilities underlies the concept of literacy.

• *Sequential combination* is "increasing linkage and integration of discrete actions to reproduce the sense, if not the precise order and detail, of some procedure or event complex" (Garvey, 1982, p. 82). Thus, a child can play with a doll in a sequence reflective of, but not necessarily faithful to, a real sequence with a baby. The ability to integrate and link discrete actions is a basic feature of organization, one of the primary aspects of planful behavior, linguistic as well as nonlinguistic. (Different strategies that relate to information organizing are discussed throughout the text.)

• *Self-other relations* is the increasing ability to recognize the characteristic qualities of self and others in order to depict these characteristic relationships in play. As children develop social role-play, these self-other relationships are elaborated into role, function, relational, occupational, and fantasy themes and patterns. Out of these patterns, children develop abilities to take others' perspectives. The ability to take another perspective is one of the important aspects of pragmatics necessary for normal functioning in a social and cultural group. It is also a major factor that enables listeners and readers to interpret both narrative and expository text.

We will return to these themes in Chapters 4 and 5.

### Social Role-Play

Most children by age four have become able to participate in mature social role-play. For these children, social role-play provides a rich context in which to manipulate, test, and transform the limits of reality and fantasy, the literal and nonliteral. Social role-play is also the context in which children experience the communicative interactions necessary to guide play across the realms of pretend and reality. These communicative interactions form yet another layer of organizational strategies children take to school. This layer of communicative interaction is woven of a metacognitive and a nonliteral strand. These strands form a pragmatic, metacognitive, and metalinguistic structure on which much of children's later language and cognitive development may rely.

The nonliteral strand of social role play is what Garvey (1982) calls "communications in role" — the comments children make as they pretend to be teachers or firefighters. This in-role communication is characterized by alterations in speech style, speech register, gestures, and content appropriate to the role and context of the play. Of course, for the role and context to work, children need willing and able partners who understand these in-role communicative alterations (Garvey, 1982). Most children utilize the metacommunicative strand to communicate about the play they wish to take place in order to incorporate a partner. Children discuss the environmental alterations necessary ("Say this is a fire hydrant") and who will take which role ("I'll be over here with the truck. You be the guy shooting the water"). Children also exhibit what Garvey calls frame breaks during their play to discuss changes or transformations ("No, no! You can't shoot the water like that. Let me show you," or "I'm tired of this. Let's pretend we're in space"). The communication of frame breaks is metaplay in that it serves to regulate and inform the play, expressing how children envision the roles and how they wish the play sequences to unfold. As metaplay, these frame break conversations are metalinguistic in character. They serve to regulate what one can say in-role and how: "You don't sound like a daddy" or "A baby can't talk!" They are metacognitive in that they serve as fluidly emerging plans for the organization of the play sequences themselves; they seem to reflect relatively universal scripts (Garvey, 1982). They are pragmatic in that they regulate psychosocial communicative aspects of the roles, content, and themes of play sequences: "Let's say that you're the dad and I'm the mom This doll is our baby. You're comin' home from work and you talk real nice to me and the baby and you ask me how I am and how she is. You ask to hold her, okay?"

## GENERAL ORGANIZING STRATEGIES

As a way of introducing the topic of information-processing styles, consider Figure 2-1. In attempting to discover what the figure depicts, each of us engages in our preferred goodness-of fit analyzing. Some of us attempt to discover a general outline; we attempt to get a big picture. We search for an overall form that serves as a guide into which we put supporting detail. This processing approach is a cognitively driven, or top-down, strategy (Miller, 1984). Top-down learners prefer finding the gestalt before moving to the detail level. Top-down learners look for a relatively general pattern. They use detail only to corroborate the good fit in the larger framework. Thus, top-down learners might see a vague outline of a figure in Figure 2-1. The outline might suggest eyes, arms, legs, face, and other body parts to corroborate the larger schema. Top-down processing is analogous to deductive thinking. In deductive thinking one formulates a general hypothesis and infers specific outcomes on the basis of the general principle.

Some of us prefer starting with the details. We search for critical details in an attempt to get the big picture. This processing approach is data-driven, or bottom-up, processing (Miller, 1984). The bottom-up

**FIGURE 2-1.** *Puzzle picture.*

learner prefers the details to fall into place before committing to a good fit at the more general level. The details are more salient than the larger concept. Thus, bottom-up learners might find an animal's leg in one of the black portions in Figure 2-1. This detail may be accompanied by a hint of a foot, leading to a search on the more general level for the rest of the animal. Bottom-up processing is analogous to inductive thinking. Inductive reasoning involves gathering examples and letting them accumulate until the goodness-of-fit analyzer can draw a general conclusion based on the accumulated and individual details. (The solution to Figure 2-1 is provided on p. 235.)

Most of us have a preferred processing style. However, we are capable of using both top-down and bottom-up strategies. Maintaining a balanced checkbook is a bottom-up approach requiring ongoing processing of detail. Academic tasks reflect elements of top-down and bottom-up processing — or some blend of the two. Getting the gist of a story is a top-down process, as is asking students to tell or write a report on a particular topic. Such tasks require students to narrow the topic through a variety of stages. Students must ultimately present a set of general points accompanied by supporting details — all related to the general topic at hand. Phonics, on the other hand, is primarily a bottom-up process. Phonics requires a focus on detail. Students must synthesize phonemes into whole words. Bottom-up processing can proceed from the more concrete to the more abstract (reading a story and retelling it in summary form) or from the more abstract to the more concrete (synthesizing phonemes into words).

A useful exercise for teachers and clinicians is to begin attending to our preferred processing style. Teachers tend to present information in the style that is the more comfortable for them. Top-down learners generally teach in a top-down style. Bottom-up learners are more likely to present information in a data-driven style. Becoming aware of the interactions among our own preferences, students' apparent preferences, and the inherent task allows us to begin fashioning a better match among these variables. We hope to help students discover their own preferences, the characteristics of task demands, and the preferences of their teachers. Such a discovery provides students with another powerful tool toward becoming self-responsible learners.

## COGNITIVE ORGANIZING STRATEGIES

There are numerous conceptualizations of human organizing principles. Most are described as models of cognition, thinking, or intelligence. These models range from descriptions of relatively discrete domains (Guilford & Hoepfner, 1971) to descriptions of more general, overarching principles thought to guide thinking (Sternberg, 1985). One of them, Gardner's multiple-frame model of intelligence (1983), provides the structural framework for many of the language-learning strategies described throughout the text. Gardner's model has been modified to reflect concerns about children's language and learning.

## Gardner's Multiple Intelligences View

Gardner (1983) conceptualizes human thinking and intelligence from a broad perspective. Although he argues that there is "persuasive evidence for the existence of several *relatively* autonomous intellectual competencies" (p. 8), all classification systems include fuzzy boundaries and areas of overlap. The basic outline of Gardner's model provides a way of organizing intervention plans with some modifications. Learners organize what and how they know as part of the *self.* The self integrates and synthesizes the knowledge individuals bring with them to tasks. The self also organizes individuals' concepts of themselves as learners, forming a major part of self-esteem. The self organizes a variety of types of perceptions, including the learning domains Gardner describes as human intelligences or frames of mind.

### Linguistic Intelligence

Gardner (1983) presents linguistic intelligence in terms of the traditional categories, including semantics, syntax, and phonology. He defines each as a primary component of linguistic intelligence. Though he includes pragmatics as one of the traditional components of linguistic intelligence, this text views pragmatics as part of the core operations of any domain of knowledge. According to Flores (as reported by Hoskins, 1987b), within each culture, there are standard practices for engaging in any given activity. Each way of organizing knowledge, linguistic or nonlinguistic, reflects these standard practices. Pragmatics entails the match between the standard practices and each individual's perceptions of how to act in a particular domain. Pragmatics can be seen as a sort of balancing act between the self and the domains of experience it integrates.

Language practitioners are most familiar with pragmatics as it relates to the linguistic domain of processing. As part of linguistic processing, pragmatics can be seen as the bridge between the self and the standard language practices of one's culture, as just said. As such, pragmatics includes the psychosocial uses to which language is put.

Humans' interpretations of the standard practices of their own language culture are reflected in the ways in which they match their own unique linguistic styles with the situations in which they function. (Chapter 3 presents a more complete description of students as language users and as social participants in the culture of schools.) The pragmatic aspects, or the core operations of language, include the following.

**1.** The intentions underlying communicating, such as arguing, presenting, pleading, stating, negating, soliciting information, and so on.

**2.** The degree of directness with which intentions are communicated, ranging from most direct, as in "Shut the window!" to the less direct, as in "Would you mind awfully if I close that window?" The degree of directness with which speakers communicate intention is related to their ability to understand the various levels and layers of language structures and forms, including the nonliteral.

**3.** The assumptions speakers make about what their communicative partners already know so that they can say just the right thing in order for their intentions to be understood. Included here is the ability to make appropriate topic assumptions in order to present the best comment for a particular listener, which involves the ability to take another's perspective. Perspective taking is also required to modify one's speech-language style/register in varying contextual situations.

**4.** The metalinguistic aspect of language, or the potential of language to explain its own activities — the ability to use language to reflect on language. (We address this aspect of language in considerable detail in the final section of this chapter, and we also return to it in several of the remaining chapters.)

Gardner (1983) and West (1983) make some interesting points about the brain. Both suggest that verbal ability, particularly the more complex interactions that characterize many of our daily exchanges, depends on a seamless flow of information from one part of the brain to another. Older and more traditional views of brain-language behaviors, i.e., left-brain for "language" and right-brain for "nonlinguistic," may be too simplistic. For example, Gardner (1983) says that sensitivity to narrative structures (see Chapter 5) depends on right-hemisphere as well as left-hemisphere mechanisms; one has to have a gestalt set to be successful with narratives. West (1983) reminds us that many higher level verbal abilities, such as making inferences (see Chapter 6), understanding humor, using figurative language (see Chapter 8), and grasping the overall social sense of situations, may also have a right-brain cast to them. Other verbal abilities, such as sentence formulation and the like, may be more analytical and, therefore, more left-brain oriented (see Chapter 7).

Gardner (1983) goes on to discuss the processing of print. He reminds us that alphabetic systems like English rely heavily on readers' abilities to process linguistic sounds. This requires, as also pointed out by Liberman and her colleagues (Liberman et al., 1980), a highly analytical verbal sense on the part of readers. Readers of English and other alphabetic systems must learn how the individual parts of words can be used to get to the complete word (as mentioned in the discussion of bottom-up processing). Both Gardner (1983) and Liberman et al. (1980) point out that Japanese Kana, which is a syllabary system, and the Kanji, which is an ideographic (pictorial) system, are more direct representations of spoken language. In an ideographic system, for example, one symbol represents the whole word; in a syllabary system, one symbol represents a combination of sounds (the syllable). Syllabary systems still give readers a large chunk of the word. In alphabetic systems like English, on the other hand, each symbol represents a letter, which is only a small piece of the word. Accessing speech from print in alphabetic systems presents early readers with quite a dilemma in view of the highly abstract and indirect connection between the written and spoken symbols (Gardner, 1983; Liberman et al., 1980). As practitioners, we might remember that some children need more of a gestalt approach to reading initially (a word-syllable approach); others can handle the more analytical approaches (letter-sound approaches). In addition, children's metalinguistic development plays a role in their preferences for accessing print (see Chapters 4, 7, and 8).

### Logical-Mathematical Intelligence

The second intellectual frame in Gardner's model is the logical-mathematical frame. This form of thought at its most basic involves "confronting [the material world of] objects, ordering and reordering them, and . . . assessing their quantity" (Gardner, 1983, p. 129). In its more abstract forms, logical-mathematical thought is removed from the material world. As Gardner writes, it entails an appreciation of the actions that one can perform on objects, the relations that obtain among these actions, the statements (or propositions) that one can make about actual or potential actions, and the relationships among those statements (Gardner, 1983, p. 129).

The development of logical-mathematical thought proceeds from knowing about objects to being able to make statements about them, from knowing about actions to knowing about the relations among them, from the action-oriented to the purely abstract, "and — ultimately to the heights of logic and science" (Gardner, 1983, p. 129). Gardner's description of logical-mathematical thought follows Piaget's theory of knowledge rather closely, and he goes on to argue that Piaget's model is one of the best descriptions of the development of logical-mathematical thought. Gardner (1983, pp. 133–134) continues, "Piaget's fundamental stages of development are like giant cognitive waves, which spontaneously spread their principal ways of knowing across all important domains of cognition. For Piaget, logical-mathematical thought is the glue that holds together all cognition."

Discussions by Carlson et al. (1982) and Saxe (1981), among others, remind us further that mathematics can be regarded as a rule-governed system involving a specific lexicon conveying meanings. Meanings are represented in printed form through linguistic or mathematical symbols. For instance, story problems are embedded in language. Children with language learning disabilities may be at a specific disadvantage in the logical-mathematical domain due to its interaction with various aspects of language.

According to Gardner (1983), logical-mathematical thinking serves as the basis for acquiring the skills of the "schooled" literate individual: entertaining abstract positions and exploring the relations among them on a hypothetical basis; making sense of a set of ideas independent of their source or emotional tone; criticizing, detecting contradictions, and resolving contradictions (1983, p. 164). These abilities form the set of skills often referred to as higher order thinking. According to Gardner, people comfortable with logical-mathematical are people who are capable of understanding the idea that knowledge can be accumulated, who can test ideas in which they have no immediate interest, and who can discern patterns of similarity across seemingly disparate bodies of knowledge. Gardner's ideas can be seen as hypotheses about the connections among logical-mathematical abilities, literacy, and schooling success.

*Musical Intelligence*

The third intellectual frame in Gardner's model is musical intelligence, or the understanding of tones (1993). He suggests that there may be a hierarchy of difficulty involved in various musical roles. For instance, performing may be more demanding than listening, and composing may be more demanding than performing. The components of musical intelligence from Gardner's framework are threefold. *Pitch* and *rhythm* involve the frequency and temporal characteristics of tones. More specifically, musical processing entails an understanding of pitch relationships — in terms of keys, chords, and harmonics —

and the temporal relationships among tones. Music is partially organized by the horizontal relationship of pitches unfolding over time and by the vertical relationships among two or more sounds emitted simultaneously (harmonics or dissonance). *Timbre,* or the characteristic qualities of a tone, constitutes the third major component of musical intelligence.

These three primary components of musical intelligence exist as the auditory characteristics of tones, the rhythmic unfolding of tonal relationships, and the affective aspects touched by the tones. Thus, musical intelligence can be understood in terms of perceptions of the nature of the piece, that is, by the appreciation of a song in comparison with a sonata, of a fugue compared with a concerto, of a symphony in comparison with an opera. The appreciation of these aspects of music may be viewed as analogous to understanding and appreciating the linguistically based narrative and expository, poetica and biographical forms of discourse, among others (see Chapter 5).

Although musical intelligence seems to be related to auditory and rhythmic knowledge, it is also closely akin to mathematics. To understand the operations of rhythm in music, one must have at least basic numerical competence (Gardner, 1983, p. 126). Also, higher level mathematical ability is necessary to understand how basic musical structures can be repeated, transformed, embedded, or otherwise organized in relation to each other. Once again, there are interactions among different intelligences, despite the special nature of each of the domains.

### Visual-Spatial Intelligence

The fourth intellectual frame in Gardner's model is spatial, or visual-spatial, intelligence. The primary skill of visual-spatial intelligence is being able to perceive the visual world accurately. Spatial abilities underlie several different arenas of human functioning ranging from the relatively concrete ability to orient oneself geographically to the relatively abstract ability to hypothesize three dimensional figures in space. Spatial abilities are required to recognize objects and scenes, both in their original form and in transformed form. Spatial abilities are invoked when confronting graphic depictions such as maps, diagrams, geometric forms, models, pictures, and so on (see Chapter 8). Gardner further describes the necessary spatial abilities in discerning resemblances across what seem to be disparate forms or domains of experience, as when Thomas (1975) likens the earth to a single-celled organism.

Gardner utilizes Piaget's model once more to describe the development of spatial intelligence, focusing on Piaget's descriptions of the child's understanding of space. The sensorimotor understanding of space is shown in the child's ability to appreciate the trajectories of objects and the ability to find his or her way between various locales. The end of the sensorimotor stage is characterized by the emergence of the capacity for mental imagery, which allows the child to envision a scene or event without having physically to be there. Piaget labeled this capacity *deferred imitation* (Piaget, 1926).

As children move into the concrete operational stage, they become capable of greater manipulation of spatial images. Children begin to take others' perspectives through *mental reversibility* and *decentration*, both of which play important roles in children's acquisition of literacy (see Chapter 5). With the transition into formal operational thinking, the adolescent becomes able to deal with the idea of abstract space and with formal rules governing space.

The spatial intellectual frame is called into play in a variety of domains across the various sciences, arts, and mathematics. The physical sciences depend more heavily on spatial abilities than do the social sciences, which seem to depend more heavily on linguistic abilities. Gardner points out that topology requires considerably more spatial facility than algebra. In the visual arts, the need for spatial ability seems more obvious, especially in sculpture and painting. Both require manipulation not only of design and form but of perspective and proportion. In culturally varied settings, spatial intelligence is critical for cultural and survival reasons and has often been developed to a fine degree. Gardner cites the Gikwe bushmen of the Kalahari, "who can deduce from the spoor of an antelope its size, sex, build, and mood" (Gardner, 1983, pp. 200–201). A Tanzanian children's game involves visualizing a complicated pattern of strung beads as they are rearranged by opponents. Eskimos find their way across seemingly featureless arctic landscapes, while the Pulawat navigate by stars among the many islands in their region.

### Bodily-Kinesthetic Intelligence

The fifth learning domain is bodily-kinesthetic intelligence. This involves the differentiated and skilled use of one's body for expressive (dancing, miming) and goal-directed (heavy equipment operation, surgery) purposes. All skilled performances exhibit and require certain characteristics such as a well-honed sense of timing, calibration of movements, a sense of direction or goal, and a point of no return triggering the final sequence. Gardner points out that Bartlett (1958) sees these characteristics as principles characterizing what we ordinarily call thinking. These characteristics apply equally to gross motor actions as to the fine motor actions that allow one to carry out more delicate movements, such as when typing or playing the piano.

Gardner (1983) raises the question of whether acquiring competence in symbolizing affects development of bodily-kinesthetic information processing. He suggests that symbolizing alters one's bodily-kinesthetic abilities. He states, "It is my guess that once human symbolic functioning has become a reality, the motor system becomes forever altered; the flowering of symbolization forges a major chasm between bodily intelligence as it is practiced in humans and bodily intelligence as deployed by other animals" (Gardner, 1983, pp. 221–222). Gardner also recalls an anecdotal report from Kaplan (1975), who told of an apraxic patient who could carry out the movement associated with holding and using an imaginary saw only until Kaplan said to him that he was sawing. The spoken word, *saw*, caused the patient to revert to the earlier apraxic movement, using his hand to saw, rather than using an imaginary saw. For this man, the linguistic symbol blocked his bodily-kinesthetic processing.

### The Self: Integrating Domains

Gardner considers the last intellectual frame, personal information processing, as being roughly equivalent to the others. As mentioned earlier, Gardner's view of personal information processing has been broadened here to include the self. The self is a global, integrative process. It synthesizes and integrates information from the other learning domains. Part of the self involves knowing self *qua* self. It involves individuals knowing that they are motivated, intentional beings experiencing desires and feelings. The self can be described as the individual's pattern-seeking, goodness-of-fit analyzer in action. Our ability to make sense out of the world, along with our perceptions about how we are doing, constitutes an important aspect of our self-concept. Self-concept is often reflective of the feedback we receive regarding our functioning across learning domains. In addition, self-concept includes the ability to access the wide range of feelings and emotions we experience. This access includes being able to discriminate among feelings, to label them and incorporate them into our other symbolic codes, and to use them to understand and guide our behavior. Examples of symbolic codes capturing this type of processing are rituals, religious codes, and mythic and totemic systems (Gardner, 1983).

Our self-concept is also defined against our relationships with others. This aspect of knowledge involves our ability to notice others' motivations, intentions, and desires. It involves knowing that others are selves, separate from our own self, with their own unique perceptions, experiences, goodness-of-fit conclusions. The externally oriented portion of our self learns to read others' behavior in order to determine how best to act toward them. A large part of our ability to interpret others' behavior comes through our facility with language, particularly our knowledge of pragmatics. How well we interpret others is largely dependent on our ability to take another's perspective, to judge what others already know, to interpret direct and indirect speech acts, and to know when others are following or violating the cooperative rules of conversing of our family and culture.

The self is an amalgam emerging from our awareness of ourselves as processors across domains. The sense of self is a "balance struck by every individual — and every culture — between the prompting of 'inner feelings' and the pressures of 'other persons' " (Gardner, 1983, p. 242). Each of us functions in relationship to our cultural community. No one exists without relationships of some sort; one cannot *not* use the self in the same way one can choose not to utilize one's bodily-kinesthetic processing skills. In short, the self is always present and functioning to integrate the diverse aspects involved in being human.

The emergence of self can be seen in terms of stages of development, beginning with infancy and including ages two to five, school-age, middle-childhood, adolescence, and maturity. Gardner (1983), in describing the two to five year old, reiterates the importance of the advent of symbol use for the continued development self-knowledge. The emergence of symbolization allows children to begin incorporating their culture's symbolic and interpretive systems into their lives. One important avenue through which this symbolic incorporation takes place is through pretend play, as described earlier in this chapter.

Gardner's depiction of the school-aged and middle-childhood individual centers on the development of an ability to take another's perspective and to understand reciprocity and justice in relationships. These abilities are shown in children's striving for their places within personal relationship networks, combined with the convergence of the ability to think about the interpersonal realm. Children come to utilize their burgeoning linguistic abilities in a variety of contexts. They symbolize and order their self-knowledge within the frame of the pragmatic characteristics of their family, culture, and school (see Chapter 3). Gardner suggests that adolescence is the period during which the individual integrates a number of aspects of information processing into the larger sense of self, or self-identity. In many cultures, the development of propositional knowledge about one's self is highly valued. This seems particularly true in Western cultures such as the United States. Gardner argues that the development of a sense of self is critical for social adjustment and functioning as a mature individual. (This important aspect of information processing and learning is discussed further in Chapter 5.)

## WHAT IT MEANS TO BE "META"

The models presented in the preceding sections describe different conceptualizations of how humans organize themselves to process the information they are continously encountering. Before leaving the subject of how humans process information, we return to one of the core pragmatic operations of language: the metalinguistic.

### Metacognition

The term *metacognition* involves knowing what one knows and understanding what one needs to know in order to learn, as pointed out in Chapter 1 (Flavell, 1981). Sternberg (1987) says that metacognition involves processes for planning, monitoring, and evaluating strategies for problem-solving. Researchers and educators who discuss metacognition make a distinction between declarative and procedural knowledge. According to Silliman (1986), declarative knowledge is one's storehouse of information, which stems from prior experience. In a sense, declarative knowledge is the know-how one brings to a task (Sternberg, 1985). Procedural knowledge, on the other hand, involves strategies acquired by individuals for accomplishing goals.

Silliman (1985) further describes declarative knowledge in terms of task, intrapersonal, and strategy variables. Task variables are that information must be processed differently depending on how one is going to use it and that material must be appreciated differently depending on how it is organized. Intrapersonal variables include knowledge about one's own strengths and weaknesses (e.g., I am better at remembering faces than I am at remembering names). Strategy variables include knowing which approach to a task or situation will work best (e.g., top-down or bottom-up strategies).

Silliman (1985) describes procedural knowledge in terms of problem-solving. Procedural knowledge includes the checks one uses while working on an approach and a solution to a problem (Brown & DeLoache, 1978). The checks include (1) developing a plan of action for solving a problem and completing a task; (2) predicting consequences of an action or event; (3) monitoring one's ongoing activity; (4) checking the results of a plan; and (5) understanding the consequences of choosing a particular strategy. Some questions we might ask about a student's procedural knowledge include the following: Does the student have an awareness of what constitutes effective and efficient problem-solving? Can the student analyze alternate plans for achieving goals? Does the student have a sense of how well an activity is going? Does the student understand where to look for an error? Does the student understand what went wrong?

Sternberg (1985) reminds us that being a new learner is different from being a proficient and experienced learner. New learners, such as beginning readers, must learn how to be selective. They must understand the kinds of information they are dealing with and they must learn how to apply new information to different situations. We often have to help children, especially children with language learning disabilities, make decisions about the relevance of various pieces of information. We also need to analyze our own intervention decisions in terms of relevance (Blank & Marquis, 1987; see Chapters 4 and 8).

Sternberg (1985) points out that automatizing information entails a transition between conscious, controlled information processing and automatic processing. He adds that the less time one has to spend consciously thinking about the mechanics of what to do, the more time one can devote to the task at hand. We might think about the phonics versus reading comprehension dilemma as related to the time factor mentioned by Sternberg (1985). We can ask ourselves whether some children spend too much time in sound-it-out exercises, sacrificing comprehension as a result. (The principles of selectivity and automaticity described by Sternberg and others are incorporated into our clinician/educator checklist in Chapter 4).

## Metalinguistic Development

To be *metalinguistic* is to be able to reflect on language as an object in the same way one reflects on tables or dogs or eggs or sitting or friends. As indicated in Chapters 1 and 7, being metalinguistic allows one to discover that linguistic labels are just that: labels. As such, labels have no inherent relationship to the referents they represent. Because language and referents are related as much by accidents of war and trade routes as by individual creativity and community custom, words, sounds, and sentences stand in arbitrary, if customary, relationship to their referents. Being metalinguistic involves an appreciation for both the arbitrariness and the custom. Being metalinguistic also involves knowing that language is a code for representation. As a code, language is rule-bound and predictable.

Miller (1986) has organized a developmental frame showing the emergence of metalinguistic awareness (Table 2-1). As Table 2-1 shows, most children do not become strictly metalinguistic until somewhere around age six or seven. Olson (1977) adds that this is precisely the time when most children begin to shift from contextualized to decontextualized language (see Chapter 1). However, children begin to show awareness of acts of communicating and of language and its parts much earlier. Kamhi (1987) points out that metalinguistic development is extremely complex and its sequence involves many stages. He presents the following sequence of metalinguistic acquisition: (1) repairing communication breakdowns; (2) making listener adjustments; (3) making judgments about language content and form; (4) analyzing language into linguistic units; (5) understanding and producing rhymes, puns, and riddles; and (6) understanding and producing figurative language. Van Kleeck and Schuele (1987) provide additional information about early metalinguistic awareness, which will be presented in Chapter 7.

As noted in Table 2-1, the developmental scheme is a compilation of information from a variety of sources, including the cognitive, LD, pragmatics, speech-language, and reading literature. In forthcoming chapters in this text, many aspects of children's development of metalingistic awareness are highlighted. Some acquisitions are based on observational evidence and other acquisitions are inferred from experimental data. As research provides us with experimental data, our understanding of metalinguistic awareness will undoubtedly expand (van Kleeck & Schuele, 1987).

Miller (1986) has arranged the information on metalinguistic development to correspond in rough approximation to Piaget's stages of cognitive development. The metalinguistic skills demonstrated by children in Stage One can be thought of as characteristic of the end of the sensorimotor period when children have become symbolic and have begun using language in a symbolic fashion to represent their world. The metalinguistic abilities of Stage Two are typical of preoperational thinking in that they reflect the child's progressive classifying and labeling of the perceived world. Preoperational thinking results in children believing that words and their referents are one and the same. Thus, the young child explains that *dog* is a word by barking like a dog (see Chapter 7). Preoperational thinking precludes being metalinguistic in the mature sense. That is, children at this stage do not yet fully understand the arbitrary nature of linguistic symbols. Their metalinguistic development during this time exhibits a growing

**TABLE 2-1**
*Stages of Children's Metalinguistic Ability*

*Stage One (Ages 1½ to 2):*

- Distinguishes print from nonprint
- Knows how to interact with books: right side up, page turning from left to right
- Recognizes some printed symbols, e.g., TV character's name, brand names, signs

*Stage Two (Ages 2 to 5½ or 6):*

- Ascertains word boundaries in spoken sentences
- Ascertains word boundaries in printed sequences
- Engages in word substitution play
- Plays with the sounds of language
- Begins to talk about language parts of about talking (speech acts)
- Corrects own speech/language to help the listener understand the message (spontaneously or in response to listener request)
- Self-monitors own speech and makes changes to more closely approximate the adult model; phonological first; lexical and semantic speech style last
- Believes that a word is an integral part of the object to which it refers (word realism)
- Able to separate words into syllables
- Inability to consider that one word could have two different meanings

*Stage Three (Ages 6 to 10):*

- Begins to take listener perspective and use language form to match
- Understands verbal humor involving linguistic ambiguity, e.g., riddles
- Able to resolve ambiguity: lexical first, as in homophones; deep structures next, as in ambiguous phrases ("Will you join me in a bowl of soup?"); phonological or morphemic next (Q: "What do you have if you put three ducks in a box?" A: "A box of quackers.")
- Able to understand that words can have two meanings, one literal and the other nonconventional or idiomatic, e.g., adjectives used to describe personality characteristics such as *hard, sweet, bitter*
- Able to resequence language elements, as in pig Latin
- Able to segment syllables into phonemes
- Finds it difficult to appreciate figurative forms other than idioms

*Stage Four (Ages 10+):*

- Able to extend language meaning into hypothetical realms, e.g., to understand figurative language such as metaphors, similes, parodies, analogies, etc.
- Able to manipulate various speech styles to fit a variety of contexts and listeners

*awareness of the acts associated with communicating:* "Ain't is not a word! and "Don't talk to me like that!" Children demonstrate the ability to play spontaneously with parts of language, such as playing with rhyming words. They can also discern the syllabic nature of spoken language (see Chapter 7 for an in-depth discussion of word awareness and word segmentation).

With the advent of concrete operational thinking, more mature metalinguistic awareness emerges. Once children are able to engage in decentering and reversibility in their thinking (see Piaget, 1954), they comprehend that language consists of several segments and interconnected levels. Concrete operational thinking allows them to understand that phonemes are part of words, that words can have more than one meaning, and that words can sound different but mean the same thing. Children during this period develop considerable facility with some forms of nonliteral language. They come to appreciate idioms and certain forms of verbal humor (knock-knock jokes and riddles, among others), though these abilities do not leap suddenly into existence (see Chapter 8). Most children exhibit these awarenesses gradually. As children become more skilled with language and communication in general, they become much better at analyzing their own language. They can sequence phonemes to produce pig Latin. They can perform many of the more difficult auditory analysis tasks on standardized tests (see Chapter 1). As discussed later in the text, many children do not begin to attend to the phonemic aspects of words until later in the concrete operational period. The lateness of this development has implications for language and central auditory-processing testing and for classroom performance. Performance on many central auditory-processing tests is dependent on metalinguistic ability (e.g., Wepman Test of Auditory Discrimination and the Lindamood Auditory Conceptualization Test). Phonics instruction also relates to children's ability to understand that words are made of phonemic segments. As indicated in Chapter 1, all formal language tests and many language intervention procedures require metalinguistic ability.

Becoming formal operational thinkers allows children to entertain the abstract-hypothetical and to manipulate language in a deductive manner. It is not until children are around ten or eleven years of age that they understand the truly metaphoric, as in satire, parody, allegory, and parable. With this metalinguistic development, children can consciously manipulate their oral language styles to fit a variety of contexts even if they have never encountered the contexts before. They become much more adept at the pragmatic aspects of communicating. Formal operational thinking allows the appreciation of literary types and styles to broaden considerably as students come to understand the delightful permutations of language favored by creative writers.

# PART TWO

Chapters 3 and 4 provide information about the planning phases of language intervention. Practitioners are encouraged to consider contextual, curricular, child, and task variables. Sample lesson plans are presented that show how research can be applied to practice.

# CHAPTER 3

# Teachers, Classrooms, and Materials

$H$ow do I know where to begin? This is a question asked frequently by speech-language pathologists, special educators, regular classroom teachers, and others involved in the management of language learning disabled students. Diagnosticians and specialists in various disciplines have been taught to focus on the child and the child's problems in attempts to decide where to begin. Language intervention decisions, as indicated in Chapter 1, have been decided frequently based on the results of standardized tests or child-oriented observations. (Billy was unable to do X or Y; Sally gave incorrect responses to questions, etc.) Fortunately, we have broadened our approaches to assessment. We are still concerned with the language and learning abilities that children bring with them to the tasks at hand, and we recognize that children come to learning situations with different inherent abilities and different levels of cognitive, language, and metalinguistic competence. However, we are much more aware of how the learning environment interacts with a student's inherent abilities and unique processing systems.

## INTRODUCTORY CONCERNS

Weade and Green (1985) remind us that developing language intervention programs for school age children and adolescents requires understanding the classroom as a communicative environment.

They point out that classroom lessons are constructed by the interaction of the classroom participants controlled by the teacher (see Chapter 5 for further discussion of the discourse characteristics of the classroom environment). Weade and Green go on to say that students must "read" both verbal and nonverbal signals of teachers in order to know how and when to respond. Students must give answers that are not only correct but that are also presented in a correct form. Teachers and students continually monitor the actions and messages of each other in order to proceed with a lesson. Many subtle communication rules, both social and academic, underlie classroom communication. Weade and Green (1985) provide us with the following questions as guidelines for classroom observations.

1. What are the personal frames of reference students bring to the lesson that might influence their participation (a television show they may have seen, a book they have read that relates to the topic)?
2. What will be the social and academic expectations for participation (lesson in the form of a game or a conversation)?
3. How will the group be organized (whole group doing one lesson, one group doing math, another doing reading, different group levels)?
4. How will turn-taking procedures be organized (bid for turns by raising hands, respond in unison)?
5. What forms of response are required (name the word, say the number, complete the sentence)?
6. What frames of reference for completing the lesson will be shared by teacher and students (the same way we did the lesson last time)? Which students did not get it the last time? (Weade & Green, 1985, p. 16)

Weade and Green also say that we need to understand how a lesson evolves. How do teachers work to assist students who may not be catching on as easily as others to the classroom routines? How do students' learning and language performances interact with the expectations made by teachers during lessons?

Silliman (in press) reiterates a number of concepts discussed by Weade and Green. She reminds us that there are many sources of variation that account for an individual's success and failure in the classroom. Two primary sources of variation are teacher expectations for performance and classroom organization. Silliman says that good students frequently match teacher expectations. They manage to complete tasks on time, they will wait their turn, and they focus on the essential information during instructional activities. Good students also adapt to the dynamics of the classroom organization, picking up on both social and academic demands as structured by individual teachers. Silliman urges us to note the ways in which teachers subgroup students within the classroom. Children from high and low reading groups, for example, may get different kinds of feedback. Teachers tend to interrupt high readers less often than they interrupt low readers during oral reading practice (Eder and Felmlee, 1984, as quoted by Silliman, in press). Classroom performance, according to Silliman, is influenced by many variables, including children's prior experience and background knowledge and their inherent abilities. As indicated in the title of this chapter, teacher, classroom, and materials variables are emphasized in this chapter. Children's inherent abilities are focused on in the next chapter.

Some of the questions we will raise in this chapter are the following:

- How does the clinician's or teacher's learning style affect the child's learning environment?
- What types of teacher language facilitate learning?
- How do we know when there is a match or mismatch between teacher talk and a student's language level?
- How does the choice of materials affect language performance and learning?
- How do we analyze curricular-child matches and mismatches?

## THE CLASSROOM CONTEXT

### Teacher Characteristics

One of the most influential contexts in which school children must function is the classroom. The classroom is organized and run according to the learning preferences and processing styles of its resident teacher. Classroom teachers develop preferred ways of doing things, which reflect their likes and dislikes, interests, learning styles, and information-processing strategies.

Most classrooms are constrained to a certain extent by the dictates of predetermined curricula. However, the ways in which teachers present content and facilitate student learning are generally an amalgam of the teachers' individual preferences for particular techniques. Most teachers choose methods and techniques with which they are most comfortable, those teaching methods and techniques that generally fit best with their existing beliefs and preferences about children's learning and its enhancement. Consequently, an examination of one's preferences and beliefs yields valuable information about how and why each of us approaches teaching in the ways we do. Figure 3-1 shows a profile of one teacher's information-processing strengths and weaknesses, utilizing individual orientation. It shows one person's relative strengths and weaknesses. It is *not* a comparison of the individual with others. (In Chapter 4 we utilize a similar model to describe a student's learning profile.)

We can begin to interpret the profile in Figure 3-1 in the following way. The learner is primarily a top-down processor. She prefers finding the general picture as an orientation from which to search out the supporting details. However, whereas she is primarily top-down in the linguistic domain, she is capable of focusing on the details, e.g., at the level of phonetics. Within the linguistic domain, she finds it relatively easy to present information from either a top-down or a bottom-up framework.

By contrast, she has little knowledge of the larger patterns in the logical-mathematical domain. She experiences considerable difficulty when required to process detail by detail. Thus, her math computational ablities are not precise. She prefers not to teach math because she has difficulty with processing mathematical information from both top-down and bottom-up approaches.

In the visual-spatial realm, this teacher's processing preferences differ according to the degree of abstractness of the information to be

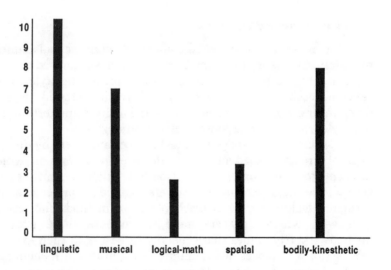

**FIGURE 3-1.** *Teacher learning profile.*

processed. In the relatively concrete realm of geography, she can utilize either top-down or bottom-up processing. In discerning patterns and relationships among seemingly disparate visual-spatial symbols, she is decidedly more top-down, preferring to focus on the overall concept rather than individual details. In the more abstract realm of geometry and topology, the teacher's visual-spatial abilities fade dramatically. She finds herself unable to teach visual-spatial abilities beyond the relatively concrete.

Musically, the teacher's processing style seems decidedly top-down. Many details of prime importance in musical processing escape her attention. For instance, she cannot discern, without great attentional effort, the chord characteristics of a musical line. She has little concept of musical keys and experiences difficulty determining the temporal measure of pieces using anything beyond the most obvious measures. On the other hand, she recognizes the general musical forms of compositions, such as songs, symphonies, and fugues. In utilizing the musical domain in her teaching, she emphasizes the similarities between musical forms and literary forms, pointing out, for instance, the relationships between songs and stories, operas and plays, symphonies and novels.

The bodily-kinesthetic frame of processing for this teacher is both top-down and bottom-up. She easily envisions the overall characteristics of bodily-kinesthetic forms but also focuses on the individual segments necessary for successful performance within any given bodily-kinesthetic domain. In learning to ski, the teacher is able to visualize herself skiing in an skilled and graceful manner. At the same time, during the learning process, she practiced individual components such as stopping, left-hand turns, right-hand turns, kick turns, and traversing. However, in bodily-kinesthetic domains requiring considerably more fine-motor differentiation, the teacher is decidedly top-down. In typing, for instance, she is much more successful (error free) when focusing attention on the overall pattern to be typed, such as a word or a sentence. Even as a beginning typist, she found a top-down approach more comfortable. Thus, this teacher's processing preference and possibly her teaching preference vary by task. When attempting to teach an eight-year-old LLD child to ride a bicycle, she experienced difficulty analyzing the necessary steps for him. Seeing the finished "product," i.e., successful riding, was quite easy for the teacher. However, the boy needed bottom-up information, and the teacher's top-down approach was not helpful to him.

The integrative self is complex, as it comprises the integration of the other processing domains. The teacher's concept of self includes knowledge of herself as an intentional, motivated, feeling person. She also has metacognitive strategies for understanding herself as a learner. As Figure 3-1 suggests, this teacher regards herself as a strong learner and linguistic processor. She feels concomitant self-esteem around these areas. Her awareness of her bodily-kinesthetic abilities includes knowing that she is relatively skilled in these areas. She feels confident using these abilities to teach. She is neither strong nor weak in the musical area. Although she listens to music frequently and regards music as an important part of her life, she does not feel she has any particular music ability. As mentioned earlier in the chapter, she uses music to teach by relating it to linguistic phenomena. Her concept of self as a logical-mathematical processor is that she is not strong in this domain. She is also not a strong processor of abstract visual-spatial information. She does not attempt to teach in mathematical and abstract visual-spatial areas because she has difficulty being creative and flexible, given her limited strength and understanding in these two domains.

The teacher's perception of her own ability to "read" others' motivations, intentions, and desires is that she is generally accurate, though not without suffering misunderstandings. She feels particularly able to understand children's portrayals of themselves, especially in learning situations. She views herself as a teacher — one who assists others in the process of discovering meaning and relevance in the world and people around them. She sees herself as perceptive of her students' puzzlements, frustrations, and joys in their learning. She believes herself to be aware of others' nonverbal feedback. However, being primarily a top-down processor, she is aware of her propensity for hurrying students by overwhelming them with information in the hope that they will extract the relevant gestalt. She finds it difficult to lay out the specific, step-by-step details for students. Thus, she must plan carefully to include bottom-up information for those who prefer it.

## Teacher Talk

There are other contextual influences particularly salient to LLD students beyond the efforts exerted on them by the learning styles of their teachers. These include the structure, content, and function of language as it is used by teachers in the classroom.

Although there are obvious exceptions, most teachers reflect middle-class values and beliefs. Whereas most teachers are aware that not every student can match their expectations, they bring into the classroom ideas about politeness, about how conversations are carried out, about atttitudes children "should" have toward teachers and education, and about what children have experienced outside of school. These expectations influence most of what transpires in the classroom. Teachers refer to things they assume their students have experienced or about which they have knowledge. They assume students can understand classroom rules, whether spoken or not, as discussed earlier. They assume students will be able to engage in conversations within the classroom, both with the teacher and with peers. They assume students will be able to follow instructions and carry out assignments arising from these instructions. They assume that students will be able to come to class prepared with the appropriate materials and information, particularly if they have been given instruction about what constitutes "appropriate."

Beyond these basic assumptions, teachers make largely unconscious presuppositions about the type and level of language to use in teaching. As discussed in Chapter 5, teachers make great use of rhetorical questioning in their teaching. Although there is evidence that teachers in the earlier grades modify their language according to the developmental level of their students, teachers after approximately fourth grade typically make frequent use of nonliteral language such as idioms, analogies, similes, sarcasm, and indirect polite forms (Nelson, 1984; Stephens & Montgomery, 1985). Many children are able to handle some aspects of nonliteral language by age eight, but many nonliteral forms are acquired as late as 13 years old (see Chapter 8). Adolescents with language learning disabilities are especially vulnerable as language becomes more abstract.

## Teacher-Child Interactions and Discourse Levels

Blank (1986) considers discourse in the following ways. First, she encourages us to assess the level of reasoning required by the discourse demands made by teachers. Second, she urges us to consider teacher-student interactions. According to Blank et al. (1978), there are four levels of discourse that can frame our interpretations of student-teacher interactions. Level 1 is matching perception, which encourages the child to focus on the immediate environment. The language is generally matched to the here and now. Demands such as, "Tell me what this is," "Point to the pencil," and "Give me the spoon," are considered Level 1 demands. Level 2 is selective analysis of perception. Level 2 demands are more refined than those of Level 1 because the child has to focus on more salient aspects of the environment. Questions such as "What color is the pencil?" "What's happening in the picture?" and "What shape is the bowl?" are at Level 2. Levels 3 and 4 require thinking beyond the immediate situation. Level 3 is reordering perception. Demands such as "Show me the ones that are not red," "Tell me what I put in the bowl before I added the eggs," and "Show me the part of the egg that we don't eat," are Level 3 demands. Level 4 is reasoning about perception. With Level 4 questions, the child must think about what could happen or what might happen. The child also has to think about cause-effect relations when asked Level 4 questions: "Why is the boy wearing a raincoat?" "Why did you pick that one?" and "What will happen to the cookies when I put them in the oven?" Discrepancies in teacher levels versus child levels might encourage us to simplify our demands so the child can complete the task; see Berlin et al. (1982) and Blank and Marquis (1987) for additional examples.

Blank (1986) recently expanded on ways to analyze the four levels of discourse. She also clarified the notion of simplifying language for children in trouble. Blank argues that we must expose children to complex language if we want to help them acquire it. Exposing children to language that is above their level is different from making unreasonable demands on them. Blank and Marquis (1987) discuss the oblige-comment distinction in relation to exposure versus demand. Obliges (such as the demands listed in the previous paragraph) require a response from the student. "Why did Christopher Columbus sail from Spain?" is a Level 4 oblige. Comments, on the other hand, are statements that accompany actions (or lessons) without requiring a response from the student. "Christopher Columbus sailed form Spain because he wanted to find a sea route from India" is a Level 4 comment that might accompany a picture of Columbus setting sail from Spain. The comment form exposes students to more sophisticated language, but they are not placed in an immediate failure situation because they do not have to respond. Obliges that might be less complex in a Christopher Columbus lesson could include, "What is Columbus doing in the picture?" (Level 2) and "What are the names of his ships?" (Level 1)

Blank (1986) suggests observing the ratio of obliges to comments that occurs in a language session or a classroom lesson. She reminds us to note whether teachers are always in an oblige mode. Do teachers continually ask students to respond to questions without giving them enough opportunities to initiate conversations at higher levels of discouse? Do teachers' lessons include a rich variety of comment levels? Is there a balance between obliges and comments with comments being given at higher levels of discourse?

Blank's system for coding discourse levels with oblige-comment components is still experimental, but we can use her formula for developing increased sensitivity to this complexity of discourse in

**TABLE 3-1**
*Discourse Oblige/Comment Analysis Outline*

|  | Obliges | Comments |
|---|---|---|
| Clinican/teacher | How many obliges occur at Levels 1 to 4 during the lesson? | How many comments occur at Levels 1 to 4 during the lesson? |
| Child/student | How many opportunities did child/student get to initiate Levels 1 to 4 obliges? | How many Level 1 to 4 comments did the child/student make? |

classrooms. The simple, yet elegant, outline in Table 3-1 represents an important dimension of discourse for analysis (see Blank and Marquis, 1987).

## Summary

It is obvious that there are many factors within the classroom that influence language intervention decisions. Our own characteristics as learners and information purveyors affect language intervention choices and outcomes. Teachers' expectations about what children know and the language they use to teach new concepts also have a tremendous effect on students' performances.

## ASKING QUESTIONS ABOUT MATERIALS

We know much more about some of the developmental milestones that occur after the age of six than we once knew. Our knowledge of information-processing and learning preferences is also more sophisticated that it was even five years ago (see Chapter 2). How might we apply this knowledge to the curriculum? To the materials we present to children in our attempts to help them learn? How do we as specialists move from the isolation of our language therapy and resource rooms into classrooms and curricula planning rooms? The following examples are suggestions for observing and modifying materials presented to students. These examples are presented as prototypes to demonstrate how theory can be applied to practice.

## Basal Readers and Narrative Structures: Decisions About "Storiness"

Brannan et al. (1986) remind us about the heavy reliance we have on commercial materials. They say that we should not assume that early readers are exposing children to the kinds of structure and content they need. Brannan et al. go on to say that publishers frequently employ readability forumulas to assess the different levels of basal readers. Readability formulas involve analyses of sentence length and vocabulary. Brannan et al. cite a study by Moskow (1980) who pointed out that of 110 first-grade reading selections, many did not meet the minimal standard for "storiness." Brannan et al. also point out that when children have difficulty recalling written passages, the problem may be arising from the texts rather than from children's cognitive abilities. Observe Passage A as provided by Brannan et al. from a typical basal reader (from Early, 1974; cited by Brannan et al., 1986).

*Passage A*

In the grass was a little hill.
On the hill was a little house.
In the house was a little witch.
On the little witch was a big hat.
It was a hat that a big witch had lost.
The big hat looked funny.
It looked funny on the little witch.
But the little witch was happy with the big hat.
The big hat had big magic.
With the hat on, the little witch jumped with grasshoppers, swam with ducks and ran fast with rabbits.
Morning after morning, the little witch went down the hill.
The little witch went to the pond to sing songs with the turtle.

Now consider Passage B, reorganized using Stein and Glenn's story grammar elements (1979; see Table 5-3, Chapter 5): setting, initiating event, internal response, attempt, consequence, and reaction (from Brannan et al., 1986, p. 103).

*Passage B*

| | |
|---|---|
| *Setting:* | The little witch lived in a house on the hills. She had a big hat. The hat was magic. |
| *Initiating Event:* | Every morning the little witch went down to the pond. When she had the hat on, she could jump with grasshoppers and run fast with the rabbits. |

| | |
|---|---|
| *Internal Response:* | One morning the witch wanted to swim with the ducks. |
| *Attempt:* | She had the big hat on when she went into the pond to swim with the ducks. |
| *Consequence:* | The big hat fell in the pond. She lost the big magic hat. The little witch was not magic without the big magic hat. |
| *Reaction:* | She looked for the magic hat, but it was lost. The little witch was not happy. |

Brannan et al. (1986) say that Passage A lacks cohesion and fails to provide the reader with any plot structure. There are no pivotal elements that cause any episodes to develop. Passage A is more like a series of individual statements, making the passage difficult to process and recall. Passage B, on the other hand, is well-formed from the point of view of "storiness." The elements described by Stein and Glenn provide a framework for analyzing the stories told by children and assessing reading materials from a broader perspective. Although one could argue that the well-formed passage might be slightly more difficult structurally than the poorly formed passage, research suggests that the well formed passage facilitates recall and comprehension (Blanchowicz, 1978; Brannan et al., 1986). In-depth information on narrative development is provided in Chapter 5, and ideas for developing cohesion across sentences are provided in Chapter 6. Suffice it to say for the moment that the Stein and Glenn (1979) story grammar format provides one way of analyzing the reading materials used with students. The basal reader example also helps us to appreciate that the problem is not always the child's (see Chapter 1).

## Reading Materials and Expository Text: Decisions About Level of Difficulty

Roller and Schreiner (1985) provide additional examples of text organization. They suggest we consider the level of difficulty of textbooks and content area materials particularly in the middle and higher elementary grades. We need to know what we are testing and teaching before we make decisions about what students can and cannot do. Roller and Schreiner provide examples of passages written in narrative and expository styles. Narrative materials are written with story formats that contain characters, events, and consequences as seen in Passage B. Expository materials involve explanation. Most textbooks are written in expository style, which tends to be more formal than narrative style. Roller and Schreiner (1985) talk about how the same content can be made more difficult by its general organization, i.e., whether it is presented in narrative or expository style. They suggest modifying classroom materials to match students' needs. They also remind diagnosticians to be well aware of the organization and style of items on standardized tests. Consider Passage C (Roller & Schreiner, 1985, p. 30–31).

### Passage C: Expository Fox

A young fox pup's life is filled with many difficulties. The pups at first live in the safety of a den with their mother and father. The babies spend most of their time eating, drinking, and tumbling and playing with one another. In the beginning they spend all of their time in the den. Within a few months they are playing in front of the den.

Even near the safety of parental care, the young fox must be wary of birds of prey. Many sets of young fox pups have hurried into the safety of the den when a gigantic hawk passed over them. When the parent foxes return from their hunting, they will know that something has happened. The scent of the hawk will be powerful near the den. The mother will find her babies huddled together for comfort. Probably one baby will be missing. (The text continued with three additional paragraphs in the Roller and Schreiner, 1985, version.)

Now consider Passage D (Roller & Schreiner, 1985, p. 30–31), which has the same content as Passage C but in narrative form.

### Passage D: Narrative Fox

Farrah was a baby fox. He had much to learn about the world he lived in. He shared a den with his mother and father and three sisters. The four babies spent most of their time either eating or sleeping or tumbling and playing with each other. As they grew older, they played in the sunlight just in front of their den.

One day as they frolicked outside, a gigantic hawk attacked the pups. The pups hurried to the safety of their den and huddled closely together for comfort. When the adult foxes returned from their hunting, they knew that something had happened. The pups were nowhere in sight, and the odor from the hawk was powerful near the den. The mother fox hurried inside and inspected her babies. One was missing. But Farrah and two of his sisters remained safe. (The narrative version is also longer in the original Roler and Schreiner, 1985, version.)

We can see by the narrative and expository examples, as we saw with Passages A and B, that the overall organization of written (and spoken) material should be considered carefully when assessing students' strengths and weaknesses. Piccolo (1987) reminds us further that school curricula are represented by many different types of expository forms. For example, there are (1) sequence paragraphs; (2) enumerative paragraphs; (3) cause-effect paragraphs; (4) descriptive paragraphs; (5) problem-solution paragraphs; and (6) comparison-contrast paragraphs. Sequence paragraphs involve a topic sentence that is supported by detail that must be conveyed in a specific order. Enumerative paragraphs have a main topic sentence followed by a list of examples that support the topic sentence. Cause-effect paragraphs include details that tell why a topic statement was made. Descriptive paragraphs present a topic and address its attributes. Problem-solving paragraphs state a problem in the topic sentence followed by descriptions of the problem, its causes, and the solutions. Comparison-contrast paragraphs address the subjects to be discussed and details that support the compare-contrast framework (Piccolo, 1987, p. 841).

Piccolo (1987) states that certain expository forms may be more difficult for some children than others. She says we should understand the type of materials we present to children, and we should find ways to heighten students' awareness of text structure. Piccolo's work (1987) is discussed in greater detail in Chapter 8, and additional examples of the different types of expository paragraphs are provided.

## The Curriculum: Decisions About Language Intervention

It is difficult to integrate speech-language resource room work and other special or remedial recommendations into students' overall educational plans without having some knowledge of what is going on in the student's classroom. We might ask ourselves: What concepts are students being asked to absorb in Grade 5? In Grade 6? What vocabulary might be required to understand the lesson? What general strategies can I work on that might generalize across content areas (Silliman, in press)? Heller (1986) points out that Grade 7 students spend a great deal of time studying the earth and learning about maps, among other topics. As specialists, might take advantage of this knowledge and combine metacognitive activities and content area work. Heller (1986) talks about using What I Know Sheets with students. Students assess their own "knows" and "don't knows" within a lesson. A brief sample is presented in Table 3-2. Each student lists the previously knowns in the "what I already knew" column. In the "what I now know" column, students list what they have gleaned from the reading itself. And in the "what I don't know" column, they

**TABLE 3-2**
*"What I Know" Sheet: Geography*

| | |
|---|---|
| **Reading topic:** | The Earth and map making |
| **Purpose for reading:** | What do we need to know in order to locate a city using a map of the earth? |

| What I already knew | What I now know | What I don't know |
|---|---|---|
| Latitude | Meridians | Grid |
| Longitude | Figuring out degrees, Kilometers, miles | Parallels of Latitude |
| Globe | | |
| | How to use the grid or system of crossing lines to locate places | Circumference |
| Map | | |

From Heller (1986), with permission.

list the concepts or words they still don't know. The "I don't know" column is the focus for each student's learning plan. In order to comprehend the content of the reading material, students build their learning plans around how to discover what they need to know. Knowing what they already know and what they have just learned narrows the task considerably and provides them with valuable feedback about themselves as capable learners who are constantly acquiring new information.

In Table 3-3, the Heller (1986) What I Know Sheet is used to guide a student's learning of specific math concepts.

We need to ask questions about what students are doing in classrooms. These questions include the following: How are students organizing or not organizing their own learning processes? What levels of organization are they using? What specific concepts are students being expected to learn? Are these concepts appropriate developmentally?

**TABLE 3-3**
*"What I Know" Sheet: Math*

| **Reading topic:** | Math story problem involving percentages |
|---|---|
| **Purpose for reading:** | What do we need to know about figure percentages of the whole? |

| What I already knew | What I now know | What I don't know |
|---|---|---|
| Whole | Whole = 100% | Smaller than 25%, 10%, 5%, 1%, 60% |
| Half | Half = 50% | |
| Quarter | Quarter = 25% | |

From Heller (1986), with permission.

Helping students discover how to organize what they know, what they are learning at present, and what they need to know in order to acquire further information provides them with tools for acquiring new information. Visual organizers such as Heller's What I Know Sheets (1986) assist students in the process of becoming responsible for their own learning. Organizers may help students' learning strategies generalize across tasks and content areas. Teachers and language practitioners can integrate more specific language plans into organizers like the ones suggested by Heller (1986). Teaching students organizational strategies may be the best approach in the long run. Intervention research will help us understand which approaches work best at which points in time. The case studies that follow provide practical examples of the concepts discussed in this chapter.

## CASE STUDIES:
## CHILD-TEACHER-MATERIAL INTERACTIONS

### Case 1: Problem Caused by Format and Structure of Items

> Students attempt to avoid using strategy (add "-ed" to words) based upon the teacher's instruction.
> Teacher's surprise at the students' incorrect responses is inappropriate.

An eighth-grade English teacher is reviewing irregular verbs with her class. The students are to give the past tense and past participle for a set of irregular verbs. The students write down their responses and then read the answers from their papers. There are 20 items in the activity. The first 18 verbs are irregular and the last 2 are regular verbs. The teacher tells the students, "Remember, we don't spell irregular verbs by adding 'ed' to the end of them." The students complete the 20 items. The teacher notices that many of the students spell the last two items incorrectly. *Drown* becomes *droun* or some other representation (instead of *drowned*) and *raise* becomes *rose* or *risen* (instead of *raised*). The teacher seems surprised that the majority of students missed the last two responses. She tells them they must have confused *raise* with *rise* for the last item (Evertson et al., 1985, pp. 143–167; quoted in Weade & Green, 1985, p. 14)

The lesson seems reasonable enough for an average classroom. What is interesting to note, as pointed out by Weade and Green (1985), is that the logic of the students' errors can be seen. They assumed that the strategy of adding "-ed" was inappropriate for the lesson. The teacher signalled to the students to do something more than just add "-ed" to the words. The teacher did not say that some words on the sheet needed "-ed" whereas others needed to be changed differently. The teacher's suggestion that the students confused *raise* with *rise* seems to indicate that the materials coupled with her specific instructions (and not a general misunderstanding of the words on the part of the students) contributed to the error.

### Case 2: Hidden Agenda

> Topic expectations are mismatched.

| Teacher: | Okay, current events. Glen? |
| Glen: | Pablo Casals, the well-known cellist, died at 96. |
| Teacher: | Okay, shush, Jim? |
| Jim: | The war in the Middle East is still going on? |
| Teacher: | Is it going on in the same way? Frank? |
| Frank: | Egypt asked Syria to intervene. They want a security meeting or a quick meeting of the U.N. Security Council. |
| Teacher: | Okay. For what reason? Do you know? Anyone know why Egypt has called a meeting of the Security Council of the U.N.? What has the Security Council just initiated? |
| Bob: | A cease fire. |

(This dialogue goes on with a discussion of the Middle East. Peshkin, 1978, p. 102, as reported by Blank, 1986).

The classroom dialogue brings to mind a number of issues raised earlier in this chapter. For one thing, students have to be sensitive to what the teacher wants. The teacher's expectations are implicit. Blank (1986) once referred to this phenomenon as the "teacher's hidden agenda." If we look at the sample, we might say that the teacher's questons are choppy, or that the vocabulary is difficult, or that he sometimes asked two questions at a time. These are valid observations, but according to Blank, they do not reflect the core of the difficulty with the dialogue. The core, in this case, is manifested in the first four exchanges. The teacher asks for contributions about current events. Glen answers with a reasonable current event. He talks about the death of a famous musician. What Glen has not "read" (and it is unclear how he could without explicit instructions) is that the teacher's desire is to talk about a specific aspect of current events. In this case, the teacher wants to talk about the war in the Middle East. Students who are prepared to talk about this specific topic are better able to participate in the classroom lesson.

## Case 3: Misunderstood Use of Materials

> Inappropriate conclusion about possible nature of child's difficulty.

A sequence of Developmental Learning Materials (DLM) cards is placed in front of a student with language learning disabilities. The clinician would like the child to "look at the pictures and tell a story about them." The child beings to tell a story but it does not "hang together." The clinician notes that the child's story is like a series of separate sentences. It seems quite fragmented and it does not seem to follow a cause-event sequence. The clinician tells the child to "tell one story for all the pictures," but this does not help. The clinician decides to work on sequence activities with the child to get her to understand how events follow from one another.

How might we reinterpret the clinician's conclusion? First, we might ask ourselves about the materials. Is the use of five separate sequence cards placed in front of the child the best way to elicit a story? Wesby (1984), Blank (1986), and others remind us about the inferring ability required by such a task. Children have to infer that the DLM pictures, though presented separately, represent one story. Children also have to infer that the pictures (depending on their content) represent one character across time, or different characters at the same time, etc. The task is not easy or as concrete as it might seem on the surface. We also need to consider whether the child would produce a better story if she were presented with one large picture with many characters. Third, we need to study narrative discourse (refer to Chapter 5 for developmental information). Fourth, we need to consider the content of the DLM pictures. Has the child had experience with the content she is being asked to discuss? Have we made too many assumptions about what is easy and what is difficult (Westby, 1984)? As in Case 1, the materials may be contributing to the child's "problem" in Case 3.

## Case 4: The Problem Is in the Text

> Text is decontextualized beyond student's ability.

Betty is asked to read this paragraph to herself:

The procedure is quite simple. First you arrange the items in two different groups. Of course, one pile may be sufficient depending on how much there is to do. If you have to go somewhere else due to lack of facilities, that is the next step; otherwise, you are pretty well set. It is important not to overdo things. That is, it is better to do a few things at once than too many. In the short run this may not seem important but complications can easily arise. A mistake can be expensive as well....(Bransford & Johnson, 1973, p. 400).

Betty understands the individual vocabulary words and the sentences are also within her syntactic repertoire. Nevertheless, she has difficulty retelling the story. She does not retain or recall very much, and her retelling is missequenced and disorganized. Her teacher

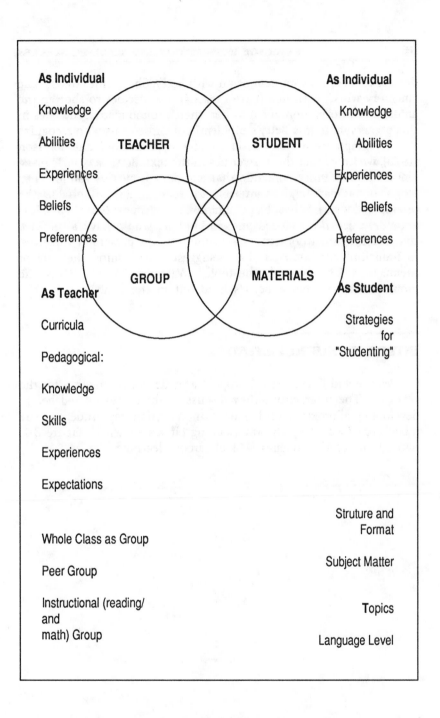

**As Individual**

Knowledge

Abilities

Experiences

Beliefs

Preferences

**As Teacher**

Curricula

Pedagogical:

Knowledge

Skills

Experiences

Expectations

Whole Class as Group

Peer Group

Instructional (reading/ and
math) Group

**As Individual**

Knowledge

Abilities

Experiences

Beliefs

Preferences

**As Student**

Strategies
for
"Studenting"

Struture and
Format

Subject Matter

Topics

Language Level

**FIGURE 3-2.** *A model of classroom interaction
(from Weade and Green, 1985, with permission).*

decides to work on comprehension with Betty. She decides to do some "memory work" with her. Betty's teacher also decides to shorten the amount of information given to her; there are too many sentences in this paragraph. Is this Betty's problem? For those of us who recognize the paragraph from the classic chapter by Bransford and Johnson (1973), we know that the answer lies in the text. Betty may have problems, but we cannot conclude that she does from *this* sample. The length of the paragraph is probably the least important variable (the original is longer). What the paragraph lacks is an explicit theme. It is extremely decontextualized and most of us would have a difficult time recalling the information. We should try the paragraph ourselves, as Bransford and Johnson (1973) suggest, after adding the title or theme to it. They provide the topic, "Washing Clothes." Thus, the problem may not be in Betty's head but in the text.

## INTERACTIONS REVISITED

Weade and Green (1975) propose a model for interaction for the classrom. The interactions they discuss might be considered before developing a program of language intervention for students. The model, represented by the interlocking circles shown in Figure 3-2, reminds us of the dynamics of classroom learning.

# C H A P T E R 4

## Child, Sequence, and Task Variables

$D$eveloping meaningful language intervention programs includes learning how to ask the right questions. These so-called right questions are formulated from research in language and information processing, while keeping sight of the larger picture described in Chapters 2 and 3. From our perspective, questions are formulated by continuous evaluation of how our language intervention goals fit in with the student's real world. In many cases, the real world is the world of the classroom, as we said in Chapter 3. We often ask our undergraduate and graduate traniees, "How does this syntax lesson, metaphor unit, or word-naming activity relate to Monday morning in the classroom?"

This chapter continues to explore ideas relating to the where-to-begin phase of language intervention, moving from the context and materials described in Chapter 3 to child-student behaviors.

### THE QUESTION PHASE

Wallach and Liebergott (1984) proposed a clinician/teacher checklist with three major sections, reminding practitioners to question themselves about (1) the information-processing demands required by the tasks and procedures being used; (2) the strategies required to complete the tasks successfully; and (3) why they have chosen to work on a particular aspect of language. As adapted from Wallach and Liebergott, practitioners might consider the following questions.

**QUESTIONS ABOUT INFORMATION-PROCESSING DEMANDS.** What are the verbal and nonverbal demands of the lesson? Have I given the student enough information? Are my instructions making the demands explicit for the student? Are the materials making the task easier or more difficult for the student to perform well? How much inferencing does the task/lesson require? Am I presenting information in the manner best suited to this student's preferred style? Am I matching the student's top-down or bottom-up preferences? Am I utilizing the student's strongest intellectual frames rather than inadvertently focusing on the least developed domains? Am I balancing the linguistic and the nonlinguistic demands of the task so that the student's learning strengths are utilized most efficiently?

**QUESTIONS ABOUT LANGUAGE AND LEARNING STRATEGIES.** How is the student organizing? Is the student an active or passive participant? How is language helping the student to organize information, script, schemas? How is language helping, or not helping, the student to re-present information and experience? Is the student focusing on the significant features of a story, word, etc., when involved in spoken and written language tasks? Does the student seem able to alter strategies, or approaches to tasks, to match the situation? How does the student process in nonlinguistic domains? How does the student re-present information nonlinguistically? Does the student utilize strategies appropriate for different types of spoken and written text? Does the student have the metacognitive know-how to complete the task (see Chapter 2)?

**QUESTIONS ABOUT THE LANGUAGE BEING TAUGHT.** Why have I chosen to work on a particular aspect of language? How does my choice relate to classroom discourse? To academic performance? Which sequence will I follow? How will I combine oral and written aspects of language? Am I trying to develop abilities for conversation or am I trying to help the student with the metalinguistic aspects of language?

There are many questions we could ask under each of the headings outlined. Blank (1986) reminds us that the creation of checklists with countless behaviors listed for observation may cause us to lose focus of the child on the other side of the desk. It helps to keep the categories and questions raised relatively brief. Clearly, a question as broad as, "How is language helping the child to re-present experience?" has many facets. Likewise, analysis of a student's metacognitive ability would go beyond the list presented here (see Chapter 2). The bottom line is to continue questioning our assumptions about what children can and cannot do. We should analyze language intervention and educational choices carefully.

Children bring abilities with them to school (see Chapter 7). Inherent abilities include children's levels of linguistic competence, their current organizational abilities (or, their declarative knowledge; see Chapter 2) and other cognitive, metacognitive, and metalinguistic abilities. Children sometimes have strategies for performing tasks, but they may not be able to articulate or demonstrate those strategies. As practitioners involved in the business of teaching children, our task is to understand the numerous possibilities that influence both language and learning success. Table 4-1 summarizes some of the critical variables influencing language intervention decisions.

## CHOOSING AN INTERVENTION SEQUENCE

After we have clarified our purposes through the questoning process described in the previous section, the next task facing us is the decision to teach a particular aspect of language. Decisions about what to teach may vary from clinician to clinician and from teacher to teacher. For example, the speech-language clinician might decide that because Billy has a word-naming and -retrieval problem, she will focus on that aspect of language for a while. Billy's teacher might decide that his bigger problem is poor word recognition for reading. It is hoped that Billy's clinician and teacher question themselves about the relevance of their teaching choices, and it is hoped that they will question each other about the possible connection between Billy's "two" problems (see Chapter 8). Billy's clinician and his teacher should evaluate the relevance of teaching word naming and word recognition at this time, in light of Billy's learning strengths and weaknesses profile. They should also think about the connection between word-naming activities and Billy's curriculum, as well as the metacognitive strategies that will facilitate the learning process. Billy's clinician might decide to combine word-naming and -retrieval activities with pragmatic activities related to conversation. She might then move on to story writing in an attempt to combine spoken and written language activities (see Chapters 5 and 8). There are numerous combinations that could lead to an integrated program for Billy.

**TABLE 4-1**
*Selected Variables Influencing Language Intervention Decisions**

| Contextual | Child Abilities | Task Strategies and Difficulty |
|---|---|---|
| Teacher/clinician | Cognitive, linguistic, and metalinguistic abilities | Linguistic and metalinguistic demands |
| *Teacher as learner*: teacher brings knowledge and beliefs to the learning; teacher has a learning style and tends to teach in that style (see Chapter 3); teacher organizes classroom material in a particular way and encourages learning in a particular way; teacher has expectations about social and academic behaviors within the classroom (see Chapters 2 and 3) | *Cognitive characteristics*: child has general learning preferences (top-down or bottom-up); child has comprehension and information-processing strategies that interact with language development (see Chapters 4, 6, and 7); child comes with strengths in particular learning domains | *Task requires*: a certain level of extralinguistic ability (context and stimuli); carried out in context with many extralinguistic cues or done without the benefit of extra cues; content and form of stimuli are at a particular level; child comes with inherent abilities in many areas that affect the structure of language intervention and classroom tasks |
| *Teacher talk*: tends to be decontextualized; is monologue-oriented and dominating, encouraging verbal participation in different ways; may involve subtle and implicit demands; varies in complexity (discourse Levels 1 through 4, Blank et al., 1978) and across teachers; may use comments and obliges at various levels (Blank, 1986; see Chapter 5) | *Communicative, linguistic, and metalinguistic competence*: child brings level of pragmatic competence to classroom; child has semantic-syntactic-phonological abilities at primary language levels (see Chapter 1); child demonstrates levels of metalinguistic awareness in pragmatic-semantic-syntactic phonological areas (see Chapter 7) | *Metalinguistic requirements*: van Kleeck hierarchy provides one example; language is matched or distanced from stimuli presented (see Chapters 3 and 4; Berlin et al., 1982); task requires appreciation for the decontextualized; task requires inference on part of student; task requires appreciation for paraphrase, double meanings, language flexibility (see Chapter 8) |

| Materials | Problem-solving (metacognitive) | Problem-solving required |
| --- | --- | --- |
| *Reading curricula:* may lack story organization in early basals (Stein and Glen) and is often fragmented and segmented; can be especially complex in expository form (consider different expository text); may encourage gestalt or analytical strategies, some of which are highly segmental (phonics); may be literal or figurative; are highly metalinguistic and inferential | *Knowledge from prior experience:* child knows how to process information based on purpose of task; child has understanding about poorly organized versus well-organized material; child recognizes own strengths and weaknesses; child can figure out which strategy works best | *Purpose of task:* Why do it? What is talker's or writer's purpose? What is teacher's purpose? |
| *Supplementary materials:* visual aids such as pictures, blocks, and diagrams should be evaluated carefully (see Chapter 8); sequence cards, picture books, and individual pictures may encourage different levels of inferential ability (see Chapter 6); aids may be concrete or abstract | *Specific strategies to complete tasks successfully (child has knowledge of these):* has a plan of action; thinks ahead regarding alternate choices and predicts consequences; monitors own activities and has a how-am-I-doing attitude; checks results of own plan and knows if consequences and solutions to problems make sense (Silliman, in press; see Chapter 2) | *Specific strategies needed to complete tasks successfully:* task requires a number of problem-solving abilities and strategies for successful completion |

*Contextual, child, and task variables overlap; the areas outlined here are samples.

*(continued)*

61

**TABLE 4-1** *(continued)*
*Selected Variables Influencing Language Intervention Decisions*[*]

| Contextual | Child Abilities | Task Strategies and Difficulty |
|---|---|---|
| *Content or curricular areas:* consider vocabulary and familiarity with content (see Chapter 8); consider metacognitive strategies needed (apply to content areas); consider language required in supposedly nonlinguistic areas such as math | | |
| Teacher/student interactions, revisited | Children have inherent cognitive and language abilities that interact with their abilities to perform successfully in the classroom | |
| *Teacher-student matches and mismatches:* student brings knowledge and beliefs to the learning situation; student brings learning style to classroom; student has to understand and adapt to teacher expectations; student brings personal frame of reference to tasks | | |

*Group dynamics:* students are involved in whole-group, small-group (math-group, work-group), and high-group or low-group activities; students have to know how to be group participants, including turn-taking and response behaviors, and bringing knowledge from previous lessons and outside experiences (see Chapter 5); students use language to participate in lessons, to add to what others have said, to compare readings, to use data and research, and to evaluate own decisions (see Chapter 5)

Group learning is different from one-to-one learning

---

*Contextual, child, and task variables overlap; the areas outlined here are samples.

Decisions about how many and which aspects of language to teach are never easy. As mentioned in Chapter 1, just because a problem, or an area of weakness, exists does not mean we automatically teach it to a child. One of our greatest challenges is to figure out which of the what-to-teach decisions will have the greatest impact on children's communication and academic progress (Blank, 1987). What-to-teach decisions might include working on one aspect of language for a time, following a particular sequence. This is sometimes referred to as vertical language intervention. On the other hand, what-to-teach might include working on a number of aspects of language at the same time. This is sometimes referred to as horizontal language intervention (Schwartz et al., 1980). Both vertical and horizontal language intervention approaches involve teaming with the classroom teacher (and other professionals) as well as working in depth on more specific concepts and content that might be relevant to communicative competence and classroom learning. Both approaches, by no means mutually exclusive, involve decisions about the sequence of teaching.

There are many sources of information that provide guidelines about the order of teaching. Developmental research, from cognitive and language camps, can provide information about where to start. Metalinguistic sequences, some of which were presented in Chapter 2, provide yet another way to decide where to begin. Finally, information about task complexity provides another source of information for developing teaching sequences. As practitioners we must use each of these pieces of information with caution. We must remember that with each decade we accumulate an enormous amount of research and clinical data. We cannot teach children everything they need to know, and so we must think about making intelligent trade-offs (Blank, 1987). We must also remember to keep in mind the heterogeneity that exists within both nondisabled and language learning disabled populations, the very long and gradual nature of language acquisition, and the relatively small amount of knowledge we have about language-learning spurts and plateaus (Maxwell & Wallach, 1984).

## Cognitive Characteristics Can Provide Guidelines

It is important to discover two things about the students we teach: (1) how they best process information and (2) which domains of information they learn most easily. To gather this information, we can draw upon the information-processing and learning models presented in Chapter 2. First, we wish to find out whether the student prefers top-down or bottom-up processing or some combination of the two. We wish to find out which types of intellectual frames, using Gardner's term, constitute strengths for the student. We wish to find out the interactions between processing style (top-down, bottom-up) and learning domain (intellectual frame). Of course, there are other important variables to consider in choosing a sequence, which are discussed in the remainder of this chapter. Focusing on the cognitive aspects affords a starting point from which to make our first teaching and intervention decisions. As stressed throughout the text, we must engage in evaluation of all aspects of children's programs in order to fine tune our teaching to match our students' learning needs more closely.

Figures 4-1 and 4-2 illustrates how learning about a child's cognitive characteristics can serve as an effective guide for teaching. Hunter, an eight-year, 11-month-old boy, currently attends a third-grade classroom after having attended a self-contained LD class during the preceding school year. Hunter's general learning profile (Figure 4-1) shows definite strengths in bodily-kinesthetic processing at the large muscle level. He also demonstrates a strength in musical processing. His weakest areas are logical-mathematical and spatial processing. Although Hunter's linguistic processing abilities are adequate when viewed as a totality, a microprofile of his linguistic processing is necessary to illustrate the strengths and weaknesses he shows within

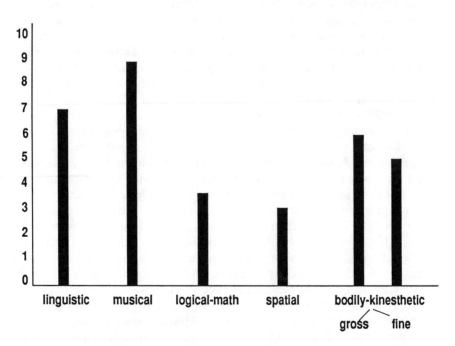

**FIGURE 4-1.** *Hunter's general learning profile.*

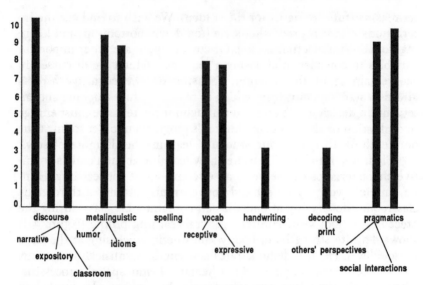

**FIGURE 4-2.** Hunter's linguistic microprofile.

the linguistic domain (Figure 4-2). The microprofile shows definite strengths in his language, particularly in receptive and expressive vocabulary, pragmatics, story constructing and storytelling, listening and reading comprehension for narrative text, and story listening. His language weaknesses are in spelling, reading decoding, handwriting, understanding classroom management language (see Chapter 5), and comprehension of expository text (see Chapter 5).

   After seeing the profiles, Hunter's teachers and clinician were able to construct an intervention program for him based on his love for hearing, reading, and writing narratives. To circumvent his poor spelling and handwriting, he was introduced to a word processor, and he was given a speller's dictonary, which he already knew how to use. In addition, his teacher capitalized on Hunter's love of music by having him listen to and transcribe lyrics from songs that were to be used for the class play. He then taught the lyrics to the students who were to perform the songs. Another aspect of the program involved having Hunter translate expository text into narrative forms, following Brannan et al. (1986; see Chapter 3). Hunter developed a series of short narrative stories from the science text his class was using. To improve Hunter's ability to follow classroom instructions, his teachers began writing all instructions on the board. Hunter tape-recorded lengthy instructions and listened to them as needed through earphones. He made the decisions about when and when not to tape.

## Language Development Can Provide Guidelines

Information from the language-acquisition literature also provides guidelines for both the focus of language intervention and the sequence of a lesson. An example from the comprehension literature shows how developmental information can be applied to practice. The example presented reveals how knowledge of specific sequences provides a way to evaluate our intervention choices. The choices are always subject to change based on feedback from the child, new information, and modifications of stimuli and lesson formats, as reflected in the cognitive guidelines presented in the previous section.

Much information is available about the comprehension strategies children use when learning language (Olson, 1982; Wallach, 1984, 1985). In the preschool period, children are quite dependent on extralinguistic cues such as facial gestures and context to understand what they hear. They are more comfortable with contextualized language (see Chapter 1). Younger children are also oriented toward "probable events." That is, they use their knowledge of the world and logic to figure out what things mean. Some people say that young children are semantically oriented (see Chapter 7). They listen to key words, piece the words together, and make some accurate guesses about connections. Young children pay little attention to the actual word order or structure of sentences unless there is a specific reason to do so (e.g., there is a communication breakdown). As children approach school age and move into the early elementary grades, they develop a more sophisticated awareness of word order and sentence structure. Older children, not as dependent on semantically oriented strategies, pay attention to word order, sentence structures, and smaller linguistic units (including conjunctions, prepositions, etc.). In a sense, school-aged children are more structurally oriented than preschool children, and they can handle language that is decontextualized (see Chapters 1 and 2).

Consider the passive sentence, "The flowers are being watered by the pretty girl." We could say that the passive sentence is more difficult structurally than an active sentence such as, "The baby is feeding the mother." However, the active sentence is somewhat improbable because mothers usually feed babies. It is difficult to say which sentence would be more difficult to comprehend. If both sentences are closely matched to the context in which they are spoken, they might be processed equally well. For example, suppose the passive sentence was used by a mother while walking in a garden with her child, as child and mother look at a girl watering flowers. The spoken sentence is matched to the situation. The sentence's word order (flowers-watered-by-girl) is less important than the context and the extralinguistic cues that accompany it (such as gesture). Likewise, the active sentence, "The baby is feeding the mother," is easier to comprehend when it is spoken in the context of a game involving a mother and baby taking turns feeding one another. Without the surrounding context, a structurally simple sentence such as, "The baby is feeding the mother," is usually misinterpreted by very young children who assume that it is the mother who must be doing the feeding (Wallach, 1984).

As context effects diminish, interpretation accuracy for sentences such as, "The flowers are watered by the girl," and "The baby feeds the mother," may change. For example, asking children to manipulate objects or point to pictures to demonstrate comprehension is a more decontextualized task. Children must use word order as well as logical guessing strategies to interpret sentences. "The flowers are watered by the girl," might be interpreted correctly by three year olds if they used their knowledge of the world to second-guess the word order. Thus, a three-year-old child might process the sentence as "flowers," "water," "girl," and then make the correct interpretation (it is the *girl* doing the watering) even though the word order suggests otherwise (see Chapter 7).

Word order strategies are more segmental and analytical than semantically oriented strategies (Bever, 1970; Wallach, 1984). Thus, the sentence, "The dog is being chased by the cat," could be interpreted as "The dog chases the cat," if a word order strategy were employed. A word order strategy involves interpreting the Noun-Verb-Noun as if it were the Actor-Action-Recipient of the sentence. Unlike the sentence, "The flowers are watered by the girl," which has a semantic constraint (girls can water flowers but flowers cannot water girls), the dog and cat sentence cannot be figured out on a semantic basis alone. Dogs and cats can both be the doers of the chase action in the sentence. Research tells us that in the earlier phases of development, children are more comfortable with both second-guessing and semantically oriented strategies; however, as they move through the early school years, children's analytical and syntactic strategies are refined (see Chapter 7). They begin to recognize that word order can make a difference and they become increasingly metalinguistic.

Metalinguistic awareness, along with refined comprehension strategies, helps children understand that word order and meaning are not always identical. Two-clause sentences provide examples. Sentences like "Brush your teeth before you go to bed" and "Pick up the plane before you pick up the block" represent word order and meaning matches. The order in which one says the sentences follows the order of events. An order-of-mention strategy means the order one hears in the clauses is the order one follows in interpreting the sentence. Sentences like, "Before you go to bed, brush your teeth," and "Before you pick up the block, pick up the plane," represent word order and meaning mismatches. The order in which one says the sentence violates the order of events. Reversing the word order in the brush and teeth sentence, e.g., "Before you go to bed brush your teeth," should not make the sentence tremendously difficult because of its real world sequence. The block and plane sentence becomes quite difficult when clause order is reversed because there is no real-world relevance to fall back on, and the spoken or written word order is the opposite of the order of events. The listener has to be aware of subordinate and main clause constructions and smaller linguistic units such as before and after to comprehend the sentence correctly (see Chapter 7).

Two principles generated from the comprehension literature provide us with useful information. One principle informs us that children use semantically oriented strategies when they are younger. They are also more dependent on context to understand messages. The second principle informs us that children progress from almost exclusive use of semantically oriented strategies to use of more structurally and syntactically oriented strategies. The strategy shifts children make in their elementary school years are excellent illustrations of a much more general process, referred to earlier as an increasing understanding of decontextualization. As pointed out in Chapter 2, children become better able to engage in decontextualized play during their preschool years, setting the stage for later acquisitions. As children advance linguistically, they learn to speak to their teachers differently from the way they speak to peers. They learn to take others' perspectives, and they learn how to handle language away from context. The concept of decontextualization and its impact on children's academic success is further discussed in Chapters 5, 6, and 7.

How can we begin to translate the information from the comprehension literature into a language-intervention plan? The example provided in this section represents what could become a cover sheet for a more detailed lesson plan. The cover sheet (which might ultimately be in the clinician's head) represents an understanding of what we are doing and why we are doing it. In other words, each clinician might ask the following questions: Is there a theoretical base for my decision to teach something and to teach it in a particular sequence? What type of language or cognitive strategy is involved in the choice? What am I trying to help the child accomplish? Am I working on contextualized or decontextualized language?

---

## COVER SHEET FOR A SEMANTIC-SYNTACTIC COMPREHENSION LESSON

*Theoretical Principle*
Children move from semantically oriented strategies to more syntactically oriented strategies. Children move from word-order and order-of-mention to an understanding that word order does not always lead directly to meaning.

*Type of Strategy*
Analytical (figuring out words and order).

*Type of Language*
Decontextualized (the language is not embedded in a natural context)

*Clinician/Educator Questions*
1. Why has this aspect of language been chosen?
2. Is it appropriate for student's language and metacognitive/metalinguistic level?
3. How do I modify or change the plan if the student is having difficulty with the sequence I have chosen?
4. How is the language lesson related to (and integrated with) classroom activities and the curriculum?

---

Modifying the concept even further, one could translate the comprehension and strategy information into a lesson plan as shown on page 71. The lesson plan reflects a decision made by a clinician or teacher to help the student with two-clause sentences (like the *before-after* sentences discussed earlier). The clinician and teacher have also thought about why teaching two-clause sentences is relevant. Perhaps the lesson is being done to introduce the student to more literate forms of language. Perhaps the purpose of the lesson is to help the student with written language. It is always important to recognize that this kind of activity may be completely irrelevant and inappropriate for some students. The cover sheet for the lesson helps the clinician to begin to specify more precisely the goals for each student. The cover sheet also helps us to evaluate our intervention decisions.

## Metalinguistic Development Can Provide Guidelines

Metalinguistic development is an important focus of this text. A specific example of metalinguistic awareness, namely phonetic seg-

# SAMPLE LESSON PLAN WITH SYNTACTIC-STRATEGY SEQUENCE

**Target on Syntactic-Semantic Combinations**
Helps student learn to manipulate complex syntax with a particular focus on sentences where the word order is the reverse of the meaning. This activity is being done to help the student master syntactically oriented strategies and language forms.

*Syntactic Forms Targeted*
1. Main then subordinate clauses
2. Subordinate then main clauses

*Specific Sequence*
1. Begin with *and* and *and then.*
2. Move to *before* and *after* (with careful attention to word order strategies first).

*Strategies Targeted*
*First level:* order of words matches the order of events and matches the meaning.
*Second level:* order of words does not match the order of events or the meaning.

*Special Instructions*
Begin with sentences with semantic constraints and real-world logic (like "brush and teeth" sentence). Proceed to more difficult sentences that cannot be second-guessed with logic (like "plane and block" sentence).

*Task and Stimuli*
Clinican/teacher needs to decide the kinds of tasks that will be used to help the student through the syntactic/strategy sequences. The clinician/teacher will also need to decide on the stimuli to be used. Whenever possible, use material (vocabulary, etc.) from the student's textbooks (look for sentence types from her or his reader, science book, etc.) and use fiction and nonfiction appropriate to the child's age, stage of development, and interests.

mentation, can be used to develop a language intervention sequence. Segmentation is defined as an "overlaid" linguistic judgment about phrase, morpheme, or phoneme boundary (Rubin, 1986). Successful segmentation demonstrates that a child is able to decontextualize and reflect on language structure by separating speech into phrases, words, syllables, and phonemes. In the normal flow of conversation, speech is unsegmented. That is, phrases, words, and sounds mesh together in a rhythmic pattern. When listening to a foreign language with which we are unfamiliar, we often have difficulty knowing where one word ends and another begins. As we become more proficient at the language, we become more sensitive to word boundaries, phrase boundaries, and phonemic boundaries. Our knowledge of these boundaries, or language segments, is developmental. It generally comes after some degree of language proficiency. Liberman and her colleagues (1980) have done extensive work on the development of segmentation abilities (see Chapter 7). Their research poses a number of questions including the following: When do children learn that speech consists of separate units? Is there a sequence of development? Why is segmentation a valid area of language study? Why might it be relevant?

The research suggests that explicit segmentation is difficult for young children. Preschoolers have difficulty showing (or telling) how many words are in a sentence, how many syllables (parts) are in a word, and how many sounds are in a word. From the general findings in the research (Allan, 1982; Liberman et al., 1980; Rubin, 1986; see also Chapter 7 for details), the following sequence emerges: Children begin with little idea that speech can be broken up into units. For instance, the three year old might say that the sentence, "There are seven ducks," has seven words. Children then begin to appreciate that phrases are separate pieces of speech, followed by words and then syllables. The latest acquisition is the ability to appreciate that words can be separated into sounds. Although age levels vary, aspects of phonemic segmentation are difficult for some seven and eight year olds (see Kamhi, 1987 for additional information).

The research suggests that there is a developmental sequence for segmentation. Children do not know automatically that words or sounds are separate parts of speech. They have to be relatively proficient at talking before they are able to talk about language units (see Jane's speech therapy session, Case 2). The sequence for segmentation awarenesss is something like this: phrase boundary, word/syllable boundary (with content words being separated before function words) and phoneme boundaries. Our task, as with the comprehension literature, is to convert this information into an intervention plan.

The examples below represent a sample lesson cover sheet and a sample intervention sequence. Our first question, as always, is, "Why am I doing this?" This question is tempered with the considerations of being certain that the student is ready for this sophisticated metalinguistic activity. The activity is especially sophisticated at the level of sound segmentation.

---

## COVER SHEET FOR A
## PHONEMIC SEGMENTATION LESSON

*Theoretical Principle*
Children appreciate larger units of speech before they are able to break up speech into its component parts. Children move from phrase, to word, to syllable, to sound segmentation abilities.

*Type of Strategy*
Analytical/bottom-up (break words into sounds)

*Type of Language*
Metalinguistic (focus on manipulating sounds of the language)

*Clinician/Educator Questions*
1. Why have segmentation activities been chosen?
2. Is the student ready for this phonemic level of speech segmentation?
3. Am I prepared to back up and do word/syllable activities if the student has difficulty with sound segmentation?
4. Are the segmentation activities related to the student's reading/writing program? Can the segmentation activities be integrated into storytelling and other meaningful language/classroom activities? Am I keeping the focus on comprehension? Am I making the purpose of reading clear to the students?
5. Are the words chosen for the segmentation activities within the student's naming repertoire? Is the vocabulary related to curricular content areas?

---

We can take the concept of phonemic segmentation further and propose the following lesson plan.

# SAMPLE LESSON PLAN WITH PHONEMIC SEGMENTATION SEQUENCE*

**Target on Segmentation Activities†**
Helps student learn to manipulate the sounds of language with a particular focus on speech-to-letter translations. This activity is being done to help the student appreciate the structural aspects of language.

*Words and Forms Targeted*
1. Content and function words
2. Consonant vowel consonant (CVC) words (singular and plural)

*Specific Sequence*
1. Begin with sentences and have student tell how many words are in the sentence; work on content and function words.
2. Introduce CVC words and break the CVC words into their sounds (singulars).
3. Move to CVC words with plurals

*Strategies Facilitated (Bottom-Up)*
*First level:* words are segments of sentences; there are different kinds of words.
*Second level:* sounds are parts of words.

*Special Instructions*
There is an intermediate step involving the segmentations of syllables. It may be appropriate to include work on syllabication. Spoken and written activities must be integrated appropriately (see Chapter 7). These analytical activities may follow gestalt-like or top-down activities or they may be done in conjunction with them.

*Tasks and Stimuli*
Clinician/teacher needs to understand the many different ways that segmentation activities can be presented to students. Whenever possible stimuli should be chosen from the student's classroom texts. (Additional sound-word activities are described in Chapters 7 and 8.)

---

*As adapted from Rubin (1986); Liberman et al. (1980); Wallach and Lee (1982).

†These segmentation activities would be considered inappropriate for Hunter, described earlier in the chapter. His learning profile suggests other priorities for him at this time. Even though Hunter displays some bottom-up abilities, they are not apparent in his decoding of print. For Hunter, phonemic segmentation would not be a priority at this time.

## Task Complexity Can Provide Guidelines

Another step in the process of developing meaningful language intervention programs involves understanding the metalinguistic nature of some of the tasks we present to children every day in our test, resource, and classroom environments. Van Kleeck (1984b) provides a task hierarchy that can be used by clinicians and teachers. Van Kleeck (1984b) points out that, as with most hierarchies and sequences, the order of presentation is flexible. We might analyze our own lessons and consider the format of some items on standardized tests using the tasks listed in the next section as guidelines for recognizing metalinguistic complexity. We might consider how to modify each task for children at different age levels and different levels of facility in the decontextualizing process. The tasks are ordered from easier (comprehension) to more difficult (relating terms). The content being taught will affect the order of difficulty.

*Various Response Expectancies Used in Metalinguistic Tasks**

**COMPREHENSION.** The student indicates nonverbally that something spoken or written has been understood. For example, we might ask a student to point to a picture from a choice of pictures to demonstrate comprehension. The comprehension task can be quite complex (asking a student to interpret an ambiguous sentence or a complex relative clause sentence) or it can be less demanding (asking a student to interpret a logical, semantically constrained sentence such as, "The flowers were watered by the girl," or "The home run was hit by Reggie Jackson"). *Note:* Many comprehension tasks using the picture-pointing. format have a metalinguistic cast to them. The Peabody Picture Vocabulary Test–Revised, which requires the child to pick the correct word from a choice of four pictures is one example.

**SEGMENTATION.** The student is asked to separate a stimulus into its component parts. For example, we might ask a student to tell how many words are in a sentence, how many syllables are in a word, or how many sounds are in a word. Segmentation tasks are generally quite difficult for children, but, as in the comprehension task example, they can be matched to the child's level of ability. Kindergarten and Grade 1 reading tasks often involve segmentation. The teacher who says to her class, "Circle all the pictures you see that begin with the /k/ sound," is asking the children to segment speech (see section

---

*For an in-depth discussion of modifications of the task hierarchy, see Wallach (1985).

on "Classic Mistakes"). Note: Many early reading programs are segmental in nature. Phonics is a classic example of a segmentation activity.

**SYNTHESIS.** The student is asked to combine parts of a stimulus into a whole. For example, we might give a student three sounds, /b/, /ae/, /t/ and ask her or him to tell us the words. We might give the student a series of words, e.g., *boy the girl kisses,* and ask her or him to put the words into a sentence. *Note:* There is the suggestion that segmentation activities might precede synthesis activities. Many "auditory-blending" activities are mislabeled. Phonics activities require synthesis (as well as segmentation) ability.

**EVALUATION.** The student is asked to compare one item with another. For example, we might ask a student whether two words sound the same or different. We might ask a student to decide whether a spoken sentence matches a written sentence. We might ask a student to decide whether a spoken sentence makes sense or whether it sounds silly. *Note:* Auditory-discrimination tasks involve the metalinguistic ability to evaluate in that they require judgments about sameness or difference of words based upon their most abstract feature, the phoneme. The Wepman Test of Auditory Discrimination is an excellent example of an evaluation task.

**CORRECTION.** The student is asked to identify errors and change them to their correct form. For example, we might ask a student to correct a semantic error in a sentence or paragraph, such as "The sun was shining brightly at night." We might ask a student to correct a syntactic or morphological error: "The boys plays football yesterday." *Note:* We would use our knowledge of development to make decisions about what types of corrections are appropriate at particular stage or age levels (see Chapter 7).

**EXPLANATION.** The student is asked to supply reasons for comprehension, segmentation, evaluation, or correction. For example, we might ask a student why *leaf-thief* are "the same." We might ask a student why a sentence such as, "The sun came out because the snowman melted" makes sense. *Note:* The reasons students give us in their responses can be very helpful to us. They can give us more information about their problem-solving and metacognitive ability. Gardner (1984) would say that explanation is an important linguistic function (see Chapter 2).

**RELATING TERMS.** The student is asked to associate and connect words and concepts. For example, we might ask a student to provide homonyms, antonyms, and synonyms for words. We might ask a student to paraphrase or provide a definition for a word (see Chapter 8). As in other tasks, relating terms can be highly complex or can be introduced to a student with familiar vocabulary, etc.

The van Kleeck (1984b) task hierarchy is used throughout this text. It is presented here as part of an introduction to the questions and knowledge used in formulating language intervention programs for children and adolescents. More information about the metalinguistic nature of the various activities will be presented in Chapters 5 through 7. How research can guide us to our intervention decisions will be shown through model lesson plans developed for specific students. As part of each lesson, the tasks and materials being used are analyzed. Case studies that demonstrate some of the points made in this chapter follow.

## CASE STUDIES: SOME CLASSIC MISTAKES

### Case 1: Misunderstood Developmental Sequence

> Misunderstood Task Level
> Misunderstood Level of Decontextualization

Billy is nine years old. He is desribed as a poor listener in the classroom. He has "general language problems." Word-finding and -retrieval problems have been noted by his teacher. He also has problems with complex syntax. He is a poor reader and speller. Generally, he is having a great deal of difficulty keeping up with his Grade 3 peers.

He is given a number of tests in the auditory processing area. Included in his battery are the Wepman Auditory Discrimination Test and the Processing Speech Sounds subtest from the Clinical Evaluation of Language Functions. Billy has trouble deciding whether words like *thief-sheaf, ship-sip, mitt-mat,* and *rope-robe* are the same or different.

*Note:* Billy has excellent articulation and normal hearing.

One of the conclusions reached about Billy is that he has an auditory discrimination problem. This "discrimination" problem is causing his reading and writing difficulties. It is suggested that he be given auditory work. A program such as the Auditory Discrimination in Depth (ADD) is recommended.

What is wrong with this interpretation? First, we need to recognize that all formal language testing involves metalinguistic ability. Thus, both the Wepman and the Processing Speech Sounds subtest are testing Billy's metalinguistic knowledge. Both tests go beyond testing auditory discrimination. In their current formats, i.e., word pairs presented to a child for a judgment, the two tests focus on Billy's ability to make an evaluation about language. Evaluation judgments, as seen in the van Kleeck (1984b) task hierarchy, are developmentally late (see Chapter 2, Table 2-1), and they are rather difficult. Second, the task is made even more difficult by the particular nature of the evaluation Billy is being asked to make. That is, Billy is being asked to make a judgment about the smallest unit of the language, the phoneme. As just explained in the section on segmentation, children's ability to deal with the phonemes of their language on a more conscious (metalinguistic) level comes after their ability to appreciate larger units such as words and syllables (Blachman, 1984; Lieberman et al., 1980; Rubin, 1986; see Chapter 2, Table 2-1, and Chapter 7). Third, many children who are metalinguistically less developed will assume the examiner is asking for a comparison of the word referents rather than asking for a comparison of the phonemic segments of the words. Billy may think that *lake-lake* ("Are they the same or different?") requires a "different" response because all the lakes he has seen are different. Fourth, consider Billy's other language abilities. How can he have bona fide auditory discrimination problems when he has perfect articulation? On some level (basic linguistic competence), he understands that /f/ is different from /θ/, that /ʃ/ is different from /sh/, etc., as reflected in his pronunciation. What he appears to be having difficulty with is demonstrating that knowledge consciously. Finally, we might take issue with the recommendation that Billy be given "auditory" work, especially in the form of the ADD program. We will not take issue with the program at this time, but we will take issue with its recommended sequence, which is developmentally reversed. For many children, particularly those with language learning disabilities, beginning with individual phonemes and "blending" those phonemes into words would be too difficult. Rubin (1986), among others, has done extensive work in the area of sound awareness (phonemic segmentation). She proposes segmentation sequences that move the child gradually from knowledge of words, to syllables, and then, finally, to awareness of sounds (see Chapter 7 for additional suggestions). We might also say that Billy's metalinguistic difficulties (should they be documented) are interacting with his reading and spelling difficulties. We would argue strongly to avoid making quick judgments that any one behavior or group of behaviors would be *causing* spoken and written language problems.

We need to know much more about Billy before making a decision about what to teach him. We would like to know more about his word-finding and -retrieval difficulties (see Chapter 8). We should be thinking about how word-finding difficulties, should they be real, interact with reading and writing difficulties. Our recommendations might involve segmentation activities at the word or syllable level (as per the van Kleeck task hierarchy). However, we would also need to decide whether any segmentation activities should be put on hold because other areas (e.g., syntactic, conversational, or narrative areas) are a priority for Billy at this time. We might opt to combine word-naming and segmentation activities with story comprehension and story-telling activities.

## Case 2: Misunderstood Aspect of Language to Teach

> Misunderstood Type of Language Activity
> (Contextualized/Decontextualized)
> Misunderstood Task Complexity

A clinician is working with a three-year-old child, Jane, who is described as having a "language delay." Jane tends to ask questions in statement form with inflection. She might say, "We are playing now?" or "We eating snack now?" and so on. It can be noted that Jane also omits the auxiliary verb.

The lesson goes something like this:

The clinician says, "Now Jane, I want you to look at the blocks on the table. (Each block has a word on it; arranged in order, they make a sentence.) We have five blocks on the table. We are going to point to the blocks and say the words for the sentence. Ready?" (Clinician points to the blocks and says the sentence.) "We are eating snacks now." (Clinican instructs the child to do the same thing. The child begins to do the task, continuing to omit the auxiliary verb. The clinican and the child touch the blocks and the child begins to repeat the auxiliary. The child needs help touching the blocks to match the words. The clinician guides the child's hand.)

"Now, Jane, watch carefully. I am going to move the blocks around. We're going to make a question out of the blocks." (Clinician proceeds to move the second block to the first position of the block sentence.)

"Now, let's say the question sentence together: 'Are we eating snacks now?'" (The child seems confused and continues to say the sentence in statement form. The clinician shows the child the "are" block. She demonstrates the statement sentence again and then moves the "are" block to the beginning of the sentence to demonstrate the question form.)

Why might this language therapy session be inappropriate? The first question we could ask is, "Why teach question form and auxiliary at this time?" We might consider working on other aspects of language for this child. As with Billy's case, we need to know much more about Jane's language and cognitive abilities. However, we should be thinking about the decision to teach form. Why was it made? Why was it thought to be the most important area for language remediation at this time? Would there be other aspects of language that would be relevant to teach at the three-year-old period? (Form work *might* be appropriate and relevant at a somewhat later level in the child's development or after mastery of other language skills.)

The second observation relates to the type of language the clinician is trying to develop. Is the clinician trying to help the child develop better contextualized language (help the child talk to her peers, say what she wants to say within a "naturalistic" environment, etc.)? The task, as it is structured, is highly decontextualized. The sentence represented by blocks is far removed from a situation in which it is likely to be used. (There are times, particularly with older school-aged children, where this type of activity might be appropriate because we want to help them with decontextualized language. We are just questioning the use of the activity in this particular situation.)

Finally, the task is extremely difficult and highly metalinguistic. It is unlikely that normal developing three year olds would make the word-to-block connection. The understanding that speech has segmented units (words, syllables, sounds), as mentioned in the previous case example and in the section on phonemic segmentation, develops after three years of age (see Chapter 2, including Table 2-1; see segmentation overview, this chapter). The choice of activities for Jane would be considered developmentally inappropriate.

# PART THREE

Chapters 5, 6, 7, and 8 contain specific intervention suggestions in a number of areas. The goal is to help students become active and responsible learners, and the activities discussed are prototypes which must be applied carefully to the broader context of communicative and academic learning.

# CHAPTER 5

## The Transition to Literacy: Narrative and Instructional Discourse

[T]he written word ... is not merely an echo of a speaking voice. It is another kind of voice altogether, a conjurer's trick of the first order. It must certainly have appeared that way to those who invented it, and that is why we should not be surprised that the Egyptian god Thoth, who is alleged to have brought writing to King Thamus, was also the god of magic. People like ourselves may see nothing wondrous in writing, but our anthropologists know how strange and magical it appears to a purely oral people — a conversation with no one and yet with everyone. What could be stranger than the silence one encounters when addressing a question to a text? What could be more metaphysically puzzling than addressing an unseen audience, as every writer of books must do? And correcting oneself because one knows that an unknown reader will disapprove or misunderstand? (Postman, 1985, p. 14).

Postman's words describe how people in print cultures conceptualize intelligence, implicitly or explicitly. That is, in print cultures, the ability to remain immobile for a fairly long time (Postman, 1985), considering black squiggles across a page, constitutes a critical piece of being intelligent. As Postman points out, those who cannot do this may be labeled as being hyperkinetic or as having some sort of intellectual deficiency. Further, as pointed out in Chapter 2, to be able to apprehend meaning from written text is one of the hallmarks of literacy. Such apprehension of text requires rather sophisticated and abstract conceptual processes, analogous to those described in Chapter 2. Text comprehension consists of distinguishing between the words themselves, with their concomitant aesthetic or lack of it, and the logic of their argument, a formidable enough task requiring some modicum of metalinguistic awareness.

Beyond basic text comprehension, readers must learn more subtle, critical processes, described by Postman (1985) as print-intelligence. First, they must understand a writer's attitudes toward their subjects and toward their readers, or as Postman puts it, they "must know the difference between a joke and an argument" (1985, p. 26). Second, readers must judge the quality of the writer's arguments, which requires the simultaneous juggling of several aspects of the printed text "delaying a verdict until the entire argument is finished" (Postman, 1985, p. 26). Readers must engage in several levels of processing at once: they must hold in mind questions to determine if the actual text answers them, and if so, how, when, and where; they must marshal their own experiences and knowledge as a counterargument to the author's; they must withhold those of their own experiences that do not pertain to what is being proposed. Third, readers must have divested themselves of the belief that words are magical; i.e., they must understand that the printed word stands for, or represents, real and imagined experiences in an arbitrary and symbolic way. In short, readers must have developed metalinguistic awareness. Finally, readers "must have learned to negotiate the world of abstractions" (Postman, 1985, p. 26). Negotiating the world of abstractions involves an understanding of and an ability to manipulate decontextualized ideas divested of whatever concrete images (visual or otherwise) they might have held. In previous chapters it was argued that becoming literate involves a continuous process of abstracting, a moving from utterance to text. The transition to literacy includes the development of knowledge about degrees of abstractness and out-of-context, or decontextualized, ideas (see Chapter 4). As children develop in the various cognitive domains described in Chapter 2, they acquire a variety of information-processing strategies for abstracting and decontextualizing. Although the knowledge they acquire across all cognitive domains is relevant to becoming literate in the general sense proposed in Chapter 1, their relative success at print literacy depends to a large extent on their ability to understand and manipulate different forms of spoken and written discourse.

## THEORETICAL BASES FOR THE INTERVENTION SEQUENCES AND TASKS

Although this text is not devoted to a description of child language development, intervention designs must begin with a section about research in the area. Aspects relevant to research are discussed before intervention ideas. However, a strict developmental approach is not being advocated. On the contrary, intervention sequences and strategies for a given child are targeted based on a wide variety of needs, including developmental considerations. Accordingly, each section in this chapter and the next three begins with a description of the theoretical foundations of a specific area of language acquisition. These descriptions serve as the skeletal framework on which the intervention strategies that follow are based.

### The "Metas"

As our profession has broadened its conceptualization of what constitutes language development and language disorders, practitioners have discovered the ubiquitous nature of the "metas." We have learned that much of what occurs in language development after most children reach the age of six is dependent on the development of *metalinguistic* awareness. The importance of meta was discussed in Chapter 1. The end of Chapter 2 pointed out that much of what is included in language arts instruction depends on children having developed the ability to reflect on language and to analyze it in relatively abstract ways.

The developmental sequence of metalinguistic awareness presented at the end of Chapter 2 is expanded in this section of the text (see also Chapter 7). Because much of children's success with narrative and instructional discourse rests on their continued metalinguistic development, frequent reference is made to the metalinguistic sequences described in Table 2-1. Throughout the intervention sections, the van Kleeck (1984b) hierarchy presented in Chapter 4, Table 4-2, is relevant.

Another important meta is *metacognition.* Readers will note that the description of the processes of text comprehension attributed to Postman in the introduction bears striking resemblance to the cognitive and metacognitive processes described by Sternberg and Baron (1987) and others. As intervention sequences pertinent to children's narrative and instructional discourse are described, reference will be made to the metalinguistic and metacognitive aspects of learning presented in Chapters 1 and 2 and summarized in Table 4-2.

## The Low-Print to High-Print Continuum

Child language practitioners have devoted considerable attention to the connections between children's oral language development and their acquisition of print literacy. One of the strongest connections is the relationship between the style and type of language children hear from their adult caretakers and the children's later academic success, which, particularly in reading comprehension, is related to their pre-schooling experiences (Bennett, 1986). Most striking is the suggestion that the single best predictor of children's success in reading comprehension in the early grades is frequency of having been read to. The second best predictor is oral language development. Children who come from homes where a literate oral language style is the norm are more likely to enter school with considerable experience using the very style of language embodied in the texts they encounter in the classroom, as pointed out in Chapter 1. Also, children who live in homes in which print is visible and valued (high-print homes) are much more likely to have interacted with print than are children who grow up in homes where print is neither visible or valued (low-print homes). Indeed, as van Kleeck and Schuele (1987) demonstrate, an important characteristic of children's literacy socialization is their knowing how to interact with books: turning books right side up, turning through the pages from left to right, and distinguishing print from nonprint (see Table 2-1). Knowing how to interact with books is largely a funtion of being in an environment in which books are valued, where adult attitudes include the expectation that important information is to be gleaned from print, and where adults regularly use print for a variety of purposes — in short, in high-print homes.

In high-print homes, adults read and write as a matter of course. They make and post lists, keep calendars, receive and send mail, and refer to journals, magazines, religious materials, books, letters, or other printed matter. Adults in high-print homes commit words to print as part of their daily lives. As part of a literate society, they know where their cultural information is stored — in libraries, museums, computers, magazines, and in videos and on television. One of their prevailing attitudes is that print is important beyond the individual. Print is seen as important for the cultural good, for its own aesthetic, and for the manner in which ideas can be generated, stated, transformed, and abstracted. In high-print homes, print is seen as a valuable vehicle for explaining, remembering, and reflecting on language. In addition, high-print homes provide experience with the specific syntactic, semantic, and phonological/graphological aspects of language characterizing literacy. Chapters 6 and 7 are devoted to a description of these literate language characteristics.

As children enter school, they enter into a tacit contract to achieve literacy. Some children arrive with pertinent literacy-based experiences. Some arrive with well-developed oral language, including a degree of metalinguistic awareness. Some come from home environments in which language is prized and talked about. For children from high-print homes, the transition from oral to literate communication has already begun (see Chapter 1). For children from low-print homes, the transition is much more difficult and occurs later in their development.

## The Oral-to-Literate Transition

Westby (1984, 1985) has suggested that children develop through a transition from being primarily oral communicators to being able to engage in literate communication. The oral-to-literate transition entails the elaboration of strategies for communicating beyond interpersonal conversational discourse. Children acquire strategies for understanding and using language in situations that contain less contextual support, that require taking another's perspective, that are relatively abstract in comparison with the cognitive demands involved in conversational discourse. Children learn how to handle discourse that includes unshared topics, that involves being a spectator rather than an active participant, and that is relatively formal in structure. Westby (1985) describes the oral-to-literate shift in great detail. Table 5–1 outlines the continuum.

As Table 5–1 shows, children move through stages of abstractness as they progress from utterance-based communicating to text-based communicating. At the most concrete levels, children's communication is marked by structures that are familiar and somewhat redundant. Their language is characterized by talking about the here and now, or the immediate context (see Chapter 4). The underlying intent of the communication is to regulate ongoing interactions, which are relatively equal in their turn-taking and length. There is frequent use of deictics and formulaic expressions (see Chapter 6). Children rely on extralinguistic cues for comprehension (see Chapter 4). Meaning is often carried through intonation and body gestures and postures (see Chapter 6). As children become more literate in their communication, they become able to use language marked by less familiar words which are more explicit in their meaning. Their syntax becomes more precise and concise (see Chapter 7). They become able to discuss events outside the immediate context, and they can maintain a relatively abstract topic over many communicative turns. Much of the meaning in literate communication comes from inference. Topic coherence is often based on the use of explicit linguistic markers, such as "moreover," "on the other hand," etc. (see Chapter 6 for a thorough discus-

**TABLE 5-1**
*The Oral-to-Literate Transition*

**Orality to Literacy**

Asking for something or telling someone to do something

↓

Reporting a personal experience to a friend face to face

↓

Writing a note to a friend

↓

Listening to a lecture on an unfamiliar topic

↓

Writing a report on a personal experience

↓

Reading or writing an imaginative story

| High Context | Low Context |
|---|---|
| Polysynchronic time | Monochronic, linear time |
| Group interaction | Individual orientation |
| Learn by observation | Learn by being taught |

**Oral Language to Literate Language**

| Language Function | Language Topic | Language Structure |
|---|---|---|
| Regulates interaction: requesting and demanding<br>Genuine questions<br>Symmetrical interaction | Here and now<br>Talks topically<br>Meaning from context | Familiar words<br>Redundant syntax<br>Deictics and formulaic expressions<br>Cohesion based on intonation |
| Regulates thinking by planning, reflecting, seeking information<br>Many pseudo-Qs (rhetorical questions or questions posed to a child who knows the adult knows the answer) | Talk to topic<br>Meaning comes from inference from text | Concise syntax<br>Explicit vocabulary<br>Cohesion based on explicit lingusitic markers |

sion of cohesion). The shift from utterance-based communicating to text-based communicating means that children become able to engage in the manipulation of the language topics, forms, and functions required in reading or writing about unfamiliar or imaginative topics and ideas.

## THE NATURE OF DISCOURSE

Garvey (1977) defined *discourse* as the reciprocal means by which at least a dyad, or two persons, organizes verbal exchanges. This broad definition encompasses a wide range of verbal exchanges, from casual conversations and stereotyped greetings to philosophical discussion and extended fiction or poetry. Discourse structures vary according to the organization they embody. That is, the discourse structures characteristic of oral conversational language are different from those characteristic of printed, nonfictional text. Similarly, the discourse characteristics of oral poetry differ considerably from the characteristic discourse structures of a dramatic piece.

Narrative discourse is one discourse type that appears to have considerable impact on children's school performance and success. Westby (1984) argues that the narrative form of discourse is of particular interest because it most likely falls midway along the oral-to-literate continuum: "Narratives are structurally midway between the language of the oral tradition and the language of the essayist literary tradition .... Narratives, the earliest literate structure that is required, arise out of the oral tradition yet have a mathetic [explaining] function and can, thus, be used to ease the transition from oral to literate language mode" (p. 124).

In recent years, a great deal of research and thinking has been done about children's narrative knowledge and its relationship with their academic experiences.

### Approaches to Narrative Discourse

In the child language and cognition literature there are two major conceptualizations of narrative discourse. One concept stems from Bruner's model (1975) of narrative and paradigmatic thinking. According to this view, narrative discourse is a reflection of a primary mode of thinking, narrative thought. According to Sutton–Smith (1986), narrative thought is what characterizes stories and drama, and it is concerned primarily with metaphor and with credibility (Sutton-

Smith, 1986). Narrative thinking is contrasted with paradigmatic thinking, which is characterized by math and logic and which involves
experiments and validity (Sutton–Smith, 1986). Van Dongen and Westby (1986) carry this view even further, arguing that narrative thinking for children is the primary mode of thinking and requires an
understanding of social cognition, or what was described in Chapter 2
as part of the pragmatic aspects involved in self-integration. Van Dongen and Westby stress that narrative thinking exists in contrast to the
thinking required to develop an understanding of the physical world,
which was described in Chapter 2 as comprising logical-mathematical
and visual-spatial information processing. In this view, narrative
thinking develops out of children's social interactions and constitutes
their prevailing mode of thinking about those social interactions until
they begin to develop a differentiated model of the specialized kinds
of discourse.

The adherents of this view of narrative as a primary mode of
thinking make a strong argument that cognitive development is gov-
erned more by narrative scripts than by the abstract processes described by Piaget and Vygotsky (see Sutton–Smith, 1986, for example).
Sutton–Smith (1986) argues further that the true meaning of children's narrative knowledge is in their performance. Thus, narrative
knowledge is seen as an unfolding process that can be accessed through
observation of children's play, itself viewed as a performance of narrative knowledge. Children's narrative knowledge can also be observed
as children relate stories, act them out, make up new ones, engage in
show-and-tell, and so on. Table 5–2 describes narrative development
from this viewpoint.

The second major conceptualization of narrative discourse is that
narratives exist in a variety of types, or genres, which vary across cultural groups. In this view, narrative discourse, is arranged according to
major types, such as fiction, nonfiction, poetry, drama, fable, myth,
etc. Heath (1986) suggests that the major narrative genres are narratives, jokes, sermons, magical rites, and poetry. These genres constitute four universal types of narratives: recounts, eventcasts, accounts,
and stories (p. 88). Recounts are probably the most common academic
genre but may be the least common form "in early language socialization outside mainstream school-oriented families" (Heath, 1986, p.
88). Recounts are narratives in which speakers relate in the present
moment their past experiences, usually in response to an adult request, for example, "tell me what happened at the grocery store today."
Recounts typically take a serial and chronological form and utilize a
consistent point of view. That is, recounts are verbal reiterations of
events. The language of recounts is typically characterized by coordinate clauses showing little or no logical relation or relative importance.

**TABLE 5-2**
*Narrative Development*

| Type of Narrative Structure | Approximate Age of Emergence (years) |
| --- | --- |
| *Heaps:* collections of unrelated ideas | 2½ |
| *Sequences:* recurring theme without specific order of events | 3 |
| *Primitive narrative:* main theme requires the child to interpret or predict events | 4 to 4½ |
| *Unfocused chains:* no central character or topic; events linked in logical or cause-effect relationships | 4 to 4½ |
| *Focused chains:* central character and true sequence of events; listener must interpret ending | 5 |
| *True narrative:* true plot, character development, and sequence; presented problem resolved in the end | 7 |

Based on Applebee (1978), from Westby, 1984.

The eventcast is a "verbal replay or explanation of activity scenes," as, for instance, in dramatic play during the frame breaks described in Chapter 2 (Heath, 1986, p. 88). As Heath points out, such "stop-action framing" is encouraged in the formal schooling process (1986, p. 89). It also requires metalinguistic and/or metacognitive awareness in order to participate. Language typical of the eventcast involves coordination, subordination, and some degree of how the events are (or will be) related.

Accounts are sharings of experiences beyond the level of basic need demands and requests. Accounts are spontaneously initiated by children and thus reflect children's individual differences. In addition, adults rarely describe explicitly the "rules" for how accounts are structured. As Heath (1986) writes, children must tailor their accounts with predictable progressions so that their listeners can predict and anticipate what is coming next. This tailoring requires that children know how to obtain and hold the floor through signaling to potential and actual listeners, first, that an account is forthcoming and then that what is being accounted for has some understandable structure.

Stories are recognizable throughout different speech communities because of their highly structured forms and structures. They are generally at least partially fictionalized, and the language used is typically constructed to reflect a consciously shaped structure different from other narrative genres. Stories reflect the implicit knowledge that an interpretive listener plays an integral role in the story-relating process. Heath (1986) points out that, although there is at present relatively little information about how different speech communities enable children to learn the differences between real and fictionalized information, teasing seems to have a considerable effect on this type of language learning. She argues that teasing involves role exchanging and the manipulation of real events — just the sorts of cognitive juggling necessary for the achievement of literacy.

Narratives have been studied according to their common characteristics. The characteristics of narratives seem to exist cross-culturally, particularly in children's literature. Using these characteristics, children's storytelling or retelling can be analyzed from two relatively different approaches: through analysis of story grammar and through the analysis of event-chains. Perhaps the most common story grammar structure is that of Stein and Glenn (1979), which is used in the basal reader example presented in Chapter 3, and summarized in Table 5-3.

Story grammar is a way of observing the hierarchical structure of stories through analysis of how the constituent categories are organized. Glenn and Stein (1980) constructed a developmental sequence of the constituent structures in children's stories (see also Hedberg & Stoel–Gammon, 1986, p. 65). The constituent organizations, listed in developmental order, are shown in Table 5-4. As Table 5-4 shows,

**TABLE 5-3**
*Story Grammar Constituents for Simple Story*

| | |
|---|---|
| Setting | Introduction of main characters: sets stage, gives context |
| Initiating event (beginning) | Action that changes the story environment, evokes formation of the goal |
| Internal response | Goal: serves as motivation for later action |
| Attempt | Overt actions that are directed toward goal attainment |
| Consequence | Result of an attempt: attainment or nonattainment of goal |
| Reaction or ending | Emotion, cognition, or end, expressing protagonist's feelings about goal generalization to some broader consequence |

After Stein and Glenn (1979).

TABLE 5-4

*Children's Development of Constituent Structures in Stories*

---

*Descriptive sequence:* describes characters, surroundings, habitual actions; no causal relationships or temporal constraints

*Action sequence:* contains chronological order for actions; has no causal relations

*Reactive sequence:* certain changes automatically cause other changes; no goal-directed behavior

*Abbreviated episode:* contains goal, though it need not be stated explicitly

*Complete episode:* describes entire goal-oriented behavioral sequence; contains consequence statement and at least two of followng: initiating event, internal response, attempt

*Complex episodes:* elaboration of complete episode; contains embedding of episodes

*Interactive episodes:* two characters influence the goals and actions of each other

---

Based on Hedberg and Stoel-Gammon (1986).

children's stories become more complex and reflect their increasing facility with language structures as children get older. Children also learn to tailor their stories to fit a naive listener's needs (see Chapter 6).

The event-chain approach is less common but equally useful in analyzing children's narrative structures. This approach allows us to examine how narratives are causally sequenced. In contrast to story grammars, the event-chain approach focuses on the unfolding sequence of temporally and causally ordered events. It thus allows a glimpse into children's understanding of causality and the linguistic means they employ to express that understanding. Kemper and Edwards (1986) describe the event-chain as "the sequence of causally and temporally ordered actions, physical states, and mental states that explains what happens, why it occurred, and what consequences resulted" (pp. 12-13). According to Kemper and Edwards, story events are organized into actions, physical states, and mental states, which are linked through specific actions and processes. Some of these specific actions and processes initiate characteristic mental states; some motivate characters' actions through their intentions, emotions, dispositions; some result in new physical states arising from characters' actions and from natural and social processes; and some enable or block characters' actions through their physical states.

Kemper and Edwards proposed a developmental unfolding in children's abilities to express causality with the event-chain model. Their proposal is summarized in Table 5–5. It shows that although two- and three-year-old children use rudimentary causal expressions, it is not until they are six that their narratives are "causally coherent in that they consist of a causally connected sequence of actions, physical states, and mental states that explain the antecedents and consequences of characters' actions" (Kemper & Edwards, 1986, p. 18).

## Instructional Discourse

Instructional discourse can be viewed as the particular way people organize their communicative interactions within educational environments, as discussed in Chapter 3. Silliman (1984) describes instructional discourse, or the language of schooling, along four dimensions: general purpose, nature of comprehension activities, coding complexity, and participant assumptions. She states that the general purpose of instructional discourse is the transmission of scientific or logically based knowledge. In contrast, everyday discourse has as its general purpose the regulation of social interactions and interpersonal functions. Everyday discourse is socially salient, whereas instructional discourse is logically salient.

To comprehend instructional discourse requires more mental complexity than is required to understand everyday discourse. Because speakers' intentional meanings are usually inherently available in the shared situation, everyday discourse is more easily apprehendable. Instructional discourse, on the other hand, requires that meaning be reconstructed almost solely from what is actually said. That is, language in the classroom context is much more decontextualized than everyday discourse. As Nelson (1987) puts it, everyday discourse is much more situated than instructional discourse, which lacks the rich contextual surroundings of everyday discourse.

Where everyday discourse is coded for the regulation of social interactions, instructional discourse is coded for logical definitions and explanations disembedded from specific real-world contexts of use (Silliman, 1984). The cognitive consequence of this disembedding of instructional discourse is that great emphasis is placed on self-regulatory metacognitive and metalinguistic means for engaging in successful classroom participation. Silliman (1984) gives the example of a teacher asking a student to define a word. The teacher's expectation is that the student will understand that her or his intent is to elicit a

**TABLE 5-5**

*Event-Chain Development of Causality*

| | Age (years) |
|---|---|
| *Plans:* Intentional action or series of actions towards prespecified ends. Child refers to own intentions and consequences. Example: *down, up* refer to general classes of plans; *there* refers to the success of plans; *oh dear* refers to the failure of plans; *no* refers to the revision or rejection of plans; *more* refers to repetition of plans. | 2 to 3 |
| *Mental states:* Words for volitions, physiological states, perception; fewer words for emotions, judgments, and cognitions. Labels own internal states before others'. | 2⅓ |
| Labels causes and consequences of emotions of others. | 3 to 4 |
| *Agency:* Treats humans as passive recipients of own actions. | < 1½ to 2 |
| Ascribes talk and action to human play figures. Attributes sensations, perceptions, and physiological states to human play figures. | 1½ to 2 |
| Attributes emotions, obligations, and moral judgments to play figures. | 2 to 3 |
| Ascribes complex cognitions (planning, knowing, wondering) to play figures. | 5 |
| *Scripts:* Event sequences ordered causally and temporally, especially in context of familiar activities, e.g., birthdays, going to McDonald's. | 3 |
| *Connectives:* Two formal devices: (1) cause and effect are serially ordered; and (2) *so, because,* and other causal connectives formally mark the relationship. First to emerge is use of sequencing of clauses with no formal causal connective. Next is use of *and,* which declines with advent of *because* and *so.* | 2 to 3½ |
| *If* labels causal relationsips. | 2 to 3 |
| Psychological causality predominates over physical. | 4 to 9 |
| *Storytelling:* Narratives are causally coherent, containing sequences of actions, physical states, and mental states explaining antecedents and consequences of characters' actions; contain simultaneous development of content and plot. | 6 |

Based on Kemper and Edwards (1986).

metalinguistic statement: explaining word meanings in terms of other word meanings, which themselves refer to superordinate or subordinate semantic relations — a complex and relatively abstract cognitive and linguistic accomplishment. In fact, much of language arts in the elementary grades requires that children talk about language: words, sounds, letters, sentences, spellings, punctuation. In addition, much of the discourse used to teach language arts assumes that children possess a level of conscious awareness of their own mental processes (that they are metacognitive). The discourse of language arts also assumes that children can talk about their problem-solving strategies, a decontextualized and disembedded process (see Table 4-2).

In everyday discourse, participants can usually recover what is meant or intended from the shared situation or activity; in instructional discourse such recovery is quite difficult. In school situations, what is meant must be explicitly stated in more precise linguistic terms. Explicit statement of meaning allows a large range of potential meaning options, which are not constrained by the specific context; explicit statement of meaning increases the coding complexity required to attain an understanding of what is meant. Children with limited language and metalinguistic abilities often find the requirements of instructional discourse beyond their abilities. They are unable to grasp the meanings and intents being presented in decontextualized and disembedded situations. Table 5-6 provides a comparison of everyday discourse and instructional discourse.

Blank (1987) points out that the central question about instructional discourse is not whether or not it is unique (it is, but so are other forms of discourse), but whether or not it is "consistent with the school's objectives" (p. 2). Blank argues that a primary objective of school is to enhance cognition and that language is critical in the meeting of this objective. They question whether instructional discourse, particularly the dominant role teachers give to questioning, meets the stated objective of developing thinking and cognition. They state that teachers use questions almost exclusively in carrying out their objectives for educating children and that teachers rarely examine the heavy cognitive loads carried by questions. They argue that teachers must modify their question-asking considerably if their instructional discourse is to succeed in meeting children's needs and the school's objectives.

Four levels of discourse and the comment-oblige distinction were discussed in Chapter 3. Blank and her colleagues (Blank, 1987; Blank & Marquis, 1987) argue that teachers must design instructional exchanges specifically for students' levels of ability; teachers must avoid asking questions that provoke failure. Blank (1986) adds that by analyzing discourse along the four levels of difficulty, the practitioner can

**TABLE 5-6**
*Everyday and Instructional Discourse*

| Everyday Discourse | Instructional Discourse |
| --- | --- |
| Informal, familiar style (declaratives predominate). | Formal style (imperatives and interrogatives) prevails. |
| Adult fine tunes language to understanding needs of child, by modifying sentence length, vocabulary level, contextual information, explanation of referents, signaling topic shift and turn-taking. | Adult adjust language to responses of a small number of students. |
| Adult and child share assumptions about experiences on which to base language content and context; more meaning is available nonverbally; language is particularistic. | Adult language demands frequent interpretation of nonshared assumptions; more meaning is coded linguistically; language is universalistic. |
| Frequent turn-taking between adult and child according to cultural rules. | High incidence of teacher monologues; low incidence of turn-taking except in the context of the teacher-student rules in the culture-at-large. |
| Comments by adult and child relevant to ongoing context or shared assumptions. | Teacher comments frequently refer to assumptions thought to be shared in the culture-at-large. |
| Discrete amount of information depending on content. | Large volume of information used to expand content. |
| Ongoing checks for at-the-moment understanding; language is situated or contextualized. | Frequent reference to previously stated information without checking for momentary understanding; language is decontextualized. |
| General purpose of language at home is to share topics, cooperatively take turns according to the rules of the culture, and share a frame of reference with the emphasis on social factors. | General purpose of classroom language is to transmit logically based knowledge of the dominant culture, which involves talking about knowledge with an emphasis on linguistic factors. |

*(continued)*

**TABLE 5-6** *(continued)*

| | |
|---|---|
| Language at home is generally mentally simple from the child's point of view; it depends on both linguistic and nonlinguistic (contextual) cues. | Classroom language is generally mentally complex and depends almost solely on what is *said* rather than on the immediate context. |
| Participants' assumption depend to a great extent on specific context and can be taken for granted. | Participants' assumptions are based almost exclusively on what is said and cannot be taken for granted. |

determine the type of cognitive and linguistic structures more likely to lead the student to understanding rather than frustration. Blank and Marquis' suggestions (1987) involve developing a set of perceptual experiences for students so that they have more — and more relevant — information with which to comprehend the language being used in instructional settings. Blank's refinement (1986) of the discourse continuum to incorporate comment and oblige components represents another alternative (see Chapter 3 for additional information).

Another useful way to view instructional discourse is through the perspective of the pragmatic and metapragmatic skills necessary to succeed in classrooms. As Blank (1987) points out, the classroom is only one of many unique conversational situations most people encounter in their lives. As a unique setting, it requires participants to engage in the usual pragmatic behaviors: recognizing the specific aspects of the situation that render it unique; possessing a linguistic repertoire that includes those speech-language characteristics required in the situation; choosing speech-language structures and processes that are relevant and appropriate in the situation. Wilkinson and Milosky (1987) suggest that the specific pragmatic abilities required in classrooms include "making requests and responding to others' requests for information, action, or materials" (p. 62). It is important to remember that most classroom requests take the form of questions, no matter what their underlying intent (Blank & White, 1986).

As pointed out in the previous chapters, success in the classroom also demands that students be metacognitive: they must be able to understand themselves as information processors and learners. To succeed in the classroom, therefore, students must be capable of a specific type of metacognitive awareness. They must be *metapragmatic*. They must be aware of the specific ways to use language in a relevant, appropriate, and effective manner in the classroom (see the Weade &

Green, 1985, checklist of questions in Chapter 3). Wilkinson and Milosky (1987) suggest that metapragmatic skills include "the ability to reflect on [pragmatic] behaviors, to judge them, and to produce and modify them in hypothetical situations" (p. 62), and they present evidence showing that children in the elementary grades become increasingly aware of the pragmatic and metapragmatic behaviors involved in the typical classroom context of peer-learning situations. By fifth grade, children perceive a continuum of directness in requests used to elicit learning task help from peers. In addition, whereas third graders seem to see the goal of peer-learning tasks to be completion of a given problem, fifth graders are more likely to view the goal of the task in terms of their long-range needs in learning. Fifth graders indicate that certain responses are much more useful to them because they contain information about the learning process(es) involved in solving a particular problem. In short, fifth graders seem more aware than third graders on both the metapragmatic and the metacognitive levels. As discussed elsewhere in this text, it is important to recognize the wide range of ages at which children acquire some of the meta-abilities. Many children do not develop some of these awarenesses until relatively late.

Focusing specifically on the components of instructional discourse that seem to hold the most difficulty for LLD students, Nelson (in press) suggests addressing three areas of classroom discourse: classroom management, peer interactions, and the language of instruction. She argues that practitioners must include all three aspects in their assessment and intervention plans, and she suggests specific objectives for each (Table 5-7).

## INTERVENTION STRATEGIES FOR NARRATIVE DISCOURSE

Regardless of the point of view practitioners take about children's narrative knowledge, the developmental or the structural, there are some general intervention principles that lend themselves to virtually any attempt to enhance literacy. The first four points in the following list provide a beginning for all the intervention strategies presented in this and the following chapters. It is also important to construct microprofiles for students in each area of intervention. The microprofile developed in Figure 4-2 for Hunter can be used as a prototype.

**1.** Establish the teacher's and student's preferred cognitive processing styles, as illustrated in Chapter 3.

**TABLE 5-7**
*Components of Instructional Discourse*

---

**Meeting classroom management abilities**

• Responds to teacher's signals of task reorienting.
• Reorients following interruption by another.
• Knows when to try for teacher's attention.
• Knows how to make appropriate tries for teacher's attention.
• Recognizes when she or he has not understood directions or content.
• Knows how and when to ask for clarification.
• Can participate in teacher-led classroom discussions without being distracted; can pass a turn or guess appropriately; can share the right amount of information during a turn; can make relevant and logical comments; can shift attention to others during their turns.
• Follows classroom rules (both spoken and unspoken) and routines.
• Organizes self to participate in the learning process (e.g., brings materials, does homework, prepares for tests, etc.).
• "Reads" the teacher's moods and attitudes appropriately.

**Peer interaction abilities**

• Can solicit help in acceptable ways and times.
• Can give appropriate help to classmates.
• Can resolve social conflict acceptably.
• Can participate in group decision-making through appropriate conversational rules of turn-taking, obtaining and keeping floor, yielding floor, etc.

**Instructional language abilities**

• Is metalinguistic
• Has strategies for learning specific content vocabulary, e.g., science or math terms.
• Has strategies for correcting misunderstood content information.
• Can successfully access textbook language.

---

Based on Nelson (in press).

**2.** Describe the teacher's learning profile, again as shown in Chapter 3.

**3.** Question language intervention choices, as discussed in Chapter 4.

**4.** Understand task complexity, as shown in Chapter 4.

**5.** Describe the student's learning profile with particular emphasis on the linguistic. Using Hunter, whose profile we constructed in Chapter 4 (Figure 4-1), we can summarize the following strengths:

- High-print home (owns his own books; subscribes to magazines)
- Wide background knowledge
- Enjoys being read aloud to
- Was read aloud to with moderate frequency
- Good oral storytelling and retelling abilities
- Good vocabulary and knows how to find definitions of unfamiliar words
- Enjoys different types of stories: myths, biographies, fiction, fantasies, etc.
- Enjoys making up own stories for dictation
- Can copy, albeit laboriously, teacher's copy of his orally told story
- Understands conventions of dialogue: changes speech and voice registers for different characters
- Good ability to take other's perspective: can hypothesize about how different characters might think and feel
- Excellent sense of humor
- Understands verbal humor and synonyms

Hunter's profile also shows these relative weaknesses:

- Inability to decode utilizing phonics beyond very simple rules
- Poor spelling
- Small sight word vocabulary
- Easily frustrated with unfamiliar text
- Low ability to apprehend nonstory narrative discourse such as expository discourse
- Unable to read grade-level content information in science, math, and social studies
- Difficulty with classroom management language

**6.** Expose the student to high quality literature. This entails someone reading aloud to the student, be it parent, sibling, peer, older student, teacher, classroom aide, clinician, or some combination of these. Van Dongen and Westby (1986) list a wide variety of quality books for children, and Jim Trelease's *The Read-Aloud Handbook* (1985) includes an annotated listing of various narrative types along with age and interest levels. Exposing the student to high-quality literature also involves providing adult models — people who value good literature, who talk about it, who read it, who share it with others, and who are visible in their interactions with literature. Van Dongen and Westby (1986) argue that exposing children to high-quality literature has an added benefit: it provides an aesthetic experience for children that is virtually nonexistent when they are confined to basal readers. Van Dongen and Westby go on to state that, in their efforts to simplify tasks, the authors of basal readers eliminate the aesthetic. Thus, they remove the "reward" of narrative — the joy in discovering its structure(s) and meaning(s).

**7.** As an adjunct to exposing children to high-quality literature, begin pointing out the macrostructure characteristics — *but not to the detriment of the story and the aesthetic experience of apprehending it.* Especially with younger children, it is important to maintain the process of experiencing the aesthetic. Older students can compare narrative and expository texts (see Chapters 3 and 6). Older students can also learn about cohesion in both narrative and expository discourse (see Chapter 6). When focusing on macrostructure characteristics, do not further decontextualize language, but rather begin making explicit who did what, who felt which ways, what happened, where the events occurred, and how the story ended.

Table 5–8 shows the typical macrostructure characteristics of various types of narratives, accompanied by the types of questions and comments a teacher or clinician can use to focus the student's attention on the narrative structures. The goal here is to lead the student to an understanding of both the content and the structure of narrative. Van Dongen and Westby (1986) state that understanding the structures authors use in narratives affords children an opportunity to comprehend the structures their culture places on experiences, to interpret these cultural structures, and to understand them. In fact, encounters with literature allow children to "bring narrative structures to their own personal experiences and to their reading of literary work years later" (Van Dongen & Westby, 1986, p. 79).

**8.** Provide shared experiences, document them (with photos, for instance, or children's illustrations of shared experiences, such as field trips, assemblies, special events), and do group description or storytelling about the experiences. Write the group story or description in a special book accompanied by the documenting visuals (perhaps in a bound blank book). Make the class/group story and description book available as part of the reading or language center.

**9.** Using the shared experience approach mentioned above, have individual children dictate their own descriptions or stories for inclusion into their own special description and story book (again, a bound blank book). Have children illustrate their stories, or give children one of the documenting photos to glue in.

---

## SAMPLE LESSON PLANS

To focus more specifically on the story grammar and event-chain components of narrative discourse, the following Cover Sheets and Lesson Plans are offered. The plans are not designed as recipes for every student. Rather, they are offered as models to assist in devising specific intervention plans.

**TABLE 5-8**

*Macrostructure Characteristics of Narrative Types*

| Narrative Type | Macrostructure Characteristics | Questions or Comments to Highlight |
| --- | --- | --- |
| *Fictional story* | Setting | Where does the story take place? |
| | Characters | Who is the story talking about? |
| | External attempts | What happended in this story? |
| | Internal attempts | How did the character feel? |
| | Consequences | What happened at the end? |
| | Outcome | What did the character feel at the end? |
| *Expository* * | First-level organizers | Find the following: title, table of contents, index, chapter titles. |
| | Second-level organizers | Find the boldface titles and subtitles; identify the topic paragraph. |
| *Poetry* | Meter | Is there a rhythm? What is it? |
| | Stanzas | Are there "clumps" of lines together? Where? (For more advanced students, ask if there are a certain number of syllables per stanza). |
| | Rhyming | Do some words rhyme? Which ones? Where are they? |
| *Drama* | Dramatis personae | Who is this play about? |
| | Setting | Where does the action take place? How do you know? |
| | Act structure | Are there noticeable episodes or acts? What are they? How do you know? |
| | Scenes | Are there different clumps of action within acts? How do you know? |
| | Music | Is there any music with this play? What is it there for? |

* See Appendix B for the complete organizational characteristics of expository discourse.

---

# COVER SHEET FOR
# NARRATIVE DISCOURSE: FICTION

*Theoretical Principle*
Development of knowledge about narrative discourse for fiction unfolds over time; children's fictional narratives show developmental changes of structure.

*Type of Strategy*
Top-down: focus on macrostructure characteristics

*Type of Language*
Discourse: focus on fictional narrative structures

*Clinician/Educator Questions*
1. Why have I chosen these particular activities?
2. Is the subject ready for this level and type of discourse?
3. Am I prepared to alter the program if the subject has difficulty?
4. Are these activities related to the subject's classroom learning needs?
5. Are the stories within the student's knowledge repertoire? — i.e., does the student have the requisite background knowledge and knowledge about causality?

---

Using this cover sheet, we can generate the following lesson plan.

---

# SAMPLE LESSON PLAN FOR
# NARRATIVE DISCOURSE: FICTION

**Target on Story Grammar Elements
and Event Chain Causality**
Helps student learn the important components of fictional narratives. This activity is done to help the student master the macrostructure characteristics of fictional narrative discourse.

*Narrative Forms Targeted*
*Setting:* Where and when does this story take place?

*(continued)*

*Characters:* Who is this story about? How do they feel?
*Episodes:* What happens in this story?
*Conclusion:* How do the events turn out in this story? How do the characters feel at the end?
*Point of view:* Who tells this story?

*Specific Sequence*
Begin with macrostructure level, identifying the global components. Look for microstructure identifiers, such as proper names, locations, dates, personal pronouns, etc.

*Strategies Facilitated*
Top-down: stories have discernible structures with signal words marking them.

*Special Instructions*
These strategies facilitate top-down processing. For the bottom-up learner, begin at the microstructure level, identifying specific linguistic markers.

*Tasks and Materials*
Use high-quality children's fictional literature (see Van Dongen & Westby, 1986) and classroom texts. *Clinician must work with classroom teacher.*

A similar format is used to develop a cover sheet and lesson plan for expository narrative text.

# COVER SHEET FOR
# EXPOSITORY NARRATIVE DISCOURSE

*Theoretical Principle*
Expository text is more abstract and requires knowledge about hierarchically arranged patterns of organization.

*Type of Strategy*
Top-down or bottom-up

*Type of Language*
Discourse focus: expository discourse organizers at macrostructure and microstructure levels

*(continued)*

## COVER SHEET FOR EXPOSITORY
## NARRATIVE DISCOURSE *(continued)*

*Clinician/Educator Questions*
1. Why have I chosen these particular activities?
2. Is the student ready for this type and level of discourse?
3. Am I prepared to alter the plan if the student has difficulty?
4. Are these activities related to the student's classroom learning needs? Am I using materials and structures that will enhance her or his learning?
5. Are the chapters/articles within the student's knowledge repertoire? Does she or he possess the requisite background knowledge of general information and causality?

This cover sheet generates the following sample lesson plan.

## SAMPLE LESSON PLAN FOR
## EXPOSITORY NARRATIVE STRUCTURE

**Target on Macrostructure Characteristics of Expository Text**
Helps student learn the salient organizational features of expository text. This activity is done to help the student master the macrostructure characteristics of expository text.

*Expository Forms Targeted*
*Primary level organizers:* title, major headings.
*Secondary level organizers:* major boldface headings.
*Tertiary level organizers:* topic paragraphs.

*Specific Sequence*
Begin with primary level organizers and have student guess what the chapter/article is about. Move to the secondary level with updated guess about gist. Move to the tertiary level with updated guess incorporating specific detail. Include microstructure information such as *first, second, next, last, finally; so, so that, because of, as a result of, in order to, since; different from, same as, alike, similar to, resembles, compared to, unlike; a*

*(continued)*

*problem is, a solution is, the problem is solved by.* (See also Chapter 8 for expository text mapping suggestions.)

*Strategies Targeted*
Abstraction of expository organizational features.

*Special Instructions*
These strategies are top-down, macrostructure strategies. For bottom-up learners, go to the microstructure features first to point out how to move to the more abstract organizational patterns.

*Tasks and Materials*
Use high-quality children's expository literature. *Again, clinician must work with the classroom teacher.*

## INTERVENTION STRATEGIES FOR INSTRUCTIONAL DISCOURSE

There are some general practices teachers and clinicians can employ in their efforts to assist students in learning about instructional discourse and how to survive in classrooms:

1. Do I utilize questioning as a primary part of my instructional language?
2. Do I assume that my students can comprehend the questions I ask?
3. Do I understand the cognitive load of instructional questioning?
4. Am I aware of the perceptual-verbal distance continuum inherent in instructional questioning? Do I understand that requesting students to label is perceptually less complex than asking them to state how things are alike or different?
5. Do I understand the simplification process that is required in matching my instructional language to the student's perceptual-verbal level?
6. Do I balance the amount of comments and obliges used with students, and am I sensitive to the levels of discourse used for comment and oblige forms (see Chapter 3)?
7. Do I understand that asking students to make judgments about language in any form implies metalinguistic awareness?
8. Do I construct my intervention plans so that I have translated the student's weakness into a plan that forces the student to use the very ability or skill I have determined she or he lacks?
9. Do I recontextualize my instructional discourse so that my language is accompanied by contextual information? Do I make clear

to the student exactly what I am referring to, in terms of topic, specific references, and inferences?

10. Am I aware of the powerful personal-social aspect of instructional discourse? Do I focus exclusively on the cognitive-linguistic aspects?

Using this checklist as a guideline for our intervention plans, we devised the following Cover Sheets and Lesson Plans. They follow Nelson's three-part model of instructional discourse (in press).

---

## COVER SHEET FOR INSTRUCTIONAL DISCOURSE: CLASSROOM MANAGEMENT

*Theoretical Principle*
Children must be pragmatic (and metapragmatic by upper elementary grades) in order to comprehend the goings-on of the typical classroom. In addition, children must possess some degree of metacognitive and metalinguistic awareness in order to understand communications (both verbal and nonverbal) about classroom management.

*Type of Strategy*
Top-down or bottom-up, depending on student preference

*Type of Language*
Discourse: focus on instructional-classroom management.

*Clinician/Educator Questions*
1. Why have I chosen these particular activities?
2. Is the student developmentally and socially ready for this type of discourse?
3. Am I prepared to alter the program if the student has difficulty?
4. Are these activities appropriate for the student's classroom needs?
5. Are these classroom management behaviors typical of most of the student's classroom needs?

---

Using this cover sheet leads to the following lesson plan.

# SAMPLE LESSON PLAN
# FOR INSTRUCTIONAL DISCOURSE:
# CLASSROOM MANAGEMENT LANGUAGE

**Target on the Verbal and Nonverbal Cues
Signaling Classroom Management Demands**
Helps the student learn what the teacher is signaling, how to indicate her or his own understanding or misunderstanding, how to participate in classroom discussions, how to understand and follow classroom routines and rules (whether spoken or not), and how to organize for successful classroom participation. This activity is done to help the student master the verbal and nonverbal cues signaling classroom processes.

*Instructional Forms Targeted*
Teacher's verbal and nonverbal signals; stated and nonstated classroom rules; self-understanding statements; self-organizing language forms.

*Specific Sequence*
Depends on top-down or bottom-up style preference: with top-down, begin with focus on student's summary of what appears to be taking place in the classroom. With bottom-up, begin with focus on specific examples of classroom management communication.

*Strategies Facilitated*
Top-down or bottom-up.

*Special Instructions*
These strategies require some metacognitive and metalinguistic awareness. Assess student's level of awareness before planning specific forms and sequences.

*Tasks and Materials*
Use video- or audiotapes of actual classroom interactions. In a consultative model, practitioner can provide classroom teacher with specific strategies for use with identified student. Might also want to assist teacher in analyzing her or his language use in classroom management situations.

## COVER SHEET FOR INSTRUCTIONAL DISCOURSE: PEER INTERACTIONS

*Theoretical Principle*
Children develop pragmatic and metapragmatic awareness of appropriate and relevant communicative strategies for peer interactions. By fifth grade, most students have acquired a set of successful peer-interaction strategies.

*Type of Strategy*
Top-down or bottom-up, depending on cognitive processing preference of student

*Type of Language*
Discourse: focus on instructional-peer interactions

*Clinician/Educator Questions*
1. Why have I chosen these particular activities?
2. Does the student need this type of instructional discourse intervention?
3. Am I prepared to alter the program if the student has difficulty?
4. Are these communicative forms and strategies within the student's developmental abilities?
5. Are these activities relevant to the student's classroom needs, both personally and linguistically?

The following lesson plan was generated from this cover sheet.

## SAMPLE LESSON PLAN FOR INSTRUCTIONAL DISCOURSE: PEER INTERACTIONS

**Target on Peer Interaction Communication Strategies**
Helps the student learn effective strategies for communicating with peers during peer-learning tasks. This activity is done to help the student master the pragmatic and metapragmatic aspects of communicating with peers in cooperative classroom activities.

*(continued)*

---

*Instructional Forms Targeted*
Request and response to peer requests during cooperative learning activities: soliciting help; responding to requests for help; helping classmates; participating in group decision-making; altering language forms and intents; appropriately given peer feedback (tacit or explicit).

*Specific Sequence*
Top-down: begin with overview of peer interactions, statements of goal in cooperative peer tasks, and statements of self-learning needs in such tasks. Bottom-up: begin with specific language forms and their immediate consequences. Choose those which seem to be most obvious to observe.

*Strategies Facilitated*
Top-down (metacognitive and metapragmatic to cognitive and pragmatic levels) or bottom-up (cognitive and pragmatic to metacognitive and metapragmatic levels).

*Special Instructions*
These strategies require at least a beginning awareness of metacognitive, metalinguistic, and metapragmatic aspects of classroom interactions with peers.

*Tasks and Materials*
Use of video- or audiotaped observations of student in classroom interactions with peers in cooperative learning task. In consultative model, provide classroom teacher with specific intervention suggestions for incorporation within the classroom.

---

To begin intervention focused on the actual instructional language used to convey content and the learning processes thought to aid in learning that content, the following cover sheet and sample lesson plan can be used.

---

## COVER SHEET FOR INSTRUCTIONAL DISCOURSE: INSTRUCTIONAL LANGUAGE

*Theoretical Principle*
To understand instructional language, children must have begun to develop metalinguistic awareness, strategies for learn-

*(continued)*

---

## COVER SHEET FOR INSTRUCTIONAL DISCOURSE: INSTRUCTIONAL LANGUAGE
*(continued)*

*Theoretical Principle (continued)*
ing specific content vocabulary, and strategies for correcting misunderstood content information and must be able to successfully access textbook language.

*Type of Strategy*
Top-down or bottom-up

*Type of Language*
Discourse: focus on instructional — the language of instruction.

*Clinician/Educator Questions*
1. Why have I chosen these particular activities and strategies?
2. Is the student ready for this type and level of discourse?
3. Am I prepared to alter the plan if the student experiences difficulty?
4. Are these strategies related to the student's classroom needs?
5. Are these strategies likely to be useful across content areas, or are they specific to one content area?
6. Does the student possess enough metalinguistic and metacognitive awareness to understand these strategies?

---

The following sample lesson plan describes an intervention plan based on this cover sheet.

---

## SAMPLE LESSON PLAN FOR INSTRUCTIONAL DISCOURSE: THE LANGUAGE OF INSTRUCTION

**Target on Metacognitive and Metalinguistic Strategies Required to Access and Understand Both Content and Instructions About the Learning Processes Involved in Learning Content**
Helps students learn strategies for organizing their learning processes. Helps students focus on how to access content areas.

*(continued)*

---

*Discourse Forms Targeted*
Organizational characteristics of textbooks (see sample lesson plan for expository narrative discourse pp. 106 & 107, for comparison) across content areas such as math, social science, science, etc.

*Specific Sequence*
Top-down or bottom-up. For top-down, begin with first-level organizational cues such as titles, headings, boldface print. Move to more detailed level — from broad picture to specific detail. For bottom-up, begin with small units such as paragraphs or sentences. Point out main ideas, instructions, definitions, explanations. Educator might want to begin with cohesion cues (see Chapter 6 for detail). Move from detail to broad picture.

*Strategies Targeted*
Accessing pertinent information in specific content areas. Accessing strategies for finding definitions and for learning new vocabulary. Accessing strategies for comprehending teacher's language when teaching new content.

*Special Instructions*
These strategies require metacognitive and metalinguistic awareness. Assess student's levels of awareness before designing intervention plan.

*Tasks and Materials*
Use student's textbooks and class materials. Use video- or audiotapes of classroom teacher's language when teaching students how to learn new content. In consultative model, assist the classroom teacher in analyzing her or his own language assumptions when teaching new content.

# CHAPTER 6

## Inference and Cohesion

Emma observed each passenger who came aboard. Every one of them was welcomed by her cheerful greeting. Looking into both mirrors, Emma drove the yellow vehicle back onto the country road. (Johnson & von Hoff Johnson, 1986, p. 622)

Each of us probably made an inference about Emma's occupation after we read the first sentence. Perhaps we thought initially that she was a flight attendant. After reading further, we may have changed or modified our initial inference and decided that she is a school bus driver. Regardless of our choice, the example shows that we were actively involved in the comprehension process (Bransford & Johnson, 1973). We linked the sentences together by inferring relations among them from our knowledge of the world and prior experience. This process of using prior experience and knowledge is goodness-of-fit analyzing (see Chapter 2). Bransford and Johnson (1973) call it constructive comprehension. As discussed later, successful discourse exchanges often occur when listeners fill in message details (Hoskins, 1987a).

Consider the next passage, taken from the Spache (1981) Diagnostic Reading Scales as quoted by Westby (1984):

Mary was on her way to school.
She came to the corner.
She saw a red light.
Then she saw a green light.
Then she went on to school.

Questions such as, "What was the girl's name?" and "Where was the girl going?" relate to information that is explicitly given in the text. In essence, one can engage in a literal translation of the items to get the correct answers. On the other hand, questions such as, "What did she do when she came to the corner?" and "Why did she stop at the corner?" are derived from implicitly stated information. The last two questions require inferential processing (or reading between the lines) and show, as Westby (1984) says, that "meaning exists in the text that is not present in the component parts" (p. 103).

The previous chapter focused on the larger pieces, or the macro-structure aspects, of discourse. This chapter and the chapter that follows discuss some of the component parts of discourse. These parts include the organization of sentences and their linguistic connectives — part of what Liles (1987) calls the local level of discourse processing. Some people refer to this level as the microstructure level of discourse.

## THEORETICAL BASES FOR INTERVENTION SEQUENCES AND PROCEDURES

### Inference

Proficient listeners and readers make inferences. They use their background knowledge, experience, and understanding of real-world relations to read between the lines. Klein-Konigsberg (1984) points out that inferential processing is an active process, a process of expansion, even a process of survival. We construct associations and we make things fit together when trying to organize, absorb, and retain information (Johnson and von Hoff Johnson, 1986, p. 622). We might ask ourselves, as we did in Chapters 3 and 4, how might the research help us in our work with children? What does the research say about memory organization and learning strategies? What are some of the developmental milestones that might help us understand the various sequences and recommendations that appear on Individual Education Programs?

The literature relating to inferential processing includes studies of adults and children. We know more about mature patterns than we know about developing patterns. Looking across the inferential literature, a number of patterns emerge. First, adults and children often have difficulty separating inferred information from literal or given information in memory tasks (Ackerman, 1986; Klein-Konigsberg, 1984; Paris & Lindauer, 1976). Second, children make inferences relatively early (at six years old) but they become much more comfortable with inferential processing during their school years, after they are seven or eight years old (Blanchowicz, 1978; Westby, 1984). Third, learning-and reading-disabled students may not necessarily be incapable of inferential processing but they may need more exposure to, and direction about, when and why inferencing would be appropriate (Smith & Elkins, 1985; Taylor & Williams, 1983).

The classic studies by Bransford and colleagues (Bransford et al., 1972; Bransford & Franks, 1971; Bransford & Johnson, 1973) were among the earliest to demonstrate inferential processing in memory. Their classic "turtle" study (Bransford et al., 1972) demonstrated how inferences were used in the normal course of language processing. Bransford et al. (1972) found that their adult subjects confused sentences such as, "Three turtles rested on the floating log and a fish swam beneath *it*" and "Three turtles rested on a floating log and a fish swam beneath *them*" on memory tasks. Subjects heard the first sentence and then were given the second sentence after a three-minute break. Subjects thought the two sentences were identical. Through careful construction of sentence lists, the experimenters ruled out the possibility that subjects were forgetting or confusing the pronouns (*it* versus *them*). Bransford et al. (1972) concluded that the confusion between the two sentences was the result of normal inferential processing. Subjects infer (while processing) that if turtles are on the log and the fish swims under the log (under *it*), it logically follows that the fish also swims beneath the turtles (under *them*). (The reader is directed to the original article for details of the study and to Klein-Konigsberg, 1984, and Johnson-Laird, 1983, for additional information about adult processing.)

Blanchowicz (1978) took the Bransford et al. (1972) investigation a bit further. She studied elementary school children's inferential processing in a silent reading task. She was interested in second graders (7-1 through 7-8), fifth graders (10-1 through 10-11), and seventh graders (12-2 through 12-10). Blanchowicz had her subjects read ten short paragraphs silently. The paragraphs consisted of three short sentences (as adapted from Paris & Carter, 1973). Sentences 1 to 3 are examples (Blanchowicz, 1978, p. 192):

1. The birds sat on the branch.
2. A hawk flew over it.
3. The birds were robins.

The subjects were told to read the paragraphs carefully. They were told that they would be asked questions about what they read later. After reading the test paragraphs, the subjects were involved in a three-minute transition task. They were then given additional instructions: "You will now read some sentences. If you saw a sentence in the stories you read, mark *yes*. Mark *yes* only for those sentences that are exactly the same as the ones you read in the stories." Sample recognition items are presented in sentences 4 to 7 (Blanchowicz, 1978, p. 192). Sentence 6 represented information that was not given in the stories but that is a true inference from the given information. That is, if the birds are on a branch and a hawk flew over it, the hawk must also fly over the birds.

4. The birds sat on the branch (*true premise; given info.*).
5. The hawk flew under it (*false premise; not given*).
6. The hawk flew over the birds (*true inference*).
7. A hawk flew under the birds (*false inference*).

Blanchowicz (1978) found that there was a strong tendency for all subjects to mark *yes* for the true inferences. These inferential errors, according to Blanchowicz, reflect the normal course of processing. In fact, second graders made the same kinds of recognition errors as fifth and seventh graders. Blanchowicz goes on to say that the inferential errors could not be attributable to poor memory because the true and false inferences had the same length and syntactic construction as the true and false premises.

Additional research is available on children's inferential processing. The studies provide information about developmental expectations. They also show that children's processing is active and dynamic. Paris and Lindauer (1976) studied children between the ages of six and 12 years. The children were told that they would be given a list of sentences. They were told to try to remember as many sentences as they could and that the examiner would give them a hint to help them remember the sentences. Sentences were constructed so that they contained what Paris and Lindauer (1976) called explicitly and implicitly stated instruments. Sentences 8 and 9 are examples:

8. The workman dug a hole in the ground with a shovel.
9. My father struck his finger instead of the nail.

Sentence 8 contains an explicitly stated instrument. The instrument is a shovel. Sentence 9 contains an implicit instrument, a hammer. The children were given instrument prompts as retrieval cues four minutes after they heard the list of sentences. The prompt or sentence 8 would be *shovel* and the prompt for sentence 9 would be *hammer*. Paris and Lindauaer (1976) hypothesized that if children were inferencing spontaneously, then explicit and implicit prompts would be equally effective. The results indicated that the six to eight year old subjects recalled more sentences with explicit instrument prompts.

Ten and eleven year old subjects, on the other hand, recalled explicit and implicit sentences equally well. The results provided some information about the possibility of developmental changes in inferential processing — on a sentence memory task with instrument references.

Paris and Lindauer (1976) instructed the six and seven year olds to act out a new list of sentences to explore the possibility that children younger than ten or 11 use inferential processing. The researchers believed that gesture might force the children to process the implied instrument. The sentence memory task was repeated with a new list of explicit and implied instrument sentences. The results were dramatic. The younger children, when prompted with explicit and implicit prompts, performed as well as the older children under the gesture condition. The finding that gesture encourages inferential processing has practical implications that might warrant further consideration.

Paris, Lindauer, and Cox (1977) were concerned about the generalizability of the Paris and Lindauer (1976) findings because there are so many types of inferences. Paris et al. (1977) completed another study using a sentence memory and prompting task similar to the one employed by Paris and Lindauer (1976) with different inferential sentences. They used sentences with explicitly and implicitly stated consequences of actions. Sentences 10 and 11 (Paris et al., 1977) are examples:

10. The kitten tipped over the dish and spilled the milk.
11. Mary dropped the vase of flowers.

Sentence 10 contains an explicit consequence; i.e., the milk was spilled. Sentence 11 contains an implicit consequence; i.e., the vase broke. Six and seven year olds, 11 year olds, and adults were given lists of sentences. They were asked to recall the sentences after being given no cues, after explicit cues, and after implied cues. The results indicated that the 11 year olds and the adults recalled sentences with explicit and implicit cues equally well. The "equally well" result required some qualification in that more sentences were recalled with explicit consequences, but the differences between explicit and implicit sentences were not significant for the older subjects. On the other hand, the performance of six and seven year olds was significantly better on the explicit sentences.

Similar to the Paris and Lindauer (1976) study, Paris et al. (1977) asked whether younger children could be "forced" to make inferences. In the second part of the experiment, they asked the younger children to make up little stories for the stimulus sentences. The results indicated that the story-generation task facilitated inferential processing for consequences even in the youngest subjects (the six year olds).

When children constructed stories that included inferred consequences, they recalled explicit and implicit cued sentences equally well. Recent research by Miller and Pressley (1987) supports the idea that inferential processing can be facilitated in different ways, e.g., with gesture, with stories, and with pictures, but indicates that inferential processing involves many developmental changes with significant improvements noted around age ten.

Studies by Liben and Posnansky (1977), Prawat and Jones (1977), Johnson and Smith (1981), Scannell-Miller (1982), Schmidt and Paris (1983), Schmidt, Schmidt, and Tomalis (1984), and Crais and Chapman (1987), to name only a few, provide us with information about inferential processing in both nondisabled and language learning disabled children. Prawat and Jones (1977), for example, replicated the Paris and Carter (1973) study with kindergarten and second- and fourth-grade students with and without learning disabilities. (The Blanchowicz, 1978, reading study was presented earlier and is a follow-up of the Paris and Carter, 1973, study.) Prawat and Jones (1977) found that their subjects also made constructive memory errors. Subjects thought that true inference sentences appeared in the stories. Prawat and Jones note that, by Grade 4 (at about nine years old), inferential errors are particularly strong in both nondisabled and learning-disabled populations.

Scannell-Miller (1982) notes some developmental lags in learning-disabled students' abilities to perform on sentence memory tasks with instrument inferences, but also notes that learning-disabled students are not without inferencing ability. Crais and Chapman (1987) point out that both nondisabled and learning-disabled children have more difficulty answering inferential questions than literal questions about stories but they go on to say that making inferences *across* sentences is more difficult than making inferences *within* sentences. Crais and Chapman (1987) remind us to consider carefully the type of inferencing being studied and the materials used to test and observe inferential processing. We might keep Crais and Chapman's point in mind when developing intervention activities for younger children and children with language learning disabilities.

Wong (1980) says that studies of sentence memory, although artificial, may help us understand some of the strategies available and used by learning-disabled students. Wong also says that we must go beyond reporting the results of studies and consider how we might help students in trouble. Wong replicated the Paris et al. (1977) study using sentences with explicitly and implicitly stated consequences with successful readers and learning-disabled students in Grade 2 (seven years old) and Grade 6 (eleven years old). As might be predicted, good readers recalled significantly more sentences with implicit consequence prompts than the learning-disabled readers at each grade level. Wong (1980) says that the good readers appeared to employ inferential strategies spontaneously. He hypothesized that the learning-disabled students have the ability to infer but that they need more direction about the nature and appropriateness of inferential strategies. To test the hypothesis, Wong (1980) used a question-prompt procedure with learning-disabled students. Instead of having them listen to the entire list of explicit and implicit sentences, he questioned them after each sentence by asking, "What do you think happens next?" Following a four-minute interval, the learning-disabled subjects were given both explicit and implicit prompt cues to recall the sentence. The results showed that the question-prompt procedure significantly increased the comprehension and retention of implied information in the learning-disabled subjects. The results, according to Wong (1980), suggest that some learning-disabled students have constructive and inferential strategies in their repertoires but they need specific help in applying these strategies.

Roth (1987) indicates that we still have much to learn about inferential processing in language learning disabled students. She cautions us about making statements regarding what children can and cannot do prematurely. Roth (1987) points out that we know relatively little about children's abilities to integrate pieces of information into a unified whole. For example, she says that the interaction between people's knowledge of story structures (the macrostructures discussed in Chapter 5) and their syntactic-structural abilities (the microstructure discussed next and in Chapter 7) is not well understood. Roth's research (1987) suggests that some learning-disabled students retell narratives with the same overall accuracy and story organization as their nondisabled peers but their narratives seem impoverished because they contain fewer details, fewer and less precise linguistic markers for time, space, and causal relations, and fewer phrase modifiers. In other words, many of Roth's learning-disabled subjects had the story gestalt, but they lacked the linguistic sophistication to fill in the narrative skeletons they had created. Liles (1987) has recently alerted us to a similar notion: i.e., the study of linguistic cohesion represents an important component of narrative and instructional discourse.

## Linguistic Cohesion and Discourse

In order to be meaningful, connected discourse must be *coherent.* Blank and Marquis (1987) write that "coherence is the linking of individual utterances ... (or sentences) ... that relate to each other in an orderly manner" (p. 17). They go on to say that coherence is not always based directly on what is said or written. Proficient listeners and readers, as pointed out throughout this chapter, make rapid shifts across sentences, meshing explicit and implicit information with relative ease (Blank & Marquis, 1987, p. 18). Skilled language users often perceive coherence in uneven or poorly structured conversations, paragraphs, stories, and other types of text by using some of the inferential strategies described earlier. Skilled communicators make implicit connections and fill in the missing pieces as a matter of course.

Topic coherence can be made explicit in both oral and written discourse through the use of meaningful and structural ties (Ripich & Spinelli, 1985). For example, we might add information to statements other people make during conversations, we might restate points to get meanings across, and we might make statements that are relevant to the topic to maintain coherence. We also use specific linguistic devices to make meaning more explicit and to express connections that go beyond utterance and sentence boundaries. Halliday and Hasan (1976) used the term *cohesive devices* to describe some of the structural aspects of discourse that contribute to a text's coherence. They used the term *text* to refer to spoken or written passages that form unified or meaningful wholes (from Liles, 1985).

According to Mentis and Prutting (1987), "cohesion is achieved through the linguistic interdependence of elements within a text" (p. 88). Cohesion arises at any point in a text where the meaning of some aspect of text can only be determined by reference to information contained somewhere else in the text (Blank & Marquis, 1987; Mentis & Prutting, 1987; Smith & Elkins, 1985). For example, the sentence pair, "I saw George yesterday. He is a nice guy." is linked by the noun and pronoun. The two sentences form a unified whole because *George* and *he* refer to the same person. Moreover, the meaning of *he* is determined by information in the previous sentence. The *George-he* type of cohesion is called *referential cohesion.* In the sentences, "He's a fine boy. He's one of the brightest kids I know," *boy* and *kid* provide *lexical cohesion. Boy* and *kid* are the same person, and the text would be misunderstood unless the relationship between words is noted and processed. "He" also remains part of the cohesion equation which may make the sentence particularly difficult.

Halliday and Hasan (1976) describe five major types of cohesion. In addition to referential and lexical cohesion, they describe substitution, ellipsis, and conjunction. Table 6-1 provides examples from each of the cohesive categories as adapted by Mentis and Prutting (1987) and Gregg (1986).

Stoel-Gammon and Hedberg (1984) suggest a tentative developmental progression that includes referential and lexical cohesion first, followed by conjunction, substitution, and ellipsis. Liles (1985) points

**TABLE 6-1**

*Cohesive Devices*

---

**References:** a semantic relation whereby the information needed for interpretation is found elsewhere in the text; cohesion lies in the continuity of reference, as the same thing is referred to more than once in the discourse (Mentis & Prutting, 1987, p. 96):

*Pronominal:* Mary is a teacher. *She* teaches second grade.

*Demonstrative:* Tom is in his *office.* You can find him *there.*

*Comparative:* John wore his *red* shirt. His *other* shirts were dirty.

**Lexical:** a relation that is achieved through vocabulary selection; cohesion is formed by using the same word, a synonym, a superordinate word, and a general item or an associated word.

*Same word:* We went to the *store.* The *store* was crowded.

*Synonym:* The *boy* is climbing the tree. The *child* could fall.

*Superordinate:* Take some *apples.* The *fruit* is delicious.

*General word:* I gave *Tom* the keys. The *jerk* lost them.

*Associated word:* I told her to call the *doctor.* She was *ill.*

**Conjunction:** a logical relation expressed between clauses that signals how what is to follow is related to what has gone before; cohesion is achieved by using various connectors that show relationships between statements.

*Additive:* I fell. *And* everything fell on top of me.

*Adversative:* All the numbers looked perfect. *Yet* the conclusion seemed incorrect.

*Causal:* I did not know. *Otherwise,* I would have stayed away.

*Temporal:* She opened the door. *Then* she put her coat away.

*Continuative:* You needn't apologize. *After all,* you did not know what happened.

Conjunctive ties include many transitional words that express a variety of relations (as pointed out by Gregg, 1986):

*Consequence: therefore, then, thus, hence, accordingly*

*Likeness: likewise, similarly*

*Contrast: but, however, nevertheless, on the other hand, yet* (adversative)

*Amplification: and, again, in addition, further, more over, also, too* (additive)

*Example: for instance, for example*

*Sequence: first, second, finally* (temporal)

*Restatement: that is, in other words, to put it differently*

**Substitution:** the cohesive bond is established by the use of one word for another but repetition of the first term is avoided. The substituted word has the same structural function as that for which it substitutes (Mentis & Prutting, 1987, p. 96).

*Nominal:* I need a bigger *cup.* I'll get *one.*

*Clausal: They've lost them?* I regret *so.*

**Ellipsis:** cohesion is established by the deletion of a phrase or a word or a clause.

*Verbal:* Who's eating? I am (eating).

*Nominal:* What kind of ice cream do you want? Chocolate (ice cream).

*Clausal:* Has she done her exercises? She has (done her exercises).

---

Adapted from Gregg (1986) and Mentis and Prutting (1987).

out that, whereas many aspects of cohesion are evidenced by age six, cohesive adequacy may not develop until after a child is seven and a half years old. We should note that developmental information is somewhat limited and, as indicated in Chapter 5, milestones are available but must be interpreted with caution. Discourse situation and purpose, text genre, number of story episodes, among other variables, affect the number and type of cohesive devices used by children and adults (Liles, 1987; see Chapters 5 and 7).

A number of researchers have begun to consider cohesion in the discourse, narratives, and reading comprehension of nondisabled and language learning disabled subjects. We already mentioned Roth's research (1987), which indicated that structural ability interacted with learning-disabled students' storytelling performances. Liles (1985) also found that learning-disabled subjects between the ages of seven and ten years old differ from their nondisabled age-mates in their manner of cohesive organization and cohesive adequacy. She reports, for example, that the language-disabled subjects in her study used relatively fewer reference ties than the nondisabled subjects, possibly because referring back to characters and events in stories by using forms such as *he, she,* and *it* requires fairly sophisticated control over ideas and linguistic structure. She goes on to say that although the language-disabled children were able to alter their use of cohesive devices as a function of a listener's needs, they still had more difficulty keeping their stories coherent than their nondisabled counterparts. Liles suggests that we assess children's knowledge of story grammar as well as their facility with specific linguistic forms. She adds that "although poor story grammar knowledge may be a predictor of poor cohesion, good story grammar knowledge is not sufficient for good cohesion" (Liles, 1985, p. 130). As practitioners interested in helping students with both spoken and written text, we might indeed consider the role of cohesion in organization and retention (see also Liles, 1987; see Chapter 7).

In addition to Liles (1985, 1987), Ackerman (1986) has begun to consider the relations between cohesion and other aspects of organization and processing. Ackerman (1986) asks whether people's ability to make accurate causal inferences relates to their ability to recognize and understand linguistic cohesion. As shown in Chapter 5, children develop knowledge of causal relationships over time. It follows that, as their understanding of causal relations increases, their understanding of causal coherence increases as well. Ackerman (1986) also asks whether the structure of paragraphs could change inferential comprehension abilities. Would inferential abilities of young children improve if connections were made very explicitly in a spoken or written text, as some of the developmental research suggests?

Ackerman (1986) studied first graders (six year olds), fourth graders (nine year olds), and adults. He constructed 15 paragraphs with varying degrees of cohesion and relatedness. The paragraphs were read to subjects who then answered both detail and inference questions. Paragraph 1 (taken from Ackerman, 1986, p. 340), with the accompanying questions, provides an example of the way paragraphs could be constructed.

1. Nancy was working around the house.
2. Nancy washed five of her shirts and wanted to dry them on low heat.
3. She put the shirts in the dryer (*clue*).
4. She turned the dryer on (*clue*).
5. Nancy (or the girl) hung the shirts out on the line.
6. She finished up the rest of her chores.

*Fillers of various kinds:*
3a. She walked downstairs (*continues story*).
3b. She got into the car (*discontinues particular event*).
3c. The cat was on the porch (*background filler*).

*Questions:*
1. Did Nancy have five or three shirts washed? (*verbatim*)
2. Had she planned to hang the shirts on the line? (*related question*)
3. Was her clothes dryer broken or working well? (*plausible inference*)
4. Were her clothes too wet for the dryer? (*implausible*)

As can be seen from the example of paragraph 1, *Nancy* can be repeated or it can be substituted with a pronoun like *she* or the lexical item *girl*. We might also note that sentences 3 and 4 are clues because they set us up for what is going to happen. Ackerman also used paragraphs that included many fillers that clarified or obscured the main idea. (Additional examples from Ackerman, 1986, are provided in the intervention section.)

Ackerman (1986) reported a number of results. First, both the explicitness of cohesive cues and the amount of clue support affected story comprehension. The first graders answered detail and inferential questions more accurately when stories had explicit cohesive markers. Fourth graders and adults performed equally well on implicit and explicit stories. One-clue stories and lexical substitutions (*Nancy* followed by *the girl* followed by *she*) were the most difficult stories for the first graders. First graders performed better with name repetitions and with two-clue stories. Second, linguistic cohesion seems to be related to causal inferencing, but linguistic accuracy alone did not insure inferential processing. The listener has to recognize that there is a need to make an inference after cohesive ties have been established. For example, the listener must recognize that *Nancy* and *she* are the same person and that *she/Nancy* turned on the dryer and then put the clothes on the line. However, the listener still has to fill in the missing part, i.e., that the dryer must have been out of order. Third, fillers affected comprehension in different ways. Event interruptions affected causal inferencing and character discontinuity affected cohesion. Fourth, both first and fourth graders had more difficulty establishing causal relations than adults when the information in the stories was disorganized. These findings support the suggestion that children's ability to make causal inferences is tied to their developing knowledge of causal relations.

The Ackerman (1986) investigation reminds us that the study of discourse processing is indeed complex. He points out that conclusions about what children can and cannot do must be studied from many perspectives. This notion has certainly been stressed throughout the text. As practitioners, we might think about the structure and content of the materials we use with children. We might also think about the appropriateness of certain kinds of sentence work for the development of cohesion if we can apply that work to the broader purpose of helping students develop better comprehension and organizational strategies (see also Chapter 7). Although we should remain cautious about the findings reported in all of the studies mentioned, there is cause for optimism about the intervention possibilities they inspire.

## Where Does Theoretical Information Take Us?

Development involves a long and gradual series of changes. We know from the studies mentioned in Chapter 5 that children as young as four have story schemas. However, it is not until the age of five or six that they improve dramatically in their ability to create stories of their own. From the inference studies mentioned in this chapter, we know that children as young as six or seven are able to make inferences on sentence memory tasks, particularly when they are encouraged to do so (as with gesture, for example). By Grade 2, most children use their knowledge of the world to make inferences, as demonstrated by the Blanchowicz (1978) study discussed in the section on inference. However, many aspects of inferential processing continue to develop through the middle grades. Grade 2 students still have difficulty with certain types of discourse. They sometimes misinterpret dialogues, particularly when characters use pronouns that are embedded in their statements. Grade 4 students find expository text difficult. They often perform better when material is presented in narrative form. Fifth graders become much more proficient at inferential processing and they recognize well-formed information more quickly and accurately than their younger peers. However, it is not until Grades 6 and 7 that students make tremendous gains in their ability to *discuss* the significant (versus less significant) aspects of stories and expository information (Piccolo, 1987). As practitioners, we need to understand the nature and, importantly, the lateness of some of the acquisitions listed in this chapter and in other chapters. The milestones and age/grade-level differences are guidelines that must be applied carefully.

## INTERVENTION SUGGESTIONS

### Developing an Inferential Set

Hansen and Pearson (1983) offer general instructional guidelines that might be applicable across content areas. *Inferential set* involves the active use of one's background knowledge and prior information when approaching tasks. Hansen and Pearson (1983) say that students with learning and reading disabilities often make inferences in their nonschool lives, but they are "taught to learn new information (in school) by just remembering it" (Hansen & Pearson, 1983, p. 821). They add that poor students spend even less time in school on inferential types of learning because teachers frequently emphasize decoding and word identification skills and spend more time correcting students' errors. Hansen and Pearson (1983) propose that by helping students develop an inferential set for learning, we may be helping them develop a general strategy for the organization and retention of material.

Hansen and Pearson (1983) offer the following suggestions, which combine oral and written language. In the Hansen and Pearson approach, students talk about how their real-life experiences relate to written texts they use in class. Students answer (and discuss) inferential questions from their reading assignments. The following activities are included:

- Students listen to (or read) assigned stories. They discuss a significant aspect of the story that relates to one of their own experiences (e.g., a character has a problem that they have had). (*Personal experience used to make predictions.*)
- Students write down their answers to preselected questions that encourage inferential processing. (*Text material used.*)
- Students talk about what story characters might do. (*Text material used.*)
- Students compare answers about the preselected questions.
- Another question is chosen and students write down their answers.
- Students weave together their answers to emphasize the notion that readers can often facilitate comprehension if they weave information from their prior experiences into the text.

An example from Hansen and Pearson (1983) is as follows.

*Important idea* (selected by teacher or students): Sometimes people are embarrassed.

*Personal experience question:* Tell us about a time when you were embarrassed about the way you looked.

*Text question related to upcoming reading passage:* In our next story, there is a man who is embarrassed about the way he looks. What do you think is the thing that embarrasses him? (Students write down various answers that might include "ragged clothes," "cane," "gray hair," "wrinkles," etc.)

*Weave questions:* Let us put all our answers together (on the board or on a table if separate strips of paper were used by each student). How could our separate answers form a unified idea?

*Follow-up:* Students read the selection on their own. They discuss how ideas fit and why. Students read and discuss inferential reading comprehension questions for the assigned story.

Hansen and Pearson (1983) remind us that the purpose of any of these activities is to (1) make students aware of the importance of drawing inferences between new information and existing information (background knowledge that is in their heads); (2) help students discover, prior to reading (or listening), that their own predictions can be helpful when trying to comprehend text; and (3) improve students' abilities to handle inferential comprehension questions after reading the selections. Some of the activities presented in Chapter 5 also help students focus on the significant information in text and help them read between the lines (see the expository text outline in Appendix B; see Chapter 8).

Wallach and Lee (1982) offer the following suggestions as inspired by the classic chapter on comprehension by Bransford and Johnson (1973). Two paragraphs containing the same information are constructed. Students read (or listen to) the paragraphs. Group A is given one title and Group B is given another title before reading (or listening to) the paragraphs. Students then answer questions about the paragraphs. Consider the paragraph below from Bransford and Johnson (1973, p. 415).

The man stood before the mirror and combed his hair. He checked his face carefully for any places he might have missed shaving and then put on the conservative tie he had decided to wear. At breakfast, he studied the newspaper carefully and, over coffee, discussed the possibility of buying a new washing machine with his wife. Then he made several phone calls. As he was leaving the house he thought about the fact that his children would probably want to go to that private camp again this summer. When the car didn't start, he got out, slammed the door, and walked down to the bus stop in a very angry mood. Now he would be late.

Consider the paragraph again with two different titles: "The Unemployed Man" and "The Stock Broker." Now consider how the answers to questions would change based on the preselected titles. Inferential questions and the possible answers could include the following:

- Where is the man going? (*job interview or his office on Wall Street*)
- What section of the newspaper might he be reading (*want ads or financial section*)
- What do you think he's going to do about the washing machine and summer camp? (*he won't be able to afford them or he'll be able to afford them if the market is up*)
- What are some of the things he is concerned about? (*getting a job or the market prices today, etc.*)

Wallach and Lee have students dicuss the different types of inferences that could be made. They also have students rewrite (or restate) paragraphs in more explicit language. In the explicit-language activities, students add information to the text that the titles and their answers would dictate. The paragraphs used may vary, but the purpose of the activity remains the same, i.e., to help students develop an awareness of the different kinds of inferences possible and to help them become more actively involved in the comprehension process. Wallach and Lee suggest using passages from students' textbooks whenever possible.

Wallach and Lee-Schachter (1984) also use topic units with students. A topic might be sports. After a topic has been chosen, a number of activities are developed within the topic area. For example, a sports unit would include passages about more familiar sports (baseball, basketball, and football) and less familiar sports (curling, cricket, and polo). Next, paragraph-analysis activities (for ten and 11 years olds) might be used to encourage students to decide which sentence does not belong in a paragraph and why. Students would also be asked to think about substituting a sentence that might be more appropriate. An example from a paragraph (taken from Wallach & Lee, 1982, p. 109), is as follows.

A hockey team puts six men on the ice. Breakfast is their first meal of the day. There is a goalie, a center, a right wing, a left wing, a right defense, and a left defense.

Students also work on narrative and expository text comparisons with sports topics. Older students, who are ready for this level, are encouraged to discuss the differences between narrative and expository paragraphs. For example, comparisons could be made between paragraphs that involve a story about a hockey player (narrative form) and paragraphs that involve descriptions about the history of hockey (expository form). (See Chapter 3 selections, "Narrative Fox" and "Expository Fox," as additional examples.)

Johnson and von Hoff Johnson (1986) provide additional suggestions for the facilitation of inferential comprehension. They present a list of ten major inference types encountered by students in their elementary school reading books. Because their work was done with average readers in Grade 2 and above, it is important to remember to assess the background and language levels of students with language learning disabilities. The ten inference types outlined by Johnson and von Hoff Johnson (1986, p. 623) are as follows.

1. Location inferences (deciding place from clues given)
   *Example:* After check-in, the bellhop helped us carry our luggage to our room. Where are we?
2. Agent inferences (deciding occupation/role of "doer")
   *Example:* With clippers in one hand and scissors in the other, Chris approached the chair. What is Chris?
3. Time inferences (deciding when things occurred)
   *Example:* When the porch light burned out, darkness was total. When did this occur?
4. Action inferences (deciding activity)
   *Example:* George was gliding above the water. His form was perfect. What was George doing?
5. Instrument inferences (deciding tool or device)
   *Example:* With a steady hand, Dr. Hoff put the buzzing device on my tooth. What tool was he using?
6. Category inferences (deciding superstructure)
   *Example:* The Saab and Volvo were in the garage and the Audi was in front. These three are members of what category?
7. Object inferences (deciding thing being spoken about)
   *Example:*The gleaming giant had 18 wheels, and it towered above lesser vehicles on the turnpike. What is the gleaming giant?
8. Cause-effect inferences (deciding reason something happened or deciding the outcome; in this example the cause needs to be inferred)
   *Example:* In the morning, the trees were uprooted and some homes had lost their roofs. What caused this situation?
9. Problem-solution inferences (deciding about the situation or the consequence; in this example the solution must be inferred)
   *Example:* The side of Ken's face was swollen and his tooth throbbed. What should Ken do about this problem?
10. Feelings-attitudes inferences (deciding how/why characters are reacting/acting in certain ways)
    *Example:*While I marched past in the junior high band, my Dad cheered and his eyes filled up with tears. What feeling was Dad experiencing?

Johnson and von Hoff Johnson (1986) show how vocabulary and inferential comprehension might be combined in various activities. Students read (or listen to) a passage. The passage below represents an agent inference.

> Mr. Garcia looked at the group. Several hands were raised. Mr. Garcia put the chalk down and asked Janet to come to the board. Her job was to explain the new pass defense. (p. 624)

The teacher highlights important vocabulary. Highlighting might be accomplished with stress (if presented orally), by writing key words on the board, and by color-coding words in students' books. Key words for the agent passage might be: *group, chalk, board, pass defense* (the number of clues or key words can be modified according to the ages and abilities of students). Students guess the type of inference and supply an appropriate word for the implied information: Mr. Garcia is a coach.

Johnson and von Hoff Johnson (1986) suggest two follow-up activities for the inference activities we just presented. In the first follow-up activity, students analyze passages. They pick out key words and decide the type of inference the passage contains. In the next activity, students read individual sentences from passages (via an overhead projector or computer, etc.). The teacher tells them the kind of inference to make. Students are told they can retain, modify, or reject the inference. An example of the sentence-by-sentence activity (taken from Johnson & von Hoff Johnson, 1986, p. 625) is presented next.

> We discovered a pit.
> We came across a pit while we were exploring a wilderness area.
> It looked as though it had been there for a long time.
> After finishing the fruit, some litterbug must have thrown it on the ground.
> *Object:* the stone or pit of a fruit (as opposed to a tar pit)
> *Key words: finishing, fruit, litterbug, thrown, ground*

Wallach and Lee-Schachter (1984) offer additional suggestions for combining sentence comprehension and inferential processing work. The suggestions also integrate oral and written activities. Wallach and Lee-Schachter constructed sentences, reminiscent of the Paris and Lindauer (1976) study mentioned earlier, that students read on index cards. Students are to read the sentences silently and then guess what tool the person in each sentence was using. In this case, students are asked to make an instrument inference. After students make their guesses, they turn over the index card to see if their spoken answers match the written ones. Examples are presented below.

*Side 1* (target sentence): The butcher cuts the steak.
*Side 2* (correct inference): with a knife.
*Side 1* (target sentence): The artist painted the picture.
*Side 2* (incorrect inference): with a potholder.

Using an example provided by Blank (1986), Wallach and Lee-Schachter (1984) asked students to analyze sentence pairs like the one that follows.

Jill was at Stan's house.
Stan and Jill sat on the grass.

Blank (1986) says that these two sentences are more difficult than they might appear to be; however, the difficulty has nothing to do with the possessive, past tense, or the two names used. Instead, comprehending the main idea requires inferential processing; the second sentence is not easily predictable from the first sentence. One must fill in the implicit information across the two sentences. Although we may be unaware of the process, we make an inference to keep the idea coherent. The inference might be "they went outside," "they are in the backyard," "they are having a picnic." Young children, even second graders, might not make the association immediately.

Wallach and Lee-Schachter used sentence pairs similar to these sentences. They added explicit information, using "sentence bridges," before expecting students to generate the inferences on their own.

Jill was at Stan's house. Jill and Stan were having a picnic. They decided to go outside in the backyard. They put down a blanket under a tree. Stan and Jill sat on the grass.

Older students may not need as much practice, and the content would be quite different as well. They are encouraged to talk about themes, e.g., "having a picnic at Stan's house," as oral warm-ups for written work. As they progress, they work with sentence pairs and add the explicit information to the sentences on their own. Older students rewrite implicit paragraphs for younger students (see Chapter 8).

Numerous variations are possible to help students move from explicit to implicit text. For example, students can be given cards with individual sentences written on them. They can be asked to use all the cards to make up the "Jill and Stan picnic story." For more advanced students, the cards written in black ink can be designated as the "must use" cards whereas the cards written in blue ink can be designated as the "can use" cards. Students can discuss different situations where the "can use" cards might be used (e.g., telling a story to someone who cannot see an accompanying picture). Students can be asked to discuss why the Stan and Jill sentence pairs, as originally presented, might be confusing.

In another example, which combines inference and cohesion activities, a target sentence is presented to students. They are asked to say a sentence that could follow logically. Then they are given four choices that may or may not match their predictions. The answers can be compared and rated for most logical matches.

*Target sentence:*
Mr. Jones missed the bus.

*Choices for matching:*
**1.** He knew he would be late for work.
**2.** The bus has four wheels.
**3.** The bus was missed by Mr. Jones again.
**4.** Mrs. Jones was angry.

Both the logical and structural aspects of the combinations can be discussed. Titles and themes can be added to help the students with their predictions. Any number of variations is possible to help students go beyond given information. The reader is directed to Wallach and Lee (1982); Klein-Konigsberg (1984); and Sundbye (1987) for additional information.

## Developing an Appreciation for Cohesion

Ackerman's research (1986) on inference and cohesion provides information that may be applicable to intervention. For younger students who are being taught from basal readers and other prepackaged programs, modification of curricular materials provides us with a beginning (see Chapter 3). We might begin by structuring materials so that (1) the cohesive ties are explicit and (2) questions are manageable in terms of the kinds of inferences required. A modification of a passage provided by Ackerman (1986, p. 340) demonstrates some possibilities.

1. It was late afternoon and Jane was getting ready to go swimming.
2. Jane reminded herself the night before to bring her lovely new yellow swimming suit to school so that she could wear it the next day.
3. Jane looked in her bag.
4. Jane hunted for her suit.
5. Jane could not find her yellow suit.
6. She put on her old red suit and went swimming. The red suit would do for today.

As suggested by Ackerman (1986) the passage could be modified in many ways. We could add fillers that make the connection between events explicit. For example: 1a. Jane was at school and classes were over. Jane hoped she had remembered to pack her yellow suit. 5a. As Jane walked to her locker, Jane realized she would have to wear her old red suit. We could also decrease the amount of name repetition used in the story. For example, instead of repeating *Jane* in a majority of the sentences, we could substitute, "she, "the student," or "Brock High School's champion swimmer." We could also add fillers that would require additional inferencing on the part of listeners and readers. Also, a series of questions could follow the different passages, including the following:

1. Was Jane happy or unhappy with the red suit?
2. Had Jane forgotten or remembered her yellow swim suit?
3. Did her red swim suit have a hole in it?
4. Why was the yellow suit important?

Students can be given the questions before reading the passage. They can also be encouraged to discuss a real-life experience that they may have had which was like Jane's (Hansen & Pearson, 1983). Students can be asked to discuss why certain questions are more difficult to answer than others. They can be asked to restate or rewrite the passage so that it makes more sense.

For more specific cohesion work, we might underline the word *Jane* throughout the passage and ask students to think about another way to say *Jane*. Students can be given choices of pronouns and lexical substitutions that might be appropriate. It is also helpful to give the students titles with the passages to facilitate a gestalt set. As presented in both Chapters 4 and 5, more advanced students can recast the passages; for instance, narratives could be translated into expository forms. With our late elementary and junior high school students (in Grade 6 and up), we work on communication style changes. We often ask students to tell Jane's story to a friend. We then ask them to retell the story with a sports page approach, focusing less on the swim suit and more on Jane's swimming ability.

### Referential Cohesion

Baumann (1986) presents more specific activities for cohesion. She developed the following activities for Grade 3 students (eight year olds) without learning problems. Baumann (1986) says that even sixth graders have difficulty with text when cohesive references are vague. For example, confusion with the pronoun *it* occurs even as late as Grade 6 (11 years old). Baumann's suggestions (1986) deal specifically with anaphoric reference. She defines *anaphora* as "linguistic devices which signal the coreferential identity, or near identity, of two concepts" (p. 75). She goes on to say that the overall theme for students is not to learn definitions but to learn that words can stand for other words.

Baumann uses prereading discussions to help students use their background knowledge to predict what might be in their readers (similar to Hansen's and Pearson's inferential set work). She shows (or reads) students different selections, pointing out that some pronouns might be more likely to occur in narrative selections whereas others might appear more frequently in expository selections. She likes to present older students with narrative and expository "boxes." Students discuss why some pronouns might be placed in one box or the other. Students use examples from their textbooks and other preselected materials to verify their predictions.

*Narrative selections: him, his, I, me, you, etc.*
*Expository selections: one, these, itself, himself, many, other, such, etc.*

Bauman's nine lesson sequence (1986, p. 75) for third graders is presented below, followed by some general procedures and sample lessons.

*Lesson 1:* personal pronoun anaphoric terms (singular and plural), except possessive pronouns and *it*
*Lesson 2:* possessive pronoun and pronoun *it*
*Lesson 3:* reviews all pronouns in lessons 1 and 2
*Lesson 4:* demonstrative anaphoric terms such as *this, that, these,* and *those* and locative anaphoric referents such as *here* and *there*
*Lesson 5:* temporal anaphoric terms such as *now, then, later,* and *earlier* and arithmetic terms such as *one, some, all, few, both,* and *couple*
*Lesson 6:* review lessons 1 through 5
*Lesson 7:* synonymous anaphora such as *boy/lad, dog/animal, bicycle/ thing:* these are taught collectively; distinctions are not made about the different types of synonymy
*Lesson 8:* verb substitutes such as *do/have* and clause substitutes such as *so* and *not*
*Lesson 9:* review of lessons 1 through 8; we like to use material from students' textbooks as shown later in this chapter

Baumann (1986) recommends that modeling and oral practice should accompany written work. The five steps used in her procedures include introduction (students are given a purpose for the lesson), example (oral and/or written texts are part of practice), direct instruction (teachers work on specific awareness activities with students), teacher-directed application (students do generalizing work), and independent practice.

Sample lessons (Baumann, 1986, pp. 87–89) that overlap with many of the concepts discussed in this chapter are listed next:

*Lesson 1:* Anaphoric lesson for personal pronouns
*Introduction:* Students listen to a story where the names of the main characters are repeated over and over again (as in the "Jane goes swimming" passage presented above); models of alternatives to the repetition are presented by the teacher, using the personal pronouns suggested in lesson 1
*Example:* Students look at two sentences on the board/or on a chart: "Tom is my best friend. He lives next door." The teacher can read the first sentence. A student can read the second sentence. They then might discuss why *Tom* and *he* represent the same person.
*Direct instruction:* Students create charts that define cohesive devices. (Table 6-2) is a sample pronoun cohesion chart.) Students then practice with oral and written combinations of the personal pronouns listed on their charts, after which they work on the examples presented below (Baumann, 1986, pp. 88). Pronouns are underlined. Students take turns discussing who the pronouns stand for.

1. Tim and Cathy are good friends. He sometimes gets angry with her but, most of the time, they play well together.
2. Dick and John are twins. They are ten years old today.
3. Tom said, "Mike, let's go to the ball game today."
   Mike answered, "No you go by yourself. I think I will stay home and play games with my cousin Jimmy."
   "Oh, come on," said Tom. "Please play with me. You can play with him anytime."

Teacher directed application and independent practice reinforce the concepts taught in the previous stages. One of the activities that is most interesting in both teacher-directed and independent aspects

**TABLE 6-2**
*Words That Stand for People (Pronoun Cohesion Chart)*

|  | Boys or Girls | Girls Only | Boys Only |
|---|---|---|---|
| One person | I, me, my, mine | she, her, hers | he, him, his |
| One person or more | you, your, yours | | |
| More than one person | we, us, our, ours, they, them, their, theirs | | |

From Baumann, 1986.

involves having students analyze their own workbooks and readers. Baumann's research suggests that third graders in her study, following some of the pronoun work described in this section, improved in their comprehension and identification of anaphoric references in their own textbooks. Bauman (1986, p. 78) presents two examples from Grade 3 materials. She shows how much anaphoric reference appears in these materials. Her suggestions certainly offer some possibilities for curricular analysis and modification.

### Selection 1: Narrative — The Big Game

"Let's go, Tim. Hit the ball out of the yard," shouted Jane. But she knew that he wouldn't. He couldn't even hit the ball. As the ball flew past Tim, he shut his eyes and swung the bat. He opened his eyes when he heard the ball land in the catcher's mitt.

As always, Bill stepped in to give Tim some help. He said, "Keep your eyes on the ball. Look at it all the way to the catcher's mitt." Tim smiled at his friend. Bill made it sound so easy. For Bill, it was easy. "Come on, Tom, hit that!"

Questions that were used by Braumann include the following:

Who knew Tim wouldn't hit the ball?
What did Bill mean when he said, "Come on, Tim, hit that"?
Whom did Tim smile at?

### Selection 2: Expository — Honeybee

Bees are the only insects that make honey. They make it in a hive. Many bees live there.Three kinds of bees live in the bee house. Each hive has one queen bee, a few hundred drones, and thousands of worker bees. The queen bee is the largest. She is also the most important. Only the queen lays eggs. She lays them in tiny cells in the hive.

Baumann (1986) has students write the referent for the underlined word in the expository selection. One can also use a modified version of the Baumann (1986) suggestions by providing students with pronoun and noun choices. Students can discuss the correctness of word choices, or they can be provided with a paragraph that appears on a worksheet. For example,

The boy is climbing up the tree. The child could fall. The child could get hurt. The child's parents would get upset. Then the child would be in trouble. Then the boy might not be allowed to play in the boy's tree house. Then the child would be depressed, etc.

Students are asked why the story sounds silly. They are then asked to find better ways of saying or writing the underlined words. Pronouns may be provided as choices, if needed.

Lee-Schachter suggests using sentences with ambiguous referents to help students become more aware of anaphoric reference. Using sentences such as the one that follows, she asks students to guess what characters might go with the pronouns, providing students with choices such as *policeman* and *motorist* if word choices are necessary:

He gave him a speeding ticket.

Stories are then created around the sentence and pronoun-noun elements:

John was driving down the turnpike and he was going over the speed limit. A policeman on a motorcycle stopped him . . . .

Murphy (1986) provides us with additional possibilities for developing awareness of cohesion. Her research combines oral and written aspects of communication. She shows us how difficult it is for children, even nondisabled eight year olds, to take someone else's perspective. Children are asked to read the following paragraphs quietly and then guess where the penny will be. The first paragraph (Murphy, 1986, p. 123) is written in the form of direct address; that is, the children are talked to by the author.

My name is Tina.
I have a friend named Suzie.
You and Suzie and I will sit down at the table.
Everyone will have a bag.
A penny will be in one of the bags.
The penny will be in her bag.

The second paragraph (Murphy, 1986, p. 122) is written in the form of overheard conversation. The children are supposed to guess who has the penny by interpreting the dialogue in the messages.

John, Sam, and Bill had a party.
They all sat down at the table.
Everyone had a plate.
A penny was under one of the plates.
"Sam," said Bill, "Get the penny under my plate."

Murphy points out that the last sentence in each of the passages contains the critical referents: *Her* and *my*. It helps to color-code the critical words or tell students to listen for a special clue. It helps to provide students with the final sentence in isolation before they read the paragraphs.

We can use Murphy's ideas in many different ways. Murphy had her second graders listen to conversations. She then asked them to guess where the penny was. Teachers can create detective teams and have students figure out a hidden message by listening to conversations involving two or more characters. We need to remember, however, that the ability to take someone else's perspective (as in the dialogue examples) is a later acquisition (see Chapters 2 and 5). Murphy reminds us that the overheard conversations, whether presented orally or visually, tend to be more difficult for average second graders who read than direct address.

Smith and Elkins (1985) provide yet another way to help students become aware of cohesion. They use mapping strategies with some of their older students (11 year olds). Consider the following passage:

> A legend of ancient Norway tells of a gigantic sea monster called a kraken. The monster was said to have many arms and to measure over a mile from the tip of one arm to the tip of another (Smith & Elkins, 1985, p. 14).

Smith and Elkins (1985) suggest using various symbols to show students how to analyze text. For example. ‖ represent relations created by lexical items; [ and ] represent relationships created by logical connectives; ( and ) represent relationships created by ellipsis where the lexical item is implied. (Figure 6-1 shows how one could map the sea monster passage.) There are many variations for the Smith and Elkins mapping strategies, some of which are discussed in Chapter 8.

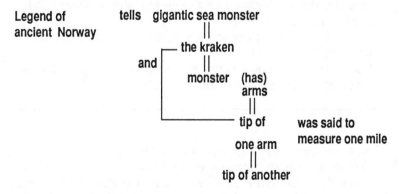

**Figure 6-1.** *Smith and Elkin's (1985, p. 14) sea monster package in visually mapped format.*

## SAMPLE LESSON PLANS

As discussed in Chapter 4 and presented in Chapter 5, the lesson plan cover sheet reminds us to consider the theoretical principles that underpin our intervention sequences and methodologies. The cover sheet also reminds us to be sensitive to the variables that affect students' performances and to be aware of the *whys* of intervention.

---

### COVER SHEET FOR COMBINING INFERENCE AND COHESION

*Theoretical Principle*
Children may have less difficulty making inferences when they recognize and understand the cohesive devices used in text. Children move from literal-explicit-redundant processing to inferential-implicit-nonredundant abilities.

*Type of Strategy*
Inferential (read between the lines and make relationships; this is the goal though we can see how analytical and metalinguistic some of the procedures are).

*Type of Language*
Decontextualized and metalinguistic (working on discussion and manipulation of sentences and sentence pairs, paragraphs, and questions).

*Clinician/Educator Questions*
1. Why has this aspect of language been chosen?
2. Is it appropriate for student's language and metacognitive/ metalinguistic level?
3. How will I modify or change the plan if the student is having difficulty?
4. How is the language lesson related to (and integrated with) classroom activities and the curriculum?

---

The clinician/educator questions should be answered in our lesson plans. We have made the decision to work on inference and cohesion after carefully considering students' communicative and language abilities within and outside of the classroom. We have listened to their narrative productions, and we have assessed their metalinguistic abilities to ensure that (within the limits of our testing and observation) the students involved in these activities can handle correction and explanation (refer to the van Kleeck [1984b] task hierarchy in Chapter 4). We have decided to begin with expository text samples taken from the students' geography and science books. Our message games, which will complement the sentence and paragraph work, will involve the overheard conversation materials. We will back up to direct-address materials if the overheard conversations present too much difficulty. The sample hierarchy that follows represents a way of summarizing intervention choices.

---

## LESSON 1:
## SAMPLE HIERARCHY FORMULATION FOR INFERENCE AND COHESION COMBINATIONS

**Target on Inference-Cohesion Combinations**
Helps students gain an appreciation for cohesive devices in their language with a particular focus on personal pronouns. The activities that follow are done to help students appreciate the way cohesive devices work in text. The ultimate purpose is to help students develop better comprehension and organizational skills.

*Cohesive Devices and Forms Targeted*
Personal pronouns (singular and plural) and individual sentences and paragraphs.

*Specific Sequence*
Begin with single sentences with two characters using ambiguous referents; students then create passages with explicit referents; students listen to passages with pronoun-noun referents, using prereading questions; students manipulate referents in expository passages from their readers.

*Strategies Facilitated*
*First level:* develop an inferential set; see how discussions help reading.

*(continued)*

---

## LESSON 1 *(continued)*

*Strategies Facilitated (continued)*

*Second level:* analyze cohesive devices; learn how they clarify and confuse relationships.
*Third level:* learn how redundant or explicit information can be translated into nonredundant or implicit information.

*Special Instructions*
These activities combine a number of areas. It may be necessary to simplify the lessons.

*Tasks and Stimuli*
(Discussed next; would be here in outline form.)

---

We would use activities like the ones suggested by Lee-Schachter. We would also incorporate the Hansen and Pearson (1983) inferential set activities into our work with students. The pronoun lessons presented here represent a small portion of the work that might be done in the area of linguistic cohesion. It helps to present paragraphs and stories in written form to our older students, who keep the written versions in front of them during listening activities. When stories have more than one character, color-coding each character provides an additional cue for cohesion (*Bill* and its referents appear in red and *John* and its referents appear in blue). The corresponding reading comprehension questions are also color-coded. It is useful to use selections from students' readers and have students write in the referent for the underlined words as suggested by Baumann (1986). Lesson 2 might take the development of cohesion a bit further by including some of Murphy's oral and written messages, which contain cohesive devices in the final sentence.

---

## CLOSING REMARKS

The bigger picture of language learning involves spoken and written text rather than isolated phrases or sentences; however, using smaller units like spoken or written sentences to help students get to the whole is important (Hoskins, 1987a). Smaller units serve as high-

---

### LESSON 2

*Cohesive Devices and Forms Targeted*
Personal pronouns (as in Lesson 1)

*Specific Sequence*
Begin with direct address; move to overheard dialogue.

*Strategies Facilitated*
*First level:* appreciate cohesive devices that are explicitly directed to the listener.
*Second level:* appreciate cohesive devices that are directed to another character.

*Special Instructions*
Combine oral and written activities whenever possible and include Pearson and Hansen's suggestions for prereading discussions; students may need much work on direct address; use overheard conversations with content very familiar and interesting to students (e.g., umpires screaming at baseball managers).

*Tasks and Stimuli*
Construct messages with content that is appropriate for age, grade, and language level.

---

lighted details that may help students approach connected discourse with a method or strategy. Recent research shows that structure still matters (Liles, 1987; Roth, 1987); at some level, students have to deal with the linguistic structures of their language, particularly as text becomes more complicated (Roth, 1987). However, it is important to remember that we are continually working in the learning domain that is most vulnerable for many language learning disabled students. The structural and decontextualized aspects of language may be particularly difficult for many of them. The research suggests that language learning disabled students are not without language abilities, and it is up to us to find ways to help those abilities grow.

# CHAPTER 7

# Analytical Strategies: From Sentences to Words to Sounds

> In the oral tradition, ideas are elaborated by stitching together...
> language .... (Language) is dependent upon prosodic features, repetitions, proverbial phrases, and shared situational knowledge. In the literate tradition, ideas are expressed in an analytical, sequential, linear manner with specific lexical items and minimal redundancy of ideas (Westby, 1984, p. 107).

The pragmatic revolution in early child language helped us move away from observing and teaching syntactic and semantic aspects of language outside of naturalistic communicative contexts. A variety of pragmatic taxonomies were developed that encouraged us to sample and to facilitate communicative interactions. We became better at encouraging conversations, reinforcing communicative intent, and modeling, stimulating, and teaching a wide range of speech acts. Language intervention of the 1980s, focusing on pragmatic competence with an emphasis on interaction, has certainly had far-reaching and positive effects on our philosophies and on the children we serve. However, as we have moved further and further away from structural concerns, we have lost some evenness of focus. The study of syntactic competence has become somewhat obscured as our interest in conversational and narrative discourse has advanced. Working on individual sentences and specific syntactic forms sometimes seems quite unacceptable (and it certainly is in many situations). Westby's words (1984) remind us, as did Postman's words (1985) at the beginning of Chapter 5, that oral and written language are different. Her words also imply that studying children's capacity to deal with language itself, i.e., specific words and syntactic forms, is an important part of understanding literate styles of communication.

There has been renewed interest in the study of syntactic abilities and other aspects of language structure for both nondisabled and language-disabled children. Although some researchers have never lost interest in studying form, the perspective from which we view syntactic growth and proficiency has broadened considerably. We always knew that children must come to grips with complex syntax as part of their overall development of spoken language, but we now know much more about how syntactic growth interfaces with the acquisition of written language (see Chapter 1). We also know more about the subtle syntactic adjustments children make when telling and when writing stories (e.g., Lee-Schachter, 1985). We understand much more about metalinguistic development, and we recognize that becoming truly proficient at one's language means becoming proficient with its structure (Kamhi, 1987; Wallach, 1985).

## THEORETICAL BASES FOR
## INTERVENTION SEQUENCES AND TASKS

We might begin our search for intervention suggestions by questioning our own knowledge of the research. What can we learn from studying children's use of complex syntax? How does the shift from semantic to syntactic strategies manifest itself as children get older? What does the developmental research say about children's growing awareness of sentence structure? Of word structure? How does any of this information relate to the student? To Monday morning in the classroom? Some of these questions remain unanswerable. Nevertheless, we might propose some connections. For example, students must use and process classroom discourse, which, as has been said throughout this text, is complex and somewhat decontextualized. Teachers and clinicians ask students to analyze and correct various aspects of their language every day. Additionally, students are asked to discuss the differences between narrative and expository text. They are asked to edit their manuscripts, to write better sentences, and to analyze their conversations. They are asked to analyze words and deal with sound-letter correspondences. Indeed, the study of children's advancing syntactic knowledge and their abilities to make metalinguistic judgments about language structures contributes to our knowledge base from a number of perspectives.

## Complex Syntax: Literate Language Forms

The majority of studies of syntactic acquisition above the age of five are studies of comprehension (Wallach, 1984). However, some researchers have discussed children's expressive abilities within the context of their narrative productions as discussed in Chapter 6. Klecan-Aker (1985) also talks about syntactic abilities in both non-disabled and language-disabled children from the perspective of story-telling. She analyzed stories told by 11- and 12-year olds about movies and TV shows and found that *and* structures were the most common sentence types used by both nondisabled and language-disabled groups followed by *because* structures. She also found that the nondisabled group used subordinate structures such as *which, after, where,* and *since,* which were absent from the narratives of the language-disabled subjects. Klecan-Aker reminds us to explore advanced syntax abilities in older children as part of narrative and discourse abilities but she also reminds us that even nondisabled sixth-grade children have much to learn about the structural complexities of their language.

Lee-Schachter (1985) also observed children's use of complex structures during storytelling. She asked superior readers and below-average readers from Grades 2 and 3 to retell stories to children who had not heard them. As inspired by Michaels and Collins (1984), Lee-Schachter described the children's use of literate syntactic and lexical forms. She found that the superior readers used many more complex structures in their stories. They used significantly more relative clause sentences, infinitives, and like forms. The superior readers tended to introduce new characters in their stories by using embeddedness. For example, one child expressed the relationship of one of the characters in the story in this way: "The man who was wearing an eye patch was the one who the children needed to be afraid of." The superior readers also tended to use what Lee-Schachter calls explicit coordination. She noted the use of *and when, and so,* and *and after* to link events in the story. She also noted that the better readers were very specific in their use of *the* and *a.* New characters were frequently introduced by *a,* indicating that this character had not appeared in the story before and signaling to the listener that more information was forthcoming. *The* frequently referred back to a character already mentioned. For example, one child expressed the relationship in this way: "There was *a*

man who came to town. *The* man would turn out to be the sheriff."
Lee-Schachter (1985) concluded that the better readers in her study
told stories that were generally less ambiguous because of syntactic
explicitness, consistent use of tense, and overall attention to details
about structure (see also Roth, 1987, discussed in Chapter 6). She indicated that the poorer readers tended to use basic syntactic forms such
as *and* constructions rather than relative clause constructions; they
overused *and then* to link events in the story and seemed more comfortable with an oral style of expression. Lee-Schachter noted *a* and
*the* confusion, frequent use of conversational and informal forms
such as *this guy here,* and tense inconsistency among the poorer readers.

Lee-Schachter's research highlights some of the interactions
among advancing syntactic and lexical abilities, storytelling, and reading proficiency. Her research also shows how acquisitions of linguistic
form can be seen from a broader perspective. Karmiloff-Smith (1979)
and Athey (1977), in earlier research, also considered structural
changes from a broader perspective. Lee-Schachter touched on Athey's
work (1977) with *and* structures when she pointed out that *and* can be
used in many ways (*and when, and so,* and *and after,* etc.). Athey
indicates that even though *and* is listed as one of the earlier developing conjunctions, *and* sentences are varied. Some *and* sentences are
more complex than others. For example, the sentence, "Jim is tall and
John is short" represents a comparative relationship, whereas the sentence, "The dog bared its teeth and Billy ran in terror" reflects a causal
relationship. According to Athey (1977), comparatives tend to be used
and processed more consistently than causal sentences among Grade 4
children. Karmiloff-Smith (1979) also pointed out that *a* and *the*
appear early in the spoken repertoires of children. However, she goes
on to say that *a* and *the* preciseness (the type described by Lee-
Schachter) is not acquired until about eight or nine years old. Similarly, causal words like *why* and *because* appear relatively early in
children's productions, but complete comprehension of causal words
and sentences occurs much later developmentally, as discussed in this
chapter (see also Table 5-5).

## Comprehension Strategies Revisited

Two points that were addressed in the discussion of comprehension in Chapter 4 should be mentioned again. One point was that
younger children tend to be semantically oriented in the earlier stages
of language development. They make decisions about what things
mean based on content, logic, and event probability. Young children
rarely attend to language form unless there is a particular reason to do

so, as when encountering a communication breakdown (Kamhi, 1987; see Chapter 2). Thus, a sentence such as, "The baby feeds the mother" might be interpreted as "mother-feeds-baby" based on real-world probability rather than on the word order of the sentence. The second point made in Chapter 4 was that sentences such as, "The home run was hit by Reggie Jackson," are easier to comprehend than sentences such as, "The cat is chased by the dog" because the Reggie sentence has a built-in semantic probability. That is, Reggie can hit home runs but home runs cannot hit Reggie. The dog-cat sentence is more difficult because dogs can chase cats and cats can chase dogs. The Reggie sentence is nonreversible whereas the dog-cat sentence is reversible.

Evidence for power of semantic–event probability strategies, particularly at younger age ranges, appears across sentence types. Keller-Cohen (1987) looked at sentences with a variety of temporal connectives including *before, after, when, while, just before that,* and *and after that.* She found that logical relationship sentences ("semantically probable") were easier for young children to process and comprehend than arbitrary relationship sentences ("reversible"). The logical sentences were thought to be easier than the arbitrary ones because children can use their extralinguistic knowledge (their knowledge of the sequence of events in the real world) to interpret them. The two sentences that follow reflect logical and arbitrary relations:

*Logical:* The boy opened the can before he poured the soup.
*Arbitrary:* The girl ate the cake after she opened the door.

Keller-Cohen (1987) also found that children become more sensitive to the specific connectives within sentences at about five or six years old. This is the point where they begin "a developmental shift from extralinguistic strategies such as event probability to syntactic interpretation of sentences" (Keller-Cohen, 1987, p. 180). Keller-Cohen adds that we can get a better picture of children's comprehension and use of temporal connectives by observing their comprehension of sentences where the events are presented in *reverse* of their logical order. If children are using probable event strategies, paying less attention to specific structural cues such as *after* and *and after that,* they should process the sentences that follow incorrectly:

*After:* After the boy poured the soup, he opened the can.
*And after that:* The boy ate the hot dog and after that he poured the ketchup.

Keller-Cohen also considered the acquisition of temporal connectives in terms of the kinds of clausal support that accompanied them.

For example, *when* can mean *after* in the first two following sentences; it can mean *after* or *while* in the third (Keller-Cohen, 1987, p. 168).

> *After:* When the boy opened the can, he poured the soup.
> *After:* The boy drank the soup when he opened the bottle.
> *After or while:* The boy ate the pancakes when he opened the soup.

Keller-Cohen (1987) observed a developmental progression among three to five year olds. She found that *before* and *after* were learned earlier than *when,* which was learned earlier than *while.* Children began interpreting more complex sentences by relying heavily on probable event and extralinguistic strategies. They also tended to interpret *when* sentences as if they were *after* sentences. *While* interpretations of *after* and *when* sentences, which were the latest acquisitions, tended to appear more frequently at the five-year-age range — the point at which children begin to shift from semantic to syntactic interpretations of sentences.

Emerson (1979, 1980) studied the semantic and structural variables in five to ten year olds' comprehension of *because* and *if* sentences. She found that sentences such as, "The snowman started to melt because the sun started to shine" were much easier to comprehend than sentences such as, "He could hear loud noises and the laughing because he went outside." The snowman sentence is nonreversible whereas the second sentence is reversible. That is, the snowman sentence has an event probability and real-world sequence (sun out = snowman melts); it becomes illogical in terms of cause and effect when reversed: "The sun comes out because the snowman melts." The second sentence, on the other hand, is unpredictable in terms of a cause and effect sequence: "He went outside because he could hear the loud noises and the laughing" and "He could hear the loud noises and the laughing because he went outside" are both logical. According to Emerson (1979, 1980), it is not until after seven and a half years of age that comprehension of reversible sentences improves (Wallach, 1984, p. 94).

Emerson (1979) also found that tasks affected comprehension performance. She used two tasks: a picture-sequence task (PST) and a first-last task (FLT). Two picture-story sequences were placed in front of the children in a cartoon strip format in the PST. Children were told a story for each cartoon sequence.

> *Cartoon sequence 1:* This is a story about a boy. The boy was feeling very happy. He went outside to play with his friends. He is playing with his friends.

*Cartoon sequence 2:* This story is a bit different. The boy is feeling lonely. He went out to play with his friends. Then he was very happy.

Children were then asked to match a spoken sentence to one of the cartoon sequences. A target sentence for cartoon sequence 2 might be, "Because he went out to play with his friends, he was feeling happy." (We might consider the lack of explicitness in the pronouns in this sentence; it might be helpful to substitute *the boy* for one of the pronouns.)

In the FLT, children sequenced pictures to match spoken sentences. Unlike the PST, where pictures were always in the child's view, children had to create their own sequence in the FLT. Children's performances, measured by correct comprehension of *because* and *if* sentences were significantly better on the PST. Emerson (1979) found that even nine and ten year olds had significant difficulty with the reversible sentences on the FLT.

Information about semantic and syntactic variables is available from other comprehension studies. Sheldon (1974) and Wallach (in preparation), for example, talk about semantic and structural strategies in relation to the processing of relative clause sentences. The research suggests that younger children, even children as young as four or five years old, are capable of processing complex sentences such as relatives, but their strategies tend to be semantically driven. Younger children tend to ignore clause boundaries, and they are less bothered by clause interruptions in sentences than older children (Sheldon, 1974; Wallach, in preparation). Somewhere between seven and nine years old, children's performance on complex sentences, including relatives, changes and improves dramatically (Fluck, 1979). Nonembedded object relatives show particularly dramatic improvements with age due to the position of the clauses in object relatives and their word-order orientation (as shown in the examples that follow). As children get older, they become much more sensitive to clause interruptions (embeddedness), word order, and particular markers (such as the temporal connectives mentioned earlier) as cues to meaning (Ferreiro et al., 1976).

An example of a semantically oriented strategy identified with children's processing of relative clause sentences is as follows. The two sentences are a subject relative and an object relative, respectively.

*Subject relative: parallel function:* The giraffe (that bites the wolf) kicks the hippo. (Giraffe bites the wolf and giraffe also kicks the hippo.)

*Object relative: nonparallel function:* The giraffe bites the wolf (that kicks the hippo). (Giraffe bites the wolf and wolf kicks hippo.)

The subject relative in the example, according to Sheldon (1974), is easier for young children to process than the second sentence because the first sentence has a semantic consistency; i.e., the giraffe is the actor or doer of all actions. Younger children, as said earlier, find the semantic consistency helpful when trying to comprehend complex relatives of this type. The clause interruption in the subject relative is ignored by younger children, who tend to pay less attention to structural variables. On the other hand, object relatives improve dramatically with age because older children (eight and nine year olds) become more comfortable with nonembedded and word-oriented strategies.

Although generally more popular among five year olds, the parallel function strategy is used by some learning- and reading-disabled children until 11 or 12 years old (Wallach, in preparation). As with the other complex sentences, some relative clause sentences, those with clause interruptions and confusing word orders, are difficult to process even after nine years old. An example of a difficult relative clause, with clause interruption and word-order confusion, follows:

The giraffe (that the hippo kicks) chases the zebra.

We might all agree that stimuli that involve animals jumping, kicking, and biting are quite absurd. Nevertheless, sentences of this type give us the opportunity to study decontextualized and highly literate language forms. The animal relatives also reflect what Keller-Cohen (1987) called arbitrary relations (i.e., they are reversible sentences). We might consider ways to lessen the processing load for students with spoken and written language problems. Fluck (1979) suggests recognizing the differences between redundant and nonredundant stimuli when working with students. Stimuli would be considered redundant if only two out of the three nouns are involved in the actions. Sentences such as, "Larry Bird who is running in front of Dr. J. is getting ready to sink the basket" and "The giraffe chases the elephant who is eating the grass" are redundant relatives. We should encourage our students to analyze their readers in terms of structural complexity and help them become more sensitive to clause boundaries and word order differences.

We are reminded by many researchers that complete proficiency with some of the syntactic forms mentioned, such as *because, if, before,* and *after,* to name only a few, may not occur until eight or nine years old (Emerson, 1980; Fluck, 1979; Wallach, 1984). We know that children use many of these constructions in their speech very early, but as said many times throughout this text, there are many levels to any acquisition (Bloom & Capatides, 1987). We also know that stimuli, task format, and instructions affect performance in different ways (see Chapters 3 and 4; Emerson, 1979). Whereas all the studies mentioned previously have a metalinguistic cast to them, some studies have focused on children's metalinguistic development specifically.

## Metalinguistics Revisited: Making Conscious Judgments About Language

### Meta and Syntax

Children's awareness of the structural aspects of their language, i.e., their ability to consciously manipulate language form, begins to develop at around six or seven years old and continues through the elementary school years (Smith & Tager-Flushberg, 1982). Ages six and seven is also about the time that children's comprehension strategies become more syntactically oriented. Tunmer and Grieve (1984) wrote that two and three year olds make judgments about the acceptability of sentences based on their ability to understand the sentences. They go on to say that four and five year olds improve in their metalinguistic abilities but they make judgments about sentences based on content or truth value. By contrast, six and seven year olds begin to separate form from content.

Tunmer and Grieve (1984) provide some interesting examples from four year olds who were asked to make grammatical judgments about sentences. The corrections by the four year olds were based on content and truth value. One four year old was asked to correct the following sentence: "Yesterday, Daddy paint the fence." The correction was made in the following way: "Daddies don't paint fences, they paint walls." Another four year old judged "The big rock was in the middle of the road" to be incorrect because "A car might run over it and get a flat tire." Van Kleeck (1984a) provides yet another example of younger children's negation of the grammatical accuracy: three and four year olds rejected the acceptability of "The men wait for the bus" on the grounds that "Only children wait for buses" (p. 145).

Emerson (1980) points out that grammatical judgment, i.e. children's ability to decide whether sentences are good or bad or silly or sensible, is a late acquisition. She says that younger children are capable of making some grammatical judgments but adds that these judgments about rightness and wrongness of sentences are more consistent above the age of eight. Emerson (1980) also points out that the younger children in her *because* and *if* sentence studies mentioned earlier tended to use different strategies than the older children to correct sentences. Five and six year olds used reduction and content change strategies when correcting *because* and *if* sentences. For example, "The river was frozen over because we went skating tonight" became "The river was all right to go skating." Nine and ten year olds used clause change strategies when correcting sentences. For example, "The river was frozen over because we wanted to go skating tonight" became "We wanted to go skating tonight because the river was frozen over." Olson (1982) reiterates Emerson's notion (1980) that structural awareness is a late acquisition by providing examples of children's responses to a simplified reasoning problem. He asked children *if* questions such as, "If John knows the milk is sour, is the milk sour?" Olson found that children as old as eight tended to use semantic-logical strategies to answer the queston. A logical response was "No, the milk isn't sour because I put it in the fridge." Nine and ten year olds, according to Olson, shifted strategies by appealing directly to the wording of the sentence. A typical response might be "Yes, the milk is sour because you just said he knew it was sour."

Evidence suggests that judgments of syntactic and morphological agreement are more difficult than lexical and word order judgments (Buday et al., 1983; Liles et al., 1977; Liles & Shulman, 1981; Wallach & Turner, 1985). Syntactic agreement violations appear in sentences such as, "John and Jim is brother." Lexical violations occur in sentences such as, "The dog writes the food." Word order violations occur in sentences such as, "Song me a sing" (Liles et al., 1977). Kamhi and Koenig (1985) provided evidence for the sequence of difficulty by studying four- to seven-year-old children's grammatical judgments and sentence corrections. They used sentences with lexical violations ("Jill eats cards"), phonological violations ("John has two tig cars"), and syntactic violations ("They throwing the stick"). They found that both nondisabled and language-disabled children between four and seven made appropriate lexical and phonological judgments, but the nondisabled children performed superiorly to the language-disabled children on the syntactic corrections. Kamhi and Koenig went on to say that the way children correct sentences is very revealing. Both nondisabled and language-disabled subjects in their study had difficulty correcting sentences with phonological errors. For example, children were correct when they said that the sentence, "John has two tig cars," was wrong, but their corrections revealed lexically oriented changes such as, "John doesn't have two cars, he only has one."

Studies of metalinguistic development have provided us with a tremendous amount of information. As practitioners, we have the difficult task of applying the research to practice. Smith and Tager-Flusberg (1982) suggest asking how early metalinguistic awareness, manifested in behaviors like repairing one's own language errors, sound play, and making up dialogue for our story characters, affects language acquisition in general. We might ask ourselves about the usefulness of some metalinguistic tasks, such as grammatical judgments, for school screenings in the early grades (Fujiki et al., 1987). We might also consider the connection between metalinguistic tasks and classroom activities (e.g., write a sentence for the new spelling word, correct your written sentences, copy sentences from the board). Indeed, can we separate the meta from the nonmeta as children get older? Certainly, many aspects of teaching, and most aspects of language intervention, involve heightening students' awareness of language. The process of becoming literate also includes, in part at least, the process of becoming metalinguistic (van Kleeck, 1984a; van Kleeck & Schuele, 1987).

### Meta and Literacy

Bowey (1986) asks us to take a hard look at metalinguistic abilities as they relate to reading because we still have much to learn about which aspects of meta have the greatest impact on reading and school learning. Evidence does suggest that oral tasks like teaching children to monitor semantic and syntactic consistency in sentences improves reading comprehension performance. Skilled readers are said to be more advanced than nonskilled readers in their ability to detect and monitor the grammatical correctness of sentences, and they are reported to have a higher level of metalinguistic ability, particularly in the area of phonemic segmentation than less skilled readers (Rubin, 1986). More advanced first-grade readers seem to be more advanced metalinguistically than the poorer readers in their grade in terms of word order awareness, word consciousness, and word and sound segmentation abilities (e.g., Allan, 1982; Warren-Leubecker, 1987; Zucchermaglio et al., 1986). Consequently, metalinguistic intervention of various types "appears worthy of consideration" (Bowey, 1986, p. 296).

### Word Order Awareness

Warren-Leubecker (1987) found that five- and six-year-old children who demonstrated word-order awareness *without* explicit instructions were advanced in reading, vocabulary, and reading readiness. Word awareness was tested by having children play a game involving two characters, Norman and Ralph (as adapted from Bohannon et al., 1984). Children were told that Norman and Ralph speak differently and that they would be required to guess who said each sentence: Norman spoke in normal order and Ralph spoke in scrambled order. A sample sentence from Norman was, "Mother told you to wash your hands." A sample sentence from Ralph was, "Told mother you hands to your wash." The more advanced children tended to perform the task rather easily. They did not need to be reminded about the different talking styles of Norman and Ralph, and they gave answers relating to sentence form when asked to state the differences between Norman and Ralph. For example, one child said, "Norman speaks English and Ralph speaks a different kind of English." Another child said, "Norman talks straight and Ralph talks backwards" (Warren-Leubecker, 1987, p. 72). Children who were less advanced in reading, vocabulary, and reading readiness needed more explicit instructions (e.g., "Norman says things the right way and Ralph says things the wrong way"); they also explained the differences between Norman and Ralph by responding with nonsyntactic strategies to explain differences. For example, one child said, "Norman has a higher voice." Another child said, "Norman is taller" (Warren-Leubecker, 1987, p. 71). Children who were the lowest in reading, vocabulary, and reading readiness had more difficulty with the task in general, frequently showing no word awareness by responding arbitrarily to Norman and Ralph choices.

Warren-Leubecker (1987) reminds us that the findings from the Norman and Ralph study are tentative because many kindergartners without problems have difficulty with word order tasks. She goes on to say that some children need more explicit instructions. Advanced first graders do quite well without explicit instructions, but average first graders seem to be helped by explicit instructions and reminders: "Remember, Ralph says things the wrong way." Warren-Leubecker states that certain instructions, e.g., "Tell me whether you heard a 'good' or a 'silly' sentence," may bias children's responses. For example, one child said that "Line up and go home" was a silly sentence because "You aren't supposed to line up; you wait for your bus to be called" (Warren-Leubecker, 1987, p. 78). Warren-Leubecker (1987) concludes by tying a number of concepts together. She says, "The child with high level word order awareness is also likely to possess high levels of other forms of metalinguistic awareness (e.g., phonemic segmentation skills), and these other forms actually may be most useful in early reading. High levels of word order awareness may also imply higher levels of metacognition in general" (Warren-Leubecker, 1987, p. 79).

### Word Consciousness and Segmentation Precursors

Van Kleeck and Schuele (1987) have done extensive work in the area of early metalinguistic development. They say that children need to learn that words are arbitrary representations of objects and experiences. Children also need to learn that the same object can have different-sounding names in various languages, that the same sound sequence can mean different things, and that language is a system of elements (sounds and words) and rules for combining these elements (van Kleeck & Schuele, 1987, p. 19).

According to van Kleeck and Schuele (1987), spontaneous manifestations of word awareness and segmentation abilities (as well as other metalinguistic skills) are indications of the very earliest emergence of metalinguistic competence. They remind us that experimental studies, standardized tests, and many school activities require that children demonstrate their metalinguistic knowledge on a conscious level (see Chapters 1 and 2). Table 7-1 highlights some of the early metalinguistic behaviors observed by van Kleeck and Schuele (1987), who wrote that some of the behaviors described in Table 7-1 may be precursors to successful performance on standardized tests and other tasks that require demonstrations of true metalinguistic ability.

This broad repertoire of metalinguistic practice outlined in Table 7-1, occurring between two and a half and three and a half, includes much variation across children. Those of us involved in the management of children with language, learning, and reading disabilities should certainly have knowledge of early metalinguistic development, which appears to be related to and interactive with primary linguistic competence as well as written language proficiency.

Children's developing metalinguistic abilities have been observed in many ways. Van Kleeck and Schuele (1987) observed spontaneous examples. Warren-Leubecker (1987) used Norman and Ralph dolls, and Emerson (1980) used puppets that talked sensibly and silly. Other researchers interviewed children directly or created games to observe children's awareness of words, syllables, and sounds (e.g., Blachman, 1984; Fox & Routh, 1984; Kamhi et al., 1985; Liberman et al., 1980; Rubin, 1986; van Kleeck, 1984b). Kamhi et al. (1985), for example, used a word interview technique (see van Kleeck, 1984). They asked three to six year olds to answer questions like, "What is a word?" or "Tell me some long words, some short words, some hard words, and some easy words." They found that younger children tended to give word referents such as *ball, table,* and *chair* when asked to define words. They also found, supporting van Kleeck (1984) and others, that younger children focus on physical attributes and real-world images when discussing various characteristics for words. For example, *wood* is a hard word and *train* is a long word. Many four year olds agree that *dog* is a real word but they often explain that they know it is a word by howling like a dog to demonstrate their understanding, as we men-

**TABLE 7-1**

*Examples of Early Metalinguistic Behaviors*

| Word Consciousness | |
|---|---|
| Changing names and rituals | Mary had a little *can.* |
| Substituting nonsense words for known words | Brush those hams before you *meep.* |
| Inventing new words by combining or overextending known words | *Ballkite* means Frisbee. |
| Foreign language awareness | I'm doing Spanish. That's called a *mindo, dindo, findo.* |
| Questions or comments about word usage | Do we have two names for that fruit, *orange* and *tangerine?* |

| Words Are Separate Segments of Language | |
|---|---|
| Word substitution play | That drives me bananas. That drives me nuts. That drives me gas stations. |
| Segmenting words and asking for meaning | What's *are* mean? |
| Figuring out word boundaries | Is it an *A-dult* or *a-NUH-dult?* |

| Phonological Awareness | |
|---|---|
| Phonological corrections | I want a cwooton, a cweeton, I want one of those, mama. |
| Nonsense sound play | Cow go moo, mommy go mamoo, daddy go dadoo. |
| Adding endings | I go get my bookie. |
| Spontaneous rhyming | Eggs are beggs. |
| Rhyming with awareness | Annie, mannie. That's the same kind. |
| Segmenting phonemes | Jonathon starts with a /dz/ sound. |

From van Kleeck and Schuele (1987), with permission.

tioned in the metalinguistic section in Chapter 2. Four year olds differ from eight year olds in word-awareness ability because eight year olds' awareness goes beyond a word's meaning. Eight year olds can focus on meaning but they can also focus on form. For example, according to eight year olds, "*dog* is a word, it is spelled *d,o,g,* and it means four-legged animal" (McGee et al., 1982). Older children's responses show, once again, how they advance from a semantic to a structural appreciation of language (see Chapter 4).

### Phonemic Segmentation

Research in the area of word, syllable, and phonemic segmentation, which was mentioned in Chapter 4 with a sample lesson, includes data about children's awareness that language is made up of units and that those units can be separated. Researchers have used many different games to observe children's knowledge about language segments. Fox and Routh (1975, 1984) examined children's segmentation abilities by providing them with spoken sentences and words and asking them, "Say just a little bit." For example, if given the stimulus "Peter jumps," an acceptable response for word segmentation would be *Peter* or *jumps;* when given the stimulus *Pete,* an appropriate response for phonemic segmentation would be /p/ or /t/ or /i/. Liberman and her colleagues (e.g., Liberman et al., 1980) used a wooden dowel and had children tap out parts of sentences, words, syllables, and sounds. Rubin (1986) used color tokens and boxes to help children with sound segmentation.

Liberman and her colleagues (e.g., Liberman et al., 1980) have probably done the most extensive work in the area of segmentation. The findings from their classic phonemic segmentation studies (e.g., Liberman & Shankweiler, 1979) have been replicated by other researchers (e.g., Blachman, 1984; Rubin, 1986) although there is still controversy regarding some of the developmental stages and the connection that phonemic segmentation abilities have to reading. Nevertheless, we know that segmentation, particularly sound (phonemic) segmentation, is quite difficult for nondisabled as well as for language-disabled students (Blachman, 1984). Some phonemic segmentation activities remain difficult until seven or eight years old, partially because they require a high degree of metalinguistic awareness and partially because of the specific tasks used to observe phonemic segmentation ability. For example, identifying initial sounds is thought to be easier than identifying final sounds. Identifying all the sounds in a word ("Tell me the three sounds in *bat*) and elision games that require identifying words when parts of the words are deleted ("If I steal the *d* from *ditch,* what do I have?") are also quite difficult. We are reminded again to be cautious about developmental progressions. While some three year olds manifest spontaneous segmentation ability, as we saw in the van Kleeck and Schuele (1987) samples, some three year olds even perform well on segmentation games that involve separating words in simple sentences. Four year olds are more likely to think that *a house* is one word than six year olds (van Kleeck, 1984b). It is not until about five or six years old that children's ability to segment words into syllables and sounds improves dramatically (Fox & Routh, 1975; Rubin, 1986, see Table 2-1). Some researchers suggest that the improved performance of six and seven year olds on sound segmentation may be a consequence of reading ability rather than a prerequisite (e.g., Allan, 1982; Backman, 1983).

## Where Does the Theoretical Information Take Us?

We are reminded to be sensitive to both the multifaceted nature of metalinguistic development and to the level of difficulty of some of the tasks and materials used to test and observe metalinguistic performance. We have seen numerous interactions across sentence-processing and metalinguistic domains. Table 7-2 provides a partial summary of some of the key points made about semantic and syntactic strategies. It reflects the kinds of information we need to have in order to develop meaningful intervention sequences.

Children are organized. They use strategies for comprehension and explanation that are semantic- and content-oriented until their late preschool years. Somewhere around seven years old, children begin to develop syntactic-structural strategies. That is, they begin to deal with language out of context. They become more sensitive to word order, and they recognize that the smaller units like connectives, articles, and prepositions make a difference. Language learning continues well into the eighth and ninth years. Children have difficulty processing reversible and nonredundant complex sentences well into their elementary school years. School-aged children also have much to learn about metalinguistics. Many metalinguistic abilities, such as detecting ambiguity, recognizing synonymy, and dealing with figurative language, continue developing until 13 and 14 years of age (see Chapters 2 and 8; Hakes, 1982; Nippold, 1985; van Kleeck, 1984a, 1984b).

Although we have a long way to go before we unravel the connections among segmentation ability, reading acquistion, and proficient reading, we do know that many children come to school *with* some knowledge of written language (Lomax & McGee, 1987; see Chapter 5). Children entering first grade with superior or above-average word awareness, rhyming and phonemic and lexical segmentation abilities maintain their superior or above-average standings in their grade in reading at the end of the school year (e.g., Zucchermaglio et al., 1986). Children who come to school with print-to-speech awareness and knowledge about sentences and words come with an advantage.

**TABLE 7-2**

*Summary of Syntactic and Semantic Strategies for Sentence Processing and Metalinguistic Awareness*

Sentence processing patterns (Semantic: logic leads the way)
1. Semantically constrained two-clause sentences that have probable events tend to be easier.
2. Sentences in which spoken word order violates event order are easier with probable event relations; use *before* or *after* conjunctions first.
3. Relative clause sentences that are redundant and subject-oriented tend to be easier initially; use subject-embedded sentences with one or two animate nouns when exposing children to difficult structures.

Specific metalinguistic awareness (corrections are easier than open-ended grammatical judgments)
1. Lexical and word-order violations may be easier.
2. Sentences that have semantic and probable event relations tend to be easier.
3. Oral-to-literate devices such as *and, and so,* and *and after that* may be added to sentence corrections.

Sentence processing patterns (structural awareness follows semantically oriented emphasis)
1. Nonconstrained sentences that follow word order with a focus on smaller linguistic units as clues to meaning might follow sentences described above; use visual cues such as pictures initially, and use familiar conjunctions such as *and then,* followed by *and so* and *because.*
2. Integrated versions of harder or unpredictable sentences should be used as spoken and written models.
3. Object relatives that follow word order may be easier and should be presented with subject relatives with parallel function; caution: this approach needs to be matched to student's strategy.

Specific metalinguistic awareness (corrections and judgments)
1. Phonological and syntactic corrections with familiar content might be introduced after lexical and word order violations.
2. Grammatical judgments with spoken and written sentences should be included as appropriate.
3. Speaker or situation style changes can be added to correction and judgment tasks; use conversation versus news reporting versus writing a report.

It is important to remember that these steps represent general guidelines and not specific sequences.

## INTERVENTION SUGGESTIONS

Individual sentences, when used creatively, may help students develop an appreciation for language structures. Although we would like to help students become more metalinguistic, we need to keep the larger picture in focus. By working on sentences and specific linguistic forms that change meaning, we hope to help children appreciate some of the differences between oral and literate styles of communication and help them make easier transitions to literacy. We also hope, as Warren-Leubecker (1987) suggested earlier, that by helping children become more aware of language — in this case, by helping them to become more analytical — we help them become more metacognitive. All the suggestions that follow represent extremely difficult and highly literate activities. *They are not appropriate for younger children with general communication problems.* The general principles that we applied to intervention in the previous chapters would apply here as well:

- Be sensitive to the teacher's and student's learning styles, as outlined in Chapter 3.
- Question intervention choices, as illlustrated in Chapters 3 and 4.
- Understand task complexity, as shown in Chapter 4.
- Describe the student's learning profile, with particular emphasis on some of the linguistic and metalinguistic strategies described in this chapter. For example, we would want to know the kinds of literate forms used by the student, the kinds of strategies he or she uses when processing sentences, and the kinds of stimuli that facilitate comprehension of more complex forms. We would also like to know about the student's grammatical judgments, sentence correction abilities, and segmentation levels.

## Appreciating Literate Forms in Use and Processing

### *Expose Students to Complex Forms: Focus on Whole to Part*

Students should be exposed to complex sentences in stories before (or in conjunction with) the following activities. The kinds of comprehension strategies used by students for particular sentences should be observed. Students can then work on complex sentences in decontextualized situations as in the activities presented below. Sentences that have a real-world sequence and that are redundant may be used initially. However, reversible sentences may be used if they are appropriate for particular students. Pictures may be used to support written sentences, or written sentences may accompany spoken sentences, again depending on the students. In the following example, the written sentence is presented to students:

The man who is wearing the red scarf is a Russian spy.

Students are asked to decide which of three ideas of the following four form the sentence. (Note that the third choice represents an inference from the given information. This is not necessarily an incorrect choice but students should discuss given and inferential information differences.)

1. The man is a spy.
2. The man is Russian.
3. The man is sneaking around the building.
4. The man is wearing a red scarf.

A variety of sentence forms can be used. Sentences can be modified to help students focus on different aspects of structure. The purpose of these types of activities is to provide students with model sentence forms. The Russian spy sentence above is a subject-embedded relative sentence with one noun (one actor). The Larry Bird sentence presented below is also a subject-embedded relative, but it has two nouns (or actors). The description of Larry as a Boston Celtic, set off by the embedded clause, is reminiscent of the literate forms described by Lee-Schachter at the beginning of this chapter. Sentences can be made more difficult by using two or three nouns (or actors) involved in different actions. The Reggie sentence below is particularly difficult because it is an embedded relative, it has three nouns, and its word order is confusing.

Larry Bird who plays for the Boston Celtics is chasing Dr. J. down the court.

1. Larry Bird is chasing someone down the court.
2. Larry Bird is chasing Dr. J. (or Dr. J. is being chased by Larry).
3. Larry Bird plays for the Celtics.
4. The Celtics are from Boston.

Reggie Jackson who is being chased by Don Mattingly is screaming instructions to the third base coach.

1. Reggie Jackson is screaming to someone.
2. Reggie is screaming to his third base coach. (note use of *his*)
3. Reggie is chasing Don Mattingly. (note word order of the clause)
4. Don Mattingly is chasing Reggie.

One can modify this activity by having students segment sentences without giving them choices (this overlaps with the segmentation activities presented a bit later). We can also have students make up contexts in which the sentences would fit different situations (as discussed in Chapter 6). A variation of the context-sentence–matching idea is to have students compare oral and literate styles. However, oral-literate style comparisons are quite difficult because they involve language evaluation. For example, students can be presented with a written sentence (Wallach, 1985):

> A woman who is in the second car of the arriving train is *the one* the authorities want to abduct.

The sentence's spoken correlate could be

> *This* woman is the person that the cops wanna pick up *and* she's hiding in the second car of the train.

Students can be asked to discuss the similarities and differences between the sentences. We like to use the conversation–casual letter to best friend–classroom–news reporting–newspaper article continuum with our older students to show how situations change our manner of presentation. (Variations of these activities are possible for younger children and for students who are not ready for this level of language analysis. Norman and Ralph puppets, as suggested earlier, can provide ways of exposing children to language differences in a somewhat more spontaneous format; see Wallach, 1985 and van Kleeck and Schuele, 1978, for additional examples.)

Emerson's picture-cartoon sequence choices (1980), mentioned earlier in this chapter, can provide students with a structure for handling complex *because* and *if* sentences. Lee-Schachter (personal communication, 1987) adapted the Emerson format for complex relatives. Emerson (1979) used the following sentence:

> Because he went out to play with his friends, he was feeling happy.

Two sets of pictures can accompany the target sentence. (For older and more advanced students, we often present written phrases in the boxes.) Students are asked to decide which set of pictures goes with the target sentence. Discussions follow as to why choices were made. To expand on the individual sentence task, students are then asked to make up dialogue for the different sequences (e.g., "What might the boy be saying to himself").

*Sequence 1:* boy happy     out to play     play with friends
*Sequence 2:* boy lonely     out to play     boy happy

Differences between *because, and so,* and *and then* sequences can also be discussed. Reminiscent of Lee-Schachter's work, we would hope to help students use coordinates and connectives more explicitly. Students can be exposed to different sentence-sequence matches. For example, one could say, "The boy was happy and then he decided to go out to play and then he was playing with his friends" for the first sequence, and one could say, "The boy was lonely and *so* he went out to play with his friends and then he was happy" for the second sequence.

Older students can be asked to make judgments about sentence-picture matches. For example, "The boy was lonely because he went out to play with his friends and then he was happy," represents an inappropriate use of *because.*

Lee-Schachter (personal communication, 1987) uses picture sequences to help students become more sensitive to embedded and nonembedded relative clause sentences. Students have pictures in front of them in a predetermined sequence. (Written stimuli in the form of phrases may be used with older students instead of pictures.)

Jumbo jet on runway      small plane still in the air

The students are given two written sentences. They are asked to decide which one might best fit the picture sequences. Students can be given hints such as, "Think about whether the jet or the small plane is on the runway." Target stimuli might include the following:

1. The jumbo jet that flew over the commuter plane landed safely on the runway.
2. The jumbo jet flew over the commuter plane that landed safely on the runway.

These sentences are somewhat redundant in that there are two nouns plus an inanimate runway. If we were going to make the sentences more difficult, we would need to be very careful about the nature of semantic and structural variables that could interfere with processing. Our purpose with any of these activities is to help students become more sensitive to some of the structural devices in language that affect meaning. We use smaller pieces of discourse (clauses and sentences) to facilitate overall comprehension (see Chapter 6).

**WORD ORDER AND ORDER OF MENTION SPECIFICS — SENTENCES AND PICTURES.** We can expand on the ideas mentioned in the previous section by considering word-order and order-of-mention strategies in relation to the connectives used in sentences (as inspired by Keller-Cohen, 1987). Students can be asked to manipulate picture sequences and discuss clause order. (We should be certain that the picture manipulation is not interfering with comprehension.) Probable event sentences should be used first. We recommend using vocabulary and content from students' readers or other curricular areas. Oral and written work may be combined. Sentences can be presented in ordered (spoken matches real-world sequence) and nonordered (spoken order is the reverse of real-world order) forms:

*Before sentence:*
The boy brushes his teeth before he goes to bed. (ordered)
Before he goes to bed the boy brushes his teeth. (nonordered)
*After sentence:*
After he opened the can the boy poured the soup. (ordered)
The boy poured the soup after he opened the can. (nonordered)
*When sentence:*
When the cake came out of the oven the girl put on the frosting. (ordered)
The girl put on the frosting when the cake came out of the oven. (nonordered)

Students listen to (or read) a target sentence and arrange pictures accordingly. With oral work, it becomes important to use stress- prosody cues to help students attend to critical pieces of the sentence. With written work, we like to color-code certain words or clauses (writing the conjunction in red or writing an entire clause in red). These crutches are used initially to help the student develop a strategy. Pictures are ordered initially so that the events make sense in terms of their real world sequence, e.g.,

Boy brushing teeth      boy getting into bed
Boy opening can      boy pouring soup

Students might also be given two sentences with one set of pictures. For example, the boy brushing teeth and boy getting into bed sequences could have the following two sentences beneath the pictures:

1. After the boy brushed his teeth, he went to bed.
2. Before the boy went to bed, he brushed his teeth.

Students can be asked to decide which sentence goes best with the pictures. Discussions of choices and *after* and *before* connectives can follow. Students are encouraged to think of other examples that might demonstrate the same patterns. Sentences become more difficult when they are reversible, e.g., "The reporters went over their notes before the President came into the press conference."

*WORD-ORDER AND ORDER-OF-MENTION SPECIFICS: SENTENCE-TO-SENTENCE MATCHES.* Meaning equivalence decisions, sometimes called synonymy judgments, are extremely difficult. The following activities can help students who read and who need help with comprehension. The content of the sentences must be considered carefully. Students can be given a written sentence that is semantically constrained (nonreversible) but that represents a more literate way of saying something, as reflected in the passive sentence below:

The Iran crisis was discussed by Sam Donaldson of NBC.

Students are given three written sentences (which can be read to them). They are asked to decide which one means the same thing as the target sentence:

1. The Iran crisis was discussed by Dan Rather of CBS.
2. Sam Donaldson of NBC discussed the Iran crisis.
3. He said the Iran crisis was a tremendously dangerous situation.

Judgments become more difficult when the stimuli are reversible:

The President congratulated the reporters.

1. The reporters congratulated the President.
2. The President was congratulated by the reporters.
3. The reporters were congratulated by the President.

Any number of variations is possible. We might color-code the doer of the actions as a clue. We might provide presentence cueing by presenting short stories before working on the target sentences. We might use some of the Hansen and Pearson (1983) inferential questions (discussed in Chapter 6) before doing these activities (do the students know who Sam Donaldson is?).

### Help Students With Smaller Linguistic Units: Focus on Parts to Whole

The following activities overlap with the ones presented in the previous section, but they are a bit more analytical. We still present the gestalt but expect students to build from the parts. As inspired by Athey's (1977) and Lee-Schachter's (1985) work on explicit coordination (as adapted from Wallach & Lee, 1982), students can be given various propositions:

| | |
|---|---|
| Getting darker | Rain coming down |
| Jim tall | John short |

Lion growled     Bob terror
Sally dreamed    Famous doctor

The students are asked to combine the ideas into a complete sentence using *and*. The possible relations that might be expressed, as described by Athey (1977) are as follows:

It was getting darker and the rain was coming down. (similarity of elements; theme of a gloomy evening)
Jim is tall and John is short. (comparison)
The lion growled and Bob ran in terror (causality)
Sally dreamed of growing up and becoming a famous doctor. (some temporal appropriateness)

Students can be given a list of connectives such as *because, but, and so, and after that, when,* and *while.* They can be asked to decide which of the conjunctions could replace the *and* in the sentences presented in the previous section. Students can also be asked to fix awkward sentences:

1. He dreamed of growing up and eating a delicious dinner that evening. (make a content change of some sort)
2. The lion growled because Bob ran in terror. (might make a content change; might change the *because* to *and* or *and then;* might change the order of propositions as per Emerson, 1980)

As suggested by Emerson (1980), we might help students with sentence changes and corrections by providing them with possible ways to correct sentences. A target sentence follows:

*Target sentence:* The glass of water spilled because the chair got very wet.

Possible corrections follow:

1. Content changes occur earlier developmentally:
The glass of water spilled because the chair *was in the way,* or the glass of water spilled because *the chair hit it,* or the glass of water spilled because *the roof was leaking.* This is meant to be illogical but students may find a reasonable way to fit it into the sentence.
2. Connective choices, such as *and* and *and then* occur at all stages developmentally. Students can be given conjunction choices: "The glass of water spilled and then the chair got very wet."
3. Clausal changes occur later developmentally. With causal changes, one reverses the propositions to make the sentence logical, i.e., "The chair got very wet because the glass of water spilled." Clausal changes may be encouraged by (a) some of the picture-to-sentence

and sentence-to-picture activities presented earlier; (b) starting the sentences for the student by saying, "The chair got very wet because — "; or (c) presenting segmented versions of sentences on index cards, e.g., The glass of water spilled because the chair got very wet.

Students can be asked to move clauses around to see if the sentence makes better sense in example(s). It is interesting to note that in certain contexts, many *because* sentences that seem illogical actually make sense. Bransford and Johnson (1973) provide an example of a *because* sentence that makes sense within a context: "John was able to go to the party tonight because his car broke down." The sentence becomes logical once we know that John intended to go home to another city when his car broke down. The consequence was that he went to the party with friends because he could not go home until his car was fixed.

In a final activity, the students listen to (and/or read) a set of simple sentences. They are asked to change the sentences so that they mean the opposite or something different. The activity can be open-ended or it can be made more specific by having students focus on the italicized forms presented in the next group of examples. Students can also be given choices of forms (written on index cards, for example) that might be used to change the sentences. The sentences can be part of a story or a paragraph.

These activities reinforce the idea that smaller linguistic units can make a difference. Forms and choices should be matched to the students' levels and interests (adapted from Wallach & Lee, 1982).

| *Stimuli* | *Possible Responses* |
|---|---|
| The boy is playing basketball. | The boy *is not* playing basketball. |
| John came to the game *without* his brother. | John came to the game *with* his brother |
| She *can* swim. | She *can't* swim. |
| Mary enjoys swimming and Mike enjoys *swimming*. | Mary enjoys swimming and Mickey *does too*. (ellipsis) |

## Appreciating Language Segements

### A Word of Caution

Rubin (1986) and Liberman et al. (1980), among others, suggest a variety of ways to enhance students' awareness that language has units and that those units can be separated. Segmentation activities are especially useful for students who have a great deal of difficulty making the transition from speech to print, who make stabs and wild guesses when reading, and who have difficulty spelling. Many students labeled as having auditory-discrimination, auditory-blending, and phonics difficulties actually have segmentation difficulties (see Chapters 1, 2, and 4). It is important to remember that many segmentation abilities are late acquisitions. The spontaneous manifestations of word consciousness and segmentation, described by van Kleeck and Schuele (1987) in the preschool period, should be observed and encouraged. It is also important to remember that segmentation activities should not be the only focus of a child's program. It helps to combine vocabulary, comprehension activities, and segmentation activities. Two of the biggest mistakes we see clinically and educationally are the overuse of segmentation activities at early ages with children who have broader communication difficulties and confusion about the sequence of difficulty surrounding segmentation units (as in the case presented at the end of Chapter 4).

### General Awareness

Word play games may enhance children's awareness of word, syllable, and sound units. Older students may engage in auditory or oral sound-play games in conjunction with written work. Oral sound-play games (done without visual support or the accompanying written word) are more useful for younger children and nonreaders. Rubin (1986) suggests a number of games, described in the following paragraphs.

**WORD COUNTING.** The teacher says a sentence and the students repeat it. The teacher holds up her or his finger for each word in the sentence if necessary or stresses certain words that the students omit. Students can use tokens or they can clap or tap out the number of words in the sentence. Word counting remains an oral activity for students who have little sense of words as units. For older students, present sentences, words, and phrases on index cards and ask the students to decide how many words are on the card. For example, use stimuli like, "ahouse," "isreporting," "con gratulations," "don't do it," etc. By organizing stimuli with certain cues, we can obtain some information about students' segmentation sets. We try to help students to use language knowledge (rather than misleading information from print) to make their segmentation decisions.

We like to include word-consciousness activities with the word-counting games. For example, we ask students to tell us about the long and short words in spoken sentences. For older students, we encourage discussions of written words. As inspired by van Kleeck (1984b), we present words to students such as, *fly, crocodile, transmitter,* and *mile,* and ask them to discuss the long and short of what they hear and see.

***SYLLABLE AWARENESS.*** Students tap out the number of syllables (or beats) to words. Oral games are used to help students become more sensitive to the units of speech. Rubin (1986) suggests an alliterating game that exposes students to words that start the same way: *ice-cube, ice-cream, ice-ing, ice-icles.* For older children, one can be more direct about definitions of syllables. One can also use more formal alliteration studies as part of literature. We like to color-code the first phoneme of written words for students who are having difficulty with multisyllabic words. It is also useful to have older students build new words by adding syllables to words they already know. For example, with more advanced students we might use word combinations: *report-reporting-reported, electric-electrician-electricity.* Fox and Routh's procedure (1984) of "Say a little bit of the word" can also be used to enhance students' abilities of syllabic units. (Rosner, 1975, should be consulted for in-depth information in this area.)

***SOUND SEGMENTATION.*** Students can be exposed to rhyming games with real words and nonsense words. Tapping procedures might also be used at the phonemic level. For example, the teacher says a series of vowel sounds such as *a a a* while clapping out the number or by making three marks on the blackboard to represent the number of sounds spoken. Rubin (1986) suggests moving from vowel sequences to consonant vowel (CV), consonant vowel consonant (CVC), and harder combinations. Words from children's readers can also serve as the segmentation stimuli. Zhurova (1973), as reported by Camp et al. (1981), used toy animals and a toy bridge to expose five year olds to phonemes. In order for the children to get their animals across the bridge, they had to give a secret password to the guard (the teacher). The password was the initial sound of the name for the animal — for example, /m/ for *mouse.* Elision games involving mystery words can also be used for phonemic awareness: for example, "Say *sheep* without the *p* to find the mystery word" (Camp et al., 1981, p. 178). Rubin (1986) outlines additional procedures for sound segmentation activities, which were adapted by Camp et al. (1981) from Elkonin (1973):

1. The student is presented with a line drawing of a person, object, etc. The word represented should be in the students' active vocabulary. It is suggested that early training periods include words beginning with

fricatives (/f/, /s/, /v/) or nasals (/m/, /n/) because these sounds are more easily produced "in isolation."

2. A picture, such as the ones presented in Figure 7-1, has a rectangle beneath it which is equivalent to the number of phonemes in the word. For instance, the word *ship* would have three boxes for the three phonemes.

3. The student is presented with counters or chips, all of one color.

4. The student says the word slowly.

5. The student places a counter in the appropriate box under the picture. Oral work with phonemic segments should make this portion relatively easy for most students.

6. After the student has done the previous portions of the phonemic segmentation activities with a variety of words and pictures, the vowel-consonant distinction can be introduced.

7. Counters or chips now have two colors: one color for consonants and one color for vowels. The student moves tokens into the appropriate

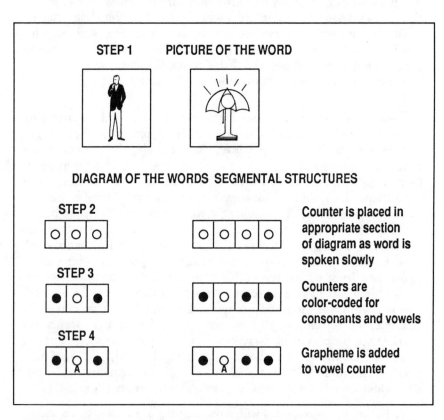

**FIGURE 7-1.** *Phonemic segmentation activities (adapted from Elkonin, 1973, by Camp et al., 1981, and by Rubin, 1986).*

boxes but now makes consonant-vowel distinctions. For the word *ship*, the first and last token would be one color and the middle token would be another color.

8. After the student can manipulate tokens for consonant and vowel combinations with considerable accuracy, graphic symbols are introduced (letters are written on the tokens). Initially, a limited number of letters are written on the tokens.
9. Eventually, letter tiles take the place of all the tokens.

Figure 7-1 represents a sequence of phonemic segmentation activities using the pictures and counters as adapted from Elkonin (1973) by Camp et al. (1981) and Rubin (1986). (See also Liberman et al., 1980, for an excellent and thorough discussion.)

---

## SAMPLE LESSON PLANS*

---

### COVER SHEET FOR
### SENTENCE AWARENESS: SUBORDINATION

*Theoretical Principle*
Children perform better on complex sentences that are probable event-oriented and predictable. They use content- and semantically oriented strategies when processing and when correcting sentences.

*Type of Strategy*
Top-down focus: pay attention to main events and use your knowledge of the real world.

*Type of Language*
Semantic-syntactic: decontextualized and metalinguistic format for comprehension and language awareness.

*Clinician/Educator Questions*
1. Why have I chosen to work on sentences?
2. Is the student ready for this level of language analysis? For these kinds of decontextualized and metacognitive activities?

*(continued)*

---

*See Chapter 4 for additional lesson plans in this area.

## COVER SHEET FOR SENTENCE AWARENESS: SUBORDINATION *(continued)*

*Clinician/Educator Questions (continued)*
3. How will I modify the program if the student performs poorly?
4. Are these activities related to the student's observed syntactic-semantic levels? What kinds of oral-to-literate forms does the student use currently? In what situations? What kinds of comprehension and sentence correction strategies have been observed?
5. Is the content within the student's repertoire? What new content am I teaching?
6. How does this lesson relate to the classroom?

## SAMPLE LESSON PLAN FOR SUBORDINATION AND META AWARENESS

**Target on Complex Syntactic Forms
With Probable Event Sequences**
Helps students become more comfortable with literate syntactic forms. The lessons are done to help students (1) approach two-clause sentences with an organized strategy; (2) understand that word order is not always identical to meaning; and (3) begin to understand that smaller units make a difference to meaning.

*Sentence Forms Targeted*
Semantically constrained two clause sentences (probable event), with *and, and after that, before, after,* and *and so,* and semantically inappropriate sentences (for sentence corrections).

*Specific Sequence*
Begin with sentences where the spoken/written order matches the meaning/events; move to where spoken order is reversed (real-world knowledge will facilitate processing); accept content and reduction changes on sentence corrections.

*(continued)*

*Strategies Facilitated*
Top-down with whole-to-part approach; bottom-up with smaller units; initially, probable event and semantic sets are encouraged.

*Special Instructions*
Some students with bottom-up preferences may be helped by focusing on smaller units initially; tasks can affect performance; comparison and evaluation are excellent to use but they require a relatively high level of meta ability; semantic constraints should be facilitative; number of connectives used should be monitored but student should be exposed to a variety of forms; students should be exposed to complex forms for a good deal of time before they are asked to analyze and create forms on their own.

*Tasks and Materials*
Use content and vocabulary appropriate for students' levels; integrate with curriculum whenever possible; focus on comprehension and segmentation of sentences initially; move to synthesis and evaluation and correction; integrate spoken-written activities whenever possible.

We can apply the cover sheet and the lesson plan checklist to relative clause sentences.

## COVER SHEET FOR SENTENCE AWARENESS: RELATIVIZATION

*Theoretical Principle*
Children begin by using semantically oriented strategies when processing relative clause sentences. Redundant relatives are easier than nonredundant relatives, and there is ambiguity about the precise age at which clause interruption presents a particular problem for children. However, embeddedness is one of the most highly literate forms reported in the literature.

*(continued)*

## COVER SHEET FOR SENTENCE AWARENESS: RELATIVIZATION *(continued)*

*Type of Strategy*
Begin with top-down focus, but the analysis of clause/form manipulation will be bottom-up; specific sentence processing strategies involve parallel function and word order strategies.

*Type of Language*
Decontextualized and metalinguistic.

*Clinician/Educator Questions*
1. Why am I working on relative clauses?
2. Is the student ready for the level of analysis and manipulation chosen?
3. How will I back up if the particular progression I have chosen is too difficult? How will I modify the plan if it is *too easy or uninteresting*?
4. How do the lesson plan and activities relate to the students' oral and written language needs and abilities?

Using the cover sheet, we can generate the following lesson plan.

## SAMPLE LESSON PLAN FOR RELATIVIZATION

**Target on Embedded and Nonembedded Relatives
With One and Two Nouns and
Word-Order Consistencies**
Helps the student with more literate syntactic forms. The activities are done to (1) help students deal with clause interruptions more effectively; (2) help them have a more sophisticated oral and written style; and (3) help them understand that structural changes make a difference.

*(continued)*

*Syntactic Forms Targeted*
Subject relatives that are redundant and parallel-function oriented; object relatives that are redundant and word-order-oriented; and coordinate (*and* sentence) versions of the relatives.

*Specific Sequence*
Start with integrated versions of sentence forms being targeted; use coordinate sentences as oral style models; move to subject redundants with one animate noun; move to object redundants with one animate noun; repeat steps with two animate nouns.

*Strategies Facilitated*
Begin with a top-down focus by presenting the entire sentence; move to bottom-up with clause analysis and discussion.

*Special Instructions*
Caution needs to be exercised regarding sequence of relative sentences; some students may do better with bottom-up approaches initially.

*Tasks and Materials*
In some cases, the subordinate and relative activities can be combined; the semantically constrained nature of the stimuli joins the different lessons; students should be reminded of connections; students' textbooks can be used for analysis of complex relatives; combine with expository work, as described in Chapters, 3, 5, 6, and 8.

Many of the structural activities presented next build on the ones described in Chapter 6. It is important to remember that a number of stages may separate the sample lessons presented here.

## COVER SHEET FOR SPECIFIC SYNTACTIC DEVICES: FOCUS ON CONJUNCTIONS

*Theoretical Principle*
Young children tend to ignore smaller units, using probable event strategies, when processing complex sentences. They

*(continued)*

---

## COVER SHEET FOR SPECIFIC SYNTACTIC DEVICES: FOCUS ON CONJUNCTIONS
*(continued)*

*Theoretical Principles (continued)*
begin to focus on structural aspects of their language in the early elementary school years. The acquisition of conjunctions and other clause connectives is a slow and gradual process. There are some suggested sequences available, but the listing of conjunctions without consideration of contextual, syntactic, and content variables is completely inappropriate.

*Type of Strategy*
Bottom-up focus; analytical and segmental.

*Type of Language*
Structural-syntactic focus, decontextualized and metalinguistic.

*Clincian/Educator Questions*
1. Why have I chosen to work on conjunctions and other connectives?
2. Do I understand the many variables related to acquisition and use of connectives?
3. How am I going to modify the plan if the student has difficulty?
4. How are these activities related to school performance? To primary linguistic competence? To metalinguistics?
5. Are the concepts reflected by the connectives chosen in the student's repertoire? How do I know?

---

Once again, we generate a lesson plan after we have questioned ourselves about our intervention choices.

---

## SAMPLE LESSON PLAN FOR STRUCTURAL AWARENESS: CONJUNCTIONS

**Target on Clausal Connectives and Conjunctions**
Helps student learn how smaller linguistic units change meanings. These activities are done to help students move from semantically oriented strategies to syntactically oriented strategies.

*(continued)*

---

*Clausal Connectives and Conjunctions Targeted*
Theme-connecting connectives; temporal connectives (*and, and after that, before/after, when*); causal connectors (*and, and so, because, if*).

*Specific Sequence*
Start with the different uses of *and;* move to changing *and* to more explicit *and* coordinates (*and when, and so, and after that*); move to logical uses of other connectors (*after/before, because, and if*).

*Strategies Facilitated*
Bottom-up: pay attention to smaller linguistic units.

*Special Instructions*
Begin with illogical/incorrect sentences to "force" a change; use stress/prosody cues and color-coding when sentences are written; provide parts of sentences to be combined (synthesis); introduce reversible sentences to demonstrate role of conjunction/connector.

*Tasks and Materials*
Move students from whole to parts; work on synthesis and grammatical judgments.

## CLOSING REMARKS

By helping students become active and self-responsible learners, practitioners can focus on academic tasks from a variety of perspectives. By assisting students in learning the discourse characteristics of school, we direct them toward discovering how teachers and students talk in classrooms, how textbooks are organized, and how their own oral and written language can be structured. In other words, students can develop strategies for discerning organizational patterns in discourse. At the same time, practitioners can direct students' attention toward the more fine-grained aspects of discourse, such as the cohesive ties holding larger organizational frames together, the specific syntactic and semantic regularities characterizing the different types of discourse, and the inferetial aspects of discourse types. At this fine-tuning level, intervention focuses on strategies for analyzing sentences, words, and sounds. By combining both top-down and bottom-up approaches to discourse, practitioners increase the likelihood that students will access school tasks more efficiently and effectively. Students will begin to understand the larger organizational patterns associated with discourse types, and they will also learn strategies for manipulating the component parts of discourse structures. Our goal is to help students discover the balance that best suits their learning needs.

# C H A P T E R   8

## Vocabulary and Word Naming, Figurative Language, and Other Meaningful Considerations

*It is not only a matter of asking what a word means, it's a matter of asking what else could the word mean (Bashir, 1987).*

Bashir's words crystalize a number of concepts about language. We must ask the right questions about language to ourselves and we must also help our students ask the right questions. Helping students to use what they know and to understand what they do not know is a critical aspect of language intervention. We know that language continues to develop throughout the school years and well into early adulthood, and we know that children become increasingly more flexible and creative with language. The increased flexibility and creativity are reflected in many ways. Children change their style of language more effectively to match situations, they give up some of their concreteness and literalness, and they use language to learn new concepts and to demonstrate their academic proficiency. We have long struggled with the question of how we help students with language learning disabilities make some of these transitions. Although practice has begun to catch up with theory, we still have much to learn about how to teach language. We also have much to learn about the specific connections between the mastery of linguistic (and nonlinguistic) strategies and academic success for different children at different points in time.

As we have learned more about the continuum of language success, we have learned more about the changing nature of language disorders through time (Bashir et al., 1983; Maxwell & Wallach, 1984; Weiner, 1985). The research discussed briefly in Chapter 1 has been powerful from a number of perspectives. We have learned, for example, that some language-disabled children use strategies that may not be as efficient or as flexible as those used by their non–language-disabled peers (see Chapter 7). We have seen how some symptoms of early language disorders, like word-naming difficulties (Leonard, 1986; Rubin & Liberman, 1983), persist over time, whereas others, such as *overt* syntactic errors and morphological omissions (Maxwell & Wallach, 1984), wash away over time. We have also learned that some language-disabled children have difficulty with aspects of figurative language and that they remain more literal and concrete in their processing and use of language (e.g., Nippold, 1985). We have all experienced the frustration of trying numerous approaches from rote memorization to spontaneous interaction to alleviate a complex and diverse group of problems, sometimes with and sometimes without the generalizability we had hoped to achieve.

## VOCABULARY AND NAMING: LANGUAGE AND LEARNING STRATEGIES

### The Theoretical Base

Information about vocabulary knowledge and naming abilities comes from many sources. Educators have been traditionally concerned about teaching students new words for both oral and written language, and reading specialists have long studied the effects of vocabulary teaching on comprehension (Stahl, 1986). The correlation between vocabulary ability and traditional measures of intelligence is also well-documented although fraught with controversy (Israel, 1984). We may not know precisely how vocabulary ability affects overall ability, but we do know, as many clinicians and educators have shown, that word proficiency of all kinds is needed to survive in clinics and classrooms. Stephens and Montgomery (1985) remind us of the wide variety of abilities needed for school success when they write, "Categorizing words, supplying synonyms and antonyms, formulating complex sentences, offering multiple definitions, recognizing ambiguity, and explaining nonliteral aspects of language are only a few of the linguistic and metalinguistic demands made by upper-grade curricula" (p. 43).

Blanchowicz (1986) gives us this typical sequence characteristic of many middle- and high-school situations: students are given new words on Monday; they look them up on Tuesday and write a dictionary definition; they write a sentence on Wednesday; they study on Thursday; they take a test on Friday (p. 643). Blank and Marquis (1987) remind us that many of our language-therapy and kindergarten-readiness classes are exercises in naming and categorization. How many of us can identify with instructions such as, "Put all the fruits in one pile and all the animals in another pile," "Name all the items of clothing you can think of in a minute," or "Tell me the colors of all the circles and squares."

There has been a tremendous amount of research in both language and reading camps in the area of word naming and word retrieval specifically (e.g., Israel, 1984; Kail, et al., 1984; Kail & Leonard, 1986; Rubin & Liberman, 1983). German's model (1986) of word-naming and word-retrieval deficits, which she terms word-finding deficits, yields a comprehensive model for building intervention plans. She argues that word finding is influenced to a considerable extent by several variables, including the situational context, the stimulus context, the nature of the target word, and the presence or absence of facilitating cues.

German found that children's word finding varies according to the situational context in which the student is expected to retrieve a particular word. For instance, in constrained situations, the student is asked to engage in picture naming (nouns, verbs, or categories), sentence completion, or description naming. These tasks call for the retrieval of a specific target word. In contrast, in a spontaneous situation, picture-simulated spontaneous language samples are analyzed for productivity and the presence of specific word-finding behaviors. German (1987) has found that productivity measures such as story length are strongly correlated to the presence of word-finding difficulties. Thirty-five percent of the students who exhibited word-finding difficulties in German's study (1987) produced stories of reduced length in comparison with the stories of their nondisabled peers. German also found that 57 percent of students exhibiting word-finding difficulties produced stories of adequate length but included many repetitions, reformulations, and substitutions. Overall, 92 percent of the students with word-finding difficulties evidenced spontaneous language differences when compared with nondisabled peers. Thus, spontaneous as well as constrained naming tasks present difficulties for many students with language learning disorders. German (1987) points out that stimulus context, nature of the word, and facilitating cues also affect how language-impaired students perform on word-retrieval tasks. For example, language-impaired students find it easier to retrieve specific words when they are asked to name pictures than when they are asked to supply a word for an open-ended sentence. German states that, although nondisabled students by age 11 can perform relatively easily no matter what the stimulus context, many language-disordered students continue to be affected by the nature of the word-finding task. She goes on the say that the nature of the word students are asked to retrieve also affects their ability to find the word. For language-impaired students, nouns are the easiest to retrieve, followed by verbs, followed by superordinate categories.

German argues that prototypic exemplars are easier to retrieve than nonprototypic words, e.g., *apple* is easier to retrieve than *pear*. German (1986) suggests that the following cues enhance the language-impaired students' word-retrieval success: phonetic prompts (/ko/ to prompt *comb*); semantic prompts ("It's not a pear; it's an _____"); and multiple choice prompts ("It's either *apple, dog, green,* or *big*").

Rubin and Liberman (1983) argue that vocabulary deficits, naming problems and retrieval problems are not necessarily synonomous terms. Goodman (1970), in earlier research (as reported by Thelen, 1986), says the same thing and discusses different situations where oral and written vocabulary intersect. She reminds practitioners to recognize the heterogeneous nature of "vocabulary problems" especially when planning intervention. Regarding terminology differences, Pearson (1984) states that vocabulary knowledge is closely related to background knowledge. He says that individuals need a conceptual base and an experiential repertoire if words are to have any real meaning and if words are going to be part of an oral and written inventory. On the other hand, naming involves the expressive representation of concepts. Names are phonological summaries of semantic information. Children can have a concept (and can show you nonverbally that they have it) but not know (or remember) the name of the concept. Naming something means coming up with a concept's phonological representation (Rubin & Liberman, 1983). Thus, naming difficulties can be related to lack of background knowledge (the semantic base) and limited verbal exposure to and practice with the word itself (the phonological structure).

Pearson (1984) states that ownership of vocabulary occurs when students relate a word to an appropriate schema they already have (Thelen, 1986; see Chapter 2). He says that educators often ask, "How can I get this word into the student's head?" when they should be asking, "What is it that the student already knows about that I can use as an anchor point, as a way of accessing this new concept?" (Thelen, 1986, p. 606). Following Pearson's line of thinking, Leonard (1986) indicates that many of the so-called retrieval problems that children appear to have may be manifestations of broader conceptual and naming problems. Leonard (1986) believes that the term *retrieval* has been overused and suggests that the inability or difficulty some children have in coming up with labels on fast naming tasks and the like is a bigger problem than accessing a word they already have. Leonard's research suggests that many naming problems are semantic elaboration problems. He believes that many language-disabled children have not had enough exposure to and practice with the words they supposedly can't retrieve. Thus, according to Leonard (1986), they seem to have forgotten the word when they never really had it (see Israel, 1984; Kail et al., 1984; and Leonard et al., 1983 for in-depth discussions).

We will see how Leonard's findings, and the findings of other researchers, relate to the intervention suggestions that follow. As always, knowledge of research is necessary if language intervention is to make any sense. We should also exercise caution when making statements about what children can and can't do from limited samples of behavior. Rubin and Liberman (1983), and German (1986), among others, argue that some naming error patterns reflect where children might be on the developmental scale, but they also say it would be a mistake to look at naming errors in a vacuum. What do the naming errors have to do with the child's real world? We might ask ourselves what naming errors say (or do not say) about children's general strategies for organizing and retaining information (see Chapter 2).

Rubin and Liberman (1983) discuss oral naming errors in relation to strategy and in relation to word-decoding errors in reading. Note the examples of word-naming errors provided by Rubin and Liberman (1983):

| Target words (picture shown to child) | Response |
|---|---|
| Wheelchair | The thing you sit on when you're sick |
| Helicopter | Airplane |
| Escalator | Elevator |
| Scissors | Sister |

According to Rubin and Liberman (1983), the response for *wheelchair* and *helicopter* are semantically oriented. Note the circumlocution for *wheelchair* and the substitution of a semantically associated word for *helicopter*. The circumlocution may be indicative of some background knowledge and experience with wheelchairs. The airplane response for *helicopter* is certainly in the semantic ballpark, and we would want to know more about the responder's knowledge of helicopters before drawing any conclusions about his or her naming abilities. The responses for *escalator* and *scissors* are especially interesting because *elevator* and *sister* are phonologically close to the target words. The *elevator-escalator* pair represents semantic and phonological closeness, whereas the *sister-scissors* pair appears to have phonological closeness alone. Rubin and Liberman (1983) say that phonological stabs like *sister* for *scissors* may be rather sophisticated because they show that the child is going for structure. Sometimes children use words they already know for words they cannot pronounce or remember (recall the goodness-of-fit discussion in Chapter 2). Indeed, the nature of phonological as well as semantic approximations for words warrants careful consideration because, as proposed by Rubin and Liberman (1983), good readers appear to develop a more efficient phonological set for word naming than poor readers.

Rubin and Liberman (1983) state that their studies with good and poor readers lend evidence to the notion that poor readers have difficulty retaining and accessing the phonological representation of words (even when they understand the concept being expressed by the word). Poor readers appear to maintain semantically oriented strategies for longer times (as suggested in the previous chapter). Rubin and Liberman (1983) go on the say that some of the word-decoding problems of poor readers may be connected to their naming difficulties because word decoding, particularly fast and efficient decoding, involves coming up with the phonological representation — the pronunciation — of the printed word.

## Intervention Options: Helping Students Become More Active Learners

Blanchowicz (1986) offers suggestions for integrating comprehension, word learning, and reading. The suggestions are excellent guidelines not only for vocabulary development, but also for structuring lessons in other areas as well. Blanchowicz outlines a number of steps for word learning, including (1) activating what students already know; (2) having students make preliminary, predictive connections between words and topics; (3) using spoken and written text contexts; (4) refining and reformulating meanings; and (5) using words in writing and additional reading.

### Techniques for Activating What Students Know

Blanchowicz (1986) suggests choosing a topic from students' readers or other curricular content areas. Her suggestion can be extended to include students' literature books as well. Blanchowicz then chooses some words from the topic area, some that do not belong to the topic, and some that are ambiguous. She calls this technique *exclusive brainstorming*. With exclusive brainstorming, students make decisions about preselected words and discuss *why* they have chosen to include or delete words from a topic. Blanchowicz (1986, p. 645) provides the following example of a topic ("Family Life in an African Bush Station") with preselected vocabulary that utilizes a multiple-choice facilitating cue:

| | | |
|---|---|---|
| *avalanche* | *tricycle* | *thicket* |
| *veldt* | *dolphin* | *pampas* |

She points out that students might want to exclude *avalanche* after discussing the terrain they associate with Africa or with avalanches. Students should be encouraged to ask about words they do not know. We like to point out to students, particularly those with language learning disabilities, that there are words *we* do not know and part of this work is to compare old and new vocabulary.

Blanchowicz (1986) also uses a knowledge rating checklist to encourage students to analyze their knowledge of words from various topics. Table 8-1 represents a word checklist used with students. Blanchowicz follows up with a modified version of some of the word-consciousness activities mentioned in the previous chapter. Students are asked questions such as, "Which are the hardest words?" "Which do you think most of us don't know?" "Which are the easiest ones?" and "Which ones will most of us know?"

**TABLE 8-1**
*How Much Do You Know About These Words?*

| | Can Define | Have Seen/Heard | Don't Know |
|---|:---:|:---:|:---:|
| *Geodesic dome* | | X | X |
| *Yurt* | | | X |
| *Mandan* | | | X |
| *Teepee* | X | | |
| *Nuraghe* | | X | |
| *Lean-to* | X | | |

From Blanchowicz, (1986), with permission.

### Techniques for Making Preliminary Connections

First, students need to become more aware of what they know and what they do not know, as discussed in Chapter 4. The next step, according to Blanchowicz (1986), is to help students make some predictions about relationships in stories (or other types of discourse selections) from words they do know. She says that we need to encourage students to hypothesize, e.g., "From the words you know, what will this chapter be about?" (Blanchowicz, 1986, p. 646; see also Chapter 5). This approach is reminiscent of the one used by Hansen and Pearson (1983) for developing an inferential set (Chapter 6). It also fits the narrative strategies described in Chapter 5. Blanchowicz (1986) also offers suggestions for helping students make predictions. She shows us how to use selected words to come to the same goal, i.e., how to get students actively involved in learning by helping them use what they know. Table 8–2 represents a Predict-O-Gram used by Blanchowicz (1986, p. 648), which combines story grammar elements with word awareness. Students use key vocabulary to construct a verbal story before they read.

### Using Oral and Written Text Reformulating and Using Words in Reading and Writing

Blanchowicz (1986) reminds us to provide students with many experiences and exposures to new words. As they listen to stories and as they read, students should be encouraged to refine their predictions and their preconceptions about words. In other words, they should be reminded to apply the principles that have been discussed above to other situations. Individual activities, such as the Predict-O-Gram, might be followed up by writing a narrative, using the Predict-O-Gram as an outline. Among the important facets of word learning and retention, according to Blanchowicz, are relating new words to current knowledge and bombarding and exposing students to words in many different contexts.

**TABLE 8–2**
*Predict How the Author Will Use These Words in the Story*

| The Setting | The Characters | The Goal or Problem | The Actions | The Resolution | Other Things |
|---|---|---|---|---|---|
| *Rolling seas* | *Fisherman* | *Rolling seas* | *Stranded* | *Wail* | *Selchie* |
| *Townsfolk* | *Townsfolk* | *Stranded* | | *Grief* | |

Predict-O-Gram, adapted from Blanchowicz (1986), with permission.

Stahl (1986) follows Blanchowicz's suggestions and reminds us that passive learning activities, such as stating definitions and providing word associations from lists out of context, appear to be ineffective teaching methods. Research suggests that children seem to learn and retain more words when they are encouraged to make connections between new and known information (Blanchowicz, 1986). Children also need to be exposed to multiple repetitions of new words *in many different contexts and settings*. Leonard (1986) makes the point that we frequently spend very little instructional time exposing children to words. He also argues that we often make assumptions about how to teach vocabulary and how to improve naming abilities without consulting research and without being knowledgeable about the levels of students' word awareness. Stahl (1986) argues that we have to make informed decisions about which words to teach and which strategies to encourage since we cannot teach students every word they will need to know in every context. We might start by assessing words that are most important in students' personal worlds; we might review their reading series or content area text to understand which words are causing the most difficulty; and, most importantly, we must understand what students know and what they do not know from the perspectives suggested by Blanchowicz (1986), German, (1986), Israel (1984), and Rubin and Liberman (1983), to name only a few.

Yoshinaga-Itano and Downey (1986) outline a powerful framework for teaching vocabulary and naming by actively involving children in constructing pictures of what they know utilizing schema theory. Following a concept presented in Chapter 2, Yoshinaga-Itano and Downey (1986) argue that schemata are efficient and adequate mechanisms for organizing, coding, storing, and retrieving knowledge. They argue further that schemata such as scripts, or action-sequenced scenarios, are typical event sequences underlying children's production and comprehension of stories or narratives. Scripts emerge out of children's real-life experiences, as do the linguistic labels children attach to those experiences and to the resulting scripts, which develop as memory structures. Because scripts form the base structure of knowledge, Yoshinaga-Itano and Downey (1986) advocate teaching verbal labels within an experiential schema approach. They describe a typical lesson in which children are asked what they know about hospitals. The teacher draws a visual map of the related concepts comprising the children's knowledge of the script *hospital,* as in Figure 8–1. The map shows how several concepts can be associated with the same script, for example, doctors, nurses, patients, x-ray, operating rooms, visitors, rooms with beds for sick people, nurseries, gift shops, wheelchairs, and so on. The children are encouraged to name each concept

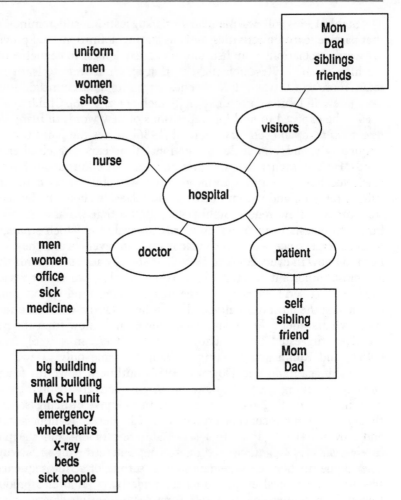

**FIGURE 8–1.** *Hospital schema, adapted from Yoshinaga-Itano and Downey (1986).*

they can think of relating to *hospital*. To demonstrate scripts embedded within scripts, the teacher can focus on a particular script within the overall *hospital* script, emphasizing the components of *doctor* or *nurse*, for instance. Using the *doctor* subscript, the focus might result in children naming the doctor's office, waiting room, stethoscope, family, hobbies, and children. To illustrate the contrasting of related scripts, the hospital can be described in terms of how it is different from a doctor's office, a medical clinic, and a mobile army surgical hospital (M.A.S.H. unit) (Yoshinaga-Itano & Downey, 1986). At each step of the process, the teacher draws a visual map to illustrate graphically the relationships under consideration. In this manner, the teacher helps children increase their vocabulary by helping them build on what they already know.

## Semantic and Phonological Awareness Revisited: Top-Down? Bottom-Up?

Pearson (1984) provides suggestions for combining word meaning, sentence structure, and decoding activities. He says that students should be encouraged to guess and to make predictions about possibilities when approaching oral and written material. However, he reminds us that at some point students are going to have to be more precise about speech-to-print matches when reading. Pearson provides some interesting suggestions for helping students make more precise guesses about words. He encourages students to use context and print to arrive at answers in sentence completion tasks. In one example (taken from Pearson & Spiro, 1982, p. 87), students are presented with sentences and a choice of words:

Susan was so happy that she _____ through the park.
*walked      trudged      skipped*

Students are asked to guess which word would be the best one to complete the sentence. They are asked to discuss all the word choices and to consider the completion of the sentence with all the choices. We like to ask students to think of other words that might be appropriate, and we also like to get them to think about words that would be totally absurd in the sentence. We sometimes provide a more restricted option by putting in the first phoneme of the correct answer in the blank:

Susan was so happy that she **sk**_____ through the park.
*walked      trudged      skipped*

This cue helps students use a critical feature from the print to trigger a word guess that might be appropriate. Any number of variations are possible with the simple, yet elegant, Pearson schema.

Vellutino (1979) says that students must learn to appreciate the linguistic nature of reading. He goes on to say that they need to become more sensitive to the verbal information in print; i.e., they have to develop a find-out-what-the-word-*says* strategy. One way to find out what words say is to use the surrounding context; another way is to develop an appreciation for the particular clues in print that help you get the word. By "get the word," we mean finding a written word's phonological representation — its pronunciation, its spoken counterpart. The "Susan skips through the park" example above shows how context can be used to help students make word guesses. The *sk* clue gives students additional information. The printed cluster is supposed to help students retrieve the word from their verbal repertoire. (This might be analogous to first-phoneme prompts used with children with oral word retrieval problems.)

It is not ideal to drill students on isolated word lists, as indicated in the previous section and implied throughout the text. Decoding at the phonemic level is only one of many strategies readers use to get to meaning. Although decoding is not the only process involved in learning to read, it is nevertheless an important one. Students need to recognize that the goal in reading is the apprehension of the meaning underlying print. Key questions to be considered include the following: What is the purpose of reading? How can word recognition and decoding activities facilitate the communication process? How can decoding activities help students appreciate bottom-up and top-down processing strategies? How can fast and efficient decoding help students become proficient readers? (By proficient readers, we mean understanding what an author has written from many perspectives; e.g., see Juel, 1983; Roth & Perfetti, 1982; and Zivian & Samuels, 1986, for fascinating discussions on comprehension and decoding in good and poor readers.)

## Learning Phoneme Clusters That Are Redundant and Popular in English

Vellutino (1979) suggests using word pairs to make students more sensitive to some of the patterns in print that represent different pronunciations. He also says that getting students to talk about the different meanings of the words makes for a nice combination of phonological (word decoding) and semantic (word meaning) strategies. Consider the following examples:

    *clam*    *calm*
    *snug*    *sung*
    *lion*    *loin*

Vellutino (1979) suggests teaching students the pronunciations of *cl, sn,* and *oi* and then having them read separate words or word pairs using those popular letter clusters. We like to use word pairs, with color-coded clusters, to help students with the letter-sound correspondences. We also like to use sentences and paragraphs to reinforce word meanings and to provide a way of bombarding students with new words in many contexts (following Blanchowicz, 1986). Many of the word-learning activities mentioned in the previous section can be combined with the decoding activities.

Juel (1983) considers both verbal and visual aspects of words when developing materials for students. Juel (1983) points out that some words are hard, particularly for children with reading problems, because their pronunciations are not easily predictable. For example, the *ea* and *ai* in *hair, pear, rain,* and *ocean* do not have consistent pronunciations. Juel (1983) points out that good readers seem to develop a sixth sense about words like these. That is, they learn very quickly that some English words have very common letter combinations like *ea* and *ai,* but that those combinations are not necessarily pronounced the same way. Juel advocates that we do some of the things Vellutino suggests but that we also expose children to large numbers of words that contain similar (and frequent) letter combinations. Juel says it might be better to help students appreciate whole word patterns *without* emphasis on some of the individual pronunciations of the separate letters. We can sometimes color-code common letter combinations using the whole-word approach to help students become sensitive to difficult orthographic-sound connections. We can warn students about certain letter clusters, telling them they will be pronounced in many different ways. Some sentence-word pairs, as adapted from Juel (1983, p. 313) might be as follows:

The girl with the long _____ is beautiful. (*legs/hair*)
The street was wet from _____. (*rain/snow*)
That isn't a frog; it's a _____. (*toad/lizard*)
The boat was in the _____. (*cove/ocean*)
My favorite fruit is a _____. (*pear/banana*)
He _____, "I want to go out!" (*said/screamed*)

Stimuli can be devised that focus on difficult letter combinations (as in *hair, rain, toad, ocean, pear*) or more predictable combinations (as in *legs, lizard,* and *cove*). We can provide students with first-phoneme or first-letter prompts, as we did in the "Susan skipped" example. In the Juel (1983) examples above, we used an embedded clause in the first sentence and a dialogue in the last one. Any number of variations is possible to expose students to the syntactic, phonological, and orthographic features of words.

## FIGURATIVE LANGUAGE: WHAT ELSE CAN IT MEAN?

As practitioners we must be very aware of the long and gradual nature of language development. An example from a child's IEP was provided in Chapter 1: "Johnny will learn fifteen metaphors by December 31st." It was pointed out that it might take nondisabled children a number of years to completely master the metaphors of a language. Our advancing knowledge of research leaves us with questions: Was this a totally invalid intervention goal for Johnny? Isn't it important for children to be able to handle figurative language? Isn't our everyday language filled with idiomatic and metaphoric expressions? The answers to these questions are "maybe not," "depends on what you mean," and "yes."

## The Theoretical Base

Understanding and using metaphors and idioms and the mastery of puns, riddles, jokes, and other aspects of humor (see Chapter 2, Table 2-1; see also Kamhi, 1987; van Kleeck, 1984a) are metalinguistic skills because they involve the understanding that language can be manipulated; they also involve the recognition that form can be separated from content and that meaning goes beyond a text's or a sentence's individual parts. Older children learn that one word can have a number of different meanings (ambiguity), that two sentences forms can have the same meaning (synonomy), and that various combinations of words and sounds can serve to have different meanings altogether (figurative interpretations).

Roth (1987) points out that nonliteral forms of language may be difficult for language learning disabled students. She provides some examples from the research on metaphors and reminds us to consider the figurative nature of both oral and written materials. For example, Lee and Kamhi (1985) studied nine- to 11-year-old children's comprehension and production of metaphors in decontextualized situations. They asked children to choose correct answers for metaphoric sentences and to complete metaphoric sentences. They observed three groups of children: nondisabled children, learning-disabled children with a history of language impairment, and reading-disabled children without a history of language impairment. Examples of the tasks by Lee and Kamhi (1985) as summarized by Roth (1987) are as follows:

1. Comprehension task
   *Target sentence:* His face turned white as a sheet and he fell to the ground.
   *Task:* Children are asked to decide what the sentence means from the following choices:
   The sheet covered his face causing him to fall to the ground.
   After his fall to the ground, someone covered him with a sheet.
   He became very pale and fainted.
   He became as scared as a ghost.

2. Production task
   *Target sentence:* The night was as dark as _____.
   *Task:* Children are asked to complete the sentence.
3. Preference task
   *Target sentence:* The volcano is _____.
   *Task:* Children are asked to decide which ending is the "best one."
   a man who is very angry (conceptual/psychological)
   a bright red fire truck (color)
   a roaring lion (sound)
   a whale spouting water (movement)
   a mountain of lava (literal translation)

Lee and Kamhi (1985) found that the learning-disabled subjects with a history of language impairment chose literal endings (such as "a mountain of lava") 94 percent of the time. The reading-disabled group chose literal endings and interpretations 44 percent of the time; the nondisabled group chose literal interpretations only 5 percent of the time. Roth (1987) points out that when the learning-disabled groups were encouraged to try metaphoric endings they felt that the sentences didn't make sense. Nippold and Fey (1983) also found that metaphors were difficult for language-disabled children to comprehend and to explain. They remind us that the acquisition of figurative language is a rather late acquisition and that significant changes in comprehension and use begin in the middle elementary school years and continue well into the older adolescent years.

Nippold (1985) provides an in-depth discussion of metaphors, idioms, and proverbs. She states that the use and understanding of figurative language is important in both academic and personal-social realms. She goes on to say that figurative language is extremely difficult to assess because so many variables — including linguistic, metalinguistic, and nonlinguistic factors — affect performance. For one thing, there are many different ways in which nonliteral relations are expressed. Metaphors are different from idioms, and idioms are different from proverbs. There are also as many different types of metaphors as there are different types of humor. Likewise, there are many ways to observe and test children's comprehension and use of figurative language. Even young children demonstrate comprehension of figurative language especially when figurative forms are used in an appropriate context, but they may not be able to demonstrate that knowledge consciously. Milestones gleaned from standardized tests and research studies should be interpreted with caution in view of the highly metalinguistic and decontextualized nature of many of the tasks employed.

## Different Types of Metaphor: What Can We Learn?

A metaphor is defined as a nonliteral usage of words in which one element, the topic, is compared to another, the vehicle, based on one or more shared features, the ground, (Nippold, 1985; Roth, 1987). Consider the metaphoric sentence, "Hair is spaghetti." The topic is hair, the vehicle is spaghetti, and the ground is thinness and length (Roth, 1987). According to Nippold (1985), there are two distinct types of metaphors: predicative (similarity metaphors) and proportional. Predicative metaphors involve one topic and one vehicle. "The giraffe was a flagpole living at the zoo" is a predicative metaphor. Giraffe is the topic and flagpole is the vehicle. Proportional metaphors contain two topics and two vehicles in an analogical relationship. One topic usually remains unstated: "Johnny's knee was a tomato that squirted juice" is a proportional metaphor. It contains the analogy "Tomato is to juice as knee is to (blood)," leaving the topic blood to be inferred (Nippold, 1985, p. 2). Nippold et al. (1984), as reported in Nippold (1985), found that nine year olds outperform seven year olds on multiple-choice problems involving metaphoric sentences, with proportional metaphors being more difficult than predicative metaphors. Nippold (1985) goes on to say that similes, which are variations of predicative metaphors, may be easier for young children to comprehend because the use of the word like makes the comparison between the topic and vehicle more explicit. "The giraffe was like a flagpole living at the zoo" is a simile. However, conflicting data indicate that caution is warranted regarding statements about the ease and difficulty of various figurative forms (Reynolds & Ortony, 1980; Winner et al., 1980).

There are other considerations that affect metaphoric comprehension. One aspect for consideration, according to Winner et al. (1976), is the conceptual aspect. Another aspect is task format. Conceptual considerations involve the relations expressed in the metaphor. Winner et al. (1976) suggest the action metaphors are easier to comprehend than static metaphors, and cross-sensory metaphors are easier than psychological metaphors. Nippold (1985) provides examples of the different types of metaphors:

> Action: The sprinter is a jet plane. (movement/speed comparison)
> Static: The basketball player was a flag pole on the court. (perceptual similarity)
> Cross-sensory: The smell of my mother's perfume was bright sunshine. (smell to color)
> Psychological: His father's anger was an erupting volcano. (emotional relation)

Winner et al. (1976) say that literal interpretations of metaphoric sentences are more common among six to eight year olds with a steady increase in comprehension accuracy through age 14. Reynolds and Ortony (1980) also say that for both metaphors and similes there is a steady improvement in comprehension with about 50 percent accuracy at Grade 2 to 80 percent accuracy at Grade 6. Winner et al. (1976) go on to say that the multiple-choice format revealed better performances than the explanation format, indicating that adequate figurative explanations were infrequent before age ten. Other researchers support the general findings of Winner et al., also pointing out that even young children have some ability to *detect* metaphoric interpretations before they can explain them. In an earlier study, Gardner (1974) found that preschoolers could match spoken words like *happy* and *sad* to color swatches like yellow-orange (happy) and violet-blue (sad) to represent metaphoric interpretations, but they could not explain their choices. Even seven year olds give literal explanations for metaphors like, "An easel is loud because you hear the brush" (Nippold, 1985). Van Kleeck (1984a) provides an example of explanation attempts by children of different ages for one of the sentences used by Winner et al. (1976, p. 293). Children were asked to tell the examiner what the following sentence means:

> After many years of working at the jail, the prison guard had become a hard rock that could not be moved.

Five and six year olds used a magical approach to explain the sentence. Younger children said thing like, "The witch turned the guard into a rock." Nine and ten year olds used a concrete/physical feature to explain the sentence: "The guard had muscles that were as hard as rocks." Twelve and 13 year olds improved dramatically in their ability to provide more accurate explanations that captured the underlying of the sentence: "The tough life in the prison made the guard a very cold and inflexible person."

The examples provided from some of the studies of metaphoric comprehension show how broad and multifaceted our knowledge of the research must be. By these examples alone, we can see that the period of metaphor acquisition is long and complex. We might now question the LEP recommendation made earlier. Why should Johnny learn 15 metaphors by December 31st? What types of metaphors is he going to be taught? In what contexts? With what types of tasks? Is the choice to teach metaphors relevant to the Monday morning classroom? To his peer group? Before attempting any work with figurative language, we must always assess its appropriateness and value for individual students.

## Intervention Suggestions: Developing Flexibility Across Language and Learning Domains

### Begin at the Perceptual Level

Nippold (1985) suggests beginning at the perceptual level and encouraging students to notice various similarities between different pairs of common objects. If action-movement metaphors appear somewhat earlier, we might consider pairing examples that exemplify action like a hopping kangaroo and a bouncing pogo stick or a twirling ice skater and a spinning top (Nippold, 1985, p. 9). For younger children, real objects might be used to encourage them to see the relationships. For older children, we might include discussions about the objects, followed by the modeling of sentences, followed by the incorporation of sentences into simple stories, followed by sentences with multiple choices, followed by the construction of sentences with the word pairs. For example, we might use the following target sentence:

The skater was a top spinning on the ice.

We could ask students to pick out the topic (*skater*) and the vehicle (*top*) (we do not have to use the labels *topic* and *vehicle*). We could ask students to pick out the "best" meaning from a choice of meanings:

1. The skater was twirling very fast.
2. She had a top next to her on the ice.
3. The skater was spinning so fast she looked like a toy.

Students can discuss the different possibilities. We like to have our older students discuss the differences between literal and nonliteral translations.

Nippold (1985) suggests doing two things to try to ensure that students understand and have enough time to practice with metaphors. She says to (1) begin with easier renditions of predicative metaphors and (2) use *like* and *as* similes to make relations more explicit. Easier predicative metaphors include topic-less metaphors such as, "The pogo stick hopped down the road." Students can talk about the use of hopping in relation to the pogo stick before relating the action and the object to the movement of a kangaroo. Nippold (1985) also suggests using riddles and quasi-analogies with students to help them generate relations among words. For example,"What is like a top but spins on the ice?" and "A top spins on the floor and something spins on the ice," represents riddle and analogy stimuli, respectively. An easier rendition of the skater metaphor (a simile) is, "The skater was like a top spinning on the ice." We like to use the most explicit version of a metaphor, as inspired by Nippold (1985). The sentence that follows represents the explicit statement of topic (*giraffe*), vehicle (*flagpole*), and ground (*tall*):

The giraffe was as tall as a flagpole living at the zoo.

We like to present students with the complete sentence. We then ask them what the words *giraffe* and *flagpole* have in common (recall that this is a static metaphor, which is believed to be more difficult than an action metaphor). We discuss the similarity of features with students and use visual supports (pictures) as needed. For older students, we use sentence comparison. We present students with written sentences and ask them to decide whether the sentences mean the same thing as the explicit giraffe sentence:

The giraffe is like a flagpole living at the zoo. (*simile*)
The giraffe is a flagpole living at the zoo. (*metaphor*)

We sometimes color-code the word *like* to give students an extra hint about the relations in the sentence (as discussed in Chapter 7). We also ask students to discuss the missing words and concepts (e.g., the implied tallness of the flagpole and the giraffe; see Chapter 6 for more on inferential processing). It is important to remember that sentence comparison is rather difficult because it involves an evaluation judgment and an appreciation for synonomy. Caution is necessary when using this type of activity, but it is useful with older students.

When students are ready, they can be presented with word pairs from which they can construct similes and metaphors. Vocabulary choices must be made carefully. (The activities presented in this section may overlap with the activities discussed in the vocabulary and naming section of this chapter.) Examples of word pairs might include the following:

*eyes-diamonds*
*mouth-cave*
*flowers-crown*
*wrestler-gorilla*

More difficult word pairs with more abstract connections might include the following:

*cold-unfriendly*
*hard-inflexible*
*anger-volcano*
*happy-bright*
*bright-smart*

Use vocabulary from students' readers and content-area textbooks whenever possible. Encourage older students to make up their own word pairs and challenge other members of the group to create original similes and metaphors.

### Moving to the More Abstract

Proportional metaphors, which are like analogies in some ways, are more difficult than predicative metaphors, which tend to be more difficult than similes. Additionally, cross-sensory and psychological metaphors are sometimes more difficult than action and static metaphors. Indeed, as we move along the scale of abstraction, we find that some concepts expressed figuratively are cognitively more complex than others. Nippold (1985) says that the statement, "Billboards are warts upon the landscape" represents a more subtle and complicated statement than some of the predicative metaphors presented in the previous section. She also says that students should have experience with similes and predicative metaphors before they work on proportional metaphors. Nippold (1985) recommended beginning with very concrete analogies when introducing students to proportional metaphors. For example, she says to start with connections like:

*picture . . . frame*
AS
*yard . . . fence*

Students should discuss the possible connections among the pairs of words; e.g., what does the frame do for a picture and what does a fence do for a yard? By presenting perceptually salient (and picturable) relations, students may have a better opportunity to abstract the relations. For older students we like to present the word pairs with the words *as* next to them. We discuss how *as* could link picture-frame to yard-fence. Sentence construction would follow a discussion period. We also like to spend a great deal of time exposing students to model sentences. Eventually, we work with proportional metaphors: "Mary's yard was a picture enclosed in a silvery-white frame."

Nippold (1985) points out that after students have spent some time with concrete analogies, they might move on to more abstract connections:

*engine . . . car*

AS

*man . . . bicycle*

She points out that even Grade 4 students begin by interpreting the analogies as if they are independent units. Nine year olds tend to say, "A car needs an engine; a bicycle needs a person." Eleven and 12 year olds explain relations more precisely by stating: "The words might go together because *engines* and *men* power cars and bicycles."

We like to use some of the sentence-combining activities discussed in the previous chapter to help students integrate information. We might present students with complete sentences like, "A car needs an engine and a bicycle needs a person" and ask them to discuss the topics and vehicles (a top-down approach). We also present students with separate words and *as* (as listed in this section) and ask them to construct sentences. We use multiple-choice activities to expose students to different sentence interpretations. We use some of the sentence completions discussed by Roth (1987):

The champion cyclist is _____.

1. a man riding a bike very fast. (*literal*)
2. a powerful engine. (*metaphoric*)
3. a streak of lightning. (*metaphoric*)
4. like a car engine because he powers the bicycle. (*simile with explicit explanation*)

Roth (1987) provides additional ideas for helping students appreciate nonliteral language. She suggests presenting metaphors, idioms, and other figurative forms in supportive contexts. One type of supporting context is a story. Roth (1987) presents short stories to children with a target sentence (underlined) at the end:

It was John's first airplane ride. He was excited and scared at the same time. The pilot announced to everyone that the plane was ready for take-off. John looked out the window. The plan was moving up off the ground. The trees disappeared like melting ice cream.

She then gives the children multiple-choice questions and asks them to pick the best answer. Any number of variations is possible to expose children to nonliteral forms of language. We might structure the target metaphors at the end of the stories so that they represent different levels of difficulty. We might ask students to choose from a list of sentences the one that would best complete the story. Sentences can also be structured so that literal and nonliteral choices are available;

different types of metaphors (cross-sensory, psychological, etc.) may also be part of the choices.

### Using Humor for Double Meanings

Roth (1987) points out that riddles, jokes, and humorous definitions can also be used to help children appreciate and enjoy language. However, she reminds us that these activities are highly metalinguistic and require fairly sophisticated language competence. We saw from Nippold's work (1985) with metaphors that explanation and discussion of word meanings improves after ten years of age. We also noted that the multiple-choice format may help children appreciate some of the double meanings of words, but it is still a rather difficult task. Roth provides examples in five areas: (1) matching riddles to answers; (2) solving riddles; (3) choosing humorous answers; (4) completing jokes; and (5) matching definitions. She says to carefully review the literature on the acquisition of metalinguistic development, assess students' linguistic competence, and ask oneself why we would choose any of these activities before using them with students with language learning disabilities. Examples in each of the areas presented by Brubaker (1985) are as follows:

1. Matching riddles to answers *
   *Choose the word that correctly answers each riddle.*
   screwdriver     bed     Mississippi     trumpet
   What kind of driver doesn't get a speeding ticket? _____
   What has four eyes? _____
   What has four legs, but only one foot? _____
   What pet makes the best music? _____
2. Solving riddles
   *Each riddle has a choice of three answers. Choose the answer that solves the riddle and circle it.*
   Which animal keeps the best time?
   lion     watchdog     hen
3. Choosing humorous answers
   *Mark the funny answer. All the answers may fit but you mark the funny one.*
   Whay did the lobster blush?
   _____ It was very hot.
   _____ It saw the salad dressing.
   _____ It was embarrassed.

---

* Some of the riddle activities are useful for improving word awareness and word segmentation skills; see Chapter 7.

**4.** Completing jokes
*Each joke has three possible endings. All the endings could fit, but only one is funny. Mark the ending that makes the sentence funny.*
Old refrigerators never die, they just
_____ wear out.
_____ stop working.
_____ lose their cool.

**5.** Matching definitions
*These definitions are funny. Choose the word from the list that fits the definition.*
*flea      silverfish      paradox      old-timer*
_____ two doctors
_____ imitation goldfish
_____ 75-year-old watch
_____ bug that's gone to the dogs

## Creative Paraphrasing and Expository Mapping as Learning Strategies

Shugarman and Hurst (1986) recommend using paraphrase writing to help students appreciate different ways that meanings can be expressed. As indicated throughout this chapter, paraphrase is an extremely difficult and sophisticated activity (also recall the van Kleeck, 1984b, hierarchy in Chapter 4). Shugarman and Hurst (1986) describe three types of paraphrasing: (1) simple rephrasing; (2) summarizing; and (3) elaborating.

Simple rephrasing is the paraphrasing of sentences, short passages, and simple stories. Many of the sentence equivalence activities presented in Chapter 7 involved rephrasing. Summarizing involves highlighting major points from a story or a paragraph or a chart or a cartoon. One generally omits more information when summarizing main ideas; one tends to keep the same information, reproduced in a different form, when rephrasing. In both rephrasing and summarizing, one concentrates on the text in order to develop a parallel form of the original meaning (Shugarman & Hurst, 1986, p. 397). Rephrasing and summarizing are highly verbal-linguistic activities in that they involve word and sentence structure manipulation. Elaboration, on the other hand, involves creating a new form to represent a writer's original message. In elaboration, linguistic material (such as a written passage) is transformed into a different symbolic representation. According to Shugarman and Hurst (1986), a written passage could be recast into a chart, cartoon, or picture. Written directions could be recast as maps.

Shugarman and Hurst (1986) go on to recommend additional activities, many of which overlap with the activities presented throughout this text. Some of the activities also reflect the authors' suggestions to use as many different learning domains as possible with students (see Chapters 2 to 4). Paraphrasing activities might include the following:

- Asking students to make judgments about the structures of passages and to paraphrase the ones that need work.
- Presenting students with games, directions, and rules and asking them to rewrite them for younger students.
- Playing popular songs and asking students to follow the song's lyrics from words on a handout for the purpose of paraphrasing the important ideas from the song.
- Having students read advertisements and paraphrase what the ads are really saying or trying to persuade people to do.

Piccolo (1987) reiterates the importance of recognizing and appreciating different ways that meanings can be expressed. The six types of expository text discussed in Chapter 3 included (1) descriptive paragraphs; (2) enumerative paragraphs; (3) sequence paragraphs; (4) cause-effect paragraphs; (5) comparison-contrast paragraphs; and (6) problem-solution paragraphs. Piccolo (1987) says that students must become sensitive to the different types of expository text, and they must also learn that certain words signal that a particular pattern of text is operating. For example, words like *first, second, third, last,* and *finally* suggest that the author is listing examples to support a topic sentence, signaling perhaps an enumerative or sequence paragraph. Words like *so, because of, as a result of, since,* and *in order to* may signal cause-effect paragraphs. *Different from, same as, alike,* and *similar to* may indicate comparison-contrast paragraphs.

Piccolo (1987) reminds us that few students, even nondisabled students, are aware of expository text structure. She goes on to say that students who have been given instruction in expository text improve in reading comprehension and recall (see Chapter 5). Piccolo (1987) suggests a number of things: First, be very sensitive to the order of acquisition of expository forms; Piccolo's experience and data suggest working on sequence, enumerative, cause-effect, descriptive, problem-solving, and comparison-contrast paragraphs in that order, although we could modify the order based on the individual needs and abilities of our students. Second, it is important to define, label, and model the structures we would like students to acquire. Students should discuss the key words that signal certain paragraph types, and they should discuss the different ways the authors present their ideas. Third, it is important to encourage students to use verbal and graphic organizers to appreciate the patterns of expository text. The verbal and graphic organizers usually follow some experience and ability with various types of expository text.

Table 8-3 is an example of a verbal organizer devised by Piccolo (1987). We can use the verbal organizer in conjunction with the expository text organizer described in Chapter 5. The graphic organizers, also developed by Piccolo (1987), are interesting because they provide a visual map for students that may alleviate some of the language overloading required by the verbal organizers (see Chapters 2 and 6).

Figures 8-2 and 8-3 are examples of the enumerative and descriptive graphic organizers used by Piccolo (1987) to help students become more sensitive to the different types of expository paragraphs. (Piccolo, 1987, should be consulted for an in-depth discussion; Carr & Wixson, 1986, should also be consulted for additional information or visual mapping ideas). Figure 8-2 shows a visual depiction providing an elaboration of a topic sentence. The elaboration can be used to develop the topic. Figure 8-3 shows another way to elaborate a topic sentence so that descriptive features are highlighted. Again, students can use the visual graphic as an aid in organizing their expository paragraphs.

The purpose of all the activities presented in the previous chapters, diverse as they might be, is to help students develop learning strategies that are flexible and applicable across situations and learning

**TABLE 8-3**

*Verbal Organizer: Questions Students Can Ask Themselves to Help Identify Text Structures When Writing Original Paragraphs*

*Descriptive*
   Do you want to tell the reader what something is?

*Sequence*
   Do you want to tell someone how to do something or make something?

*Enumerative*
   Do you want to give a specific list of things related to a topic?

*Cause-effect*
   Do you want to give reasons why something happens?

*Problem-solution*
   Do you want to discuss a problem and propose solutions?

*Comparison-contrast*
   Do you want to talk about likenesses and differences?

From Piccolo (1987), with permission.

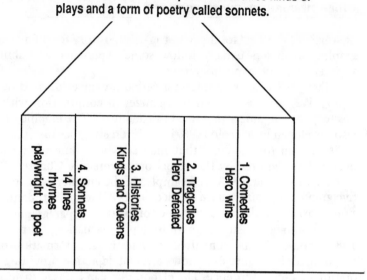

**FIGURE 8-2.** *Visual graphic, from Piccolo (1987).*

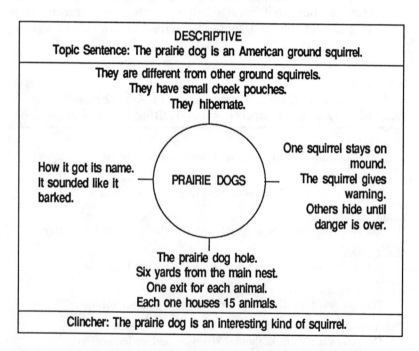

**FIGURE 8-3.** *Visual mapping, from Piccolo (1987).*

domains. However, our knowledge is not advanced to the point where we know what is generalizable and what is not generalizable. The artificial tasks that we construct need to be used and modified with caution. We must continually ask ourselves why we are doing what we are doing and we must find ways to get students to talk about the whys of lessons and tasks. We should try to keep the purpose of our lessons in mind as a yardstick for evaluating our language intervention choices.

# PART FOUR

The epilogue concludes the discussion of language
intervention. The focus is on the big picture
surrounding language intervention in academic
settings. Practitioners are encouraged to work to make
a difference for students, in spite of the road blocks
they may encounter.

# E P I L O G U E

## Reflections on Reflections, or Metatextual Remarks

$A$s indicated in the preface of this text, we gave much thought to the decision to write an intervention text. Part of our hesitation came from our concerns about how to strike a balance between theory and practice. We wanted to present practical information, but we were fearful about ending up with a 1980s cookbook. We have all been frustrated by the less-than-desired progress that some of our children make and so have been tempted by prepackaged programs., standardized tests, intervention textbooks, and workshop speakers who promise quick and easy answers to complex problems. We hope that this text represents a departure from the easy-answers orientation. We have tried to approach the subject of language intervention by using current research from language development and language disorders, information processing and cognitive psychology, and reading theory. We have attempted to bring theory and practice closer by using our own experience with children and adolescents. We have also called upon our colleagues in speech and language pathology, education, and reading to provide us with intervention suggestions.

## EVALUATING LANGUAGE INTERVENTION

Blank (1986) and Blank and Marquis (1987) ask us to evaluate carefully the goals, tasks, and stimuli we include in language intervention sessions and in classroom lessons. We highlight the following points:

• We should think about the difference between validity and relevance when developing language intervention programs (Blank & Marquis, 1987; see Chapter 1, Principle 4). Many aspects of language, including the aspects discussed in this text, represent valid areas of study. For example, children learn words, they learn that words have different meanings, and they learn to be funny. However, as we pointed out earlier, just because ambiguity and humor exist does not mean we automatically teach them (Blank, 1987). Similarly, it may be valid to know the names of fruits, vegetables, animals, and colors, but it may be ridiculous to teach children to recite lists of these items because reciting lists may have very little communicative or academic relevance. We have argued throughout the text that perhaps the most critical thing students can learn in school is how to learn. The other side of the coin is that students must be presented with relevant and meaningful content in order to learn the information comprising their intellectual and social heritage (Hirsch, 1987). Learning how to learn is a critical part of the process of becoming an active member of one's community. To become a *literate* member, one engages in the next process: learning the history, literature, art, language, math, and so on, of one's society.

• We ought to reevaluate the truisms that permeate language- and learning-disabilities training programs (Blank & Marquis, 1987). Statements like, "Say less to children," "Encourage them to talk about anything they like," and "Repeat questions to facilitate verbal processing," are misleading and have little to do with the way children learn language. We need to think about ways of avoiding discourse scenarios that have the bizarre quality unknowingly encouraged in some of our lessons. We must learn how to structure discourse experiences for children that encourage language exchanges that are more closely matched to the situation as well as to their inherent abilities (see Chapters 3 and 5).

• In general, we must make the implicit explicit for leanguage learning disabled students (Blank & Marquis, 1987). We need to highlight the critical features of spoken and written text for students when they do not make such critical observations themselves. Highlighting critical features can occur in many different ways (see Chapters 5 through 8). A basic question we might keep in mind is: "What principle do I want the student to glean from this lesson?" We add: "How can I help the student develop and use a strategy that might generalize across language and curricular areas?"

In our own evolution as clinicians, we have begun to move in two directions: considering broader educational issues and refining the principles of language intervention outlined at the end of Chapter 1. Language- learning- and reading-disabled students present us with an enormous educational challenge. We recognize the pervasive and long-term nature of their problems, and we recognize that language-disabled preschoolers do not outgrow their early language disorders (Bashir, 1987). Bashir's (1987) statement. "We may be itinerant in children's lives but their disorder is not," has brought to the forefront, once again, the need to restructure school curricula. What seems evident to us is that school curricula must change, not only for the language learning disabled student, but also for many nondisabled students. In a nation that theoretically encourages individual differences, we are struck by public school curricula that appear to reflect continued attempts to homogenize a heterogeneous population.

We are concerned with educational systems that make assumptions about what all children should and should not be doing at certain grade levels without apparent understanding of some of the developmental variables that influence academic performance. Although school systems and school personnel vary, educators seem to have little understanding of the linguistic nature of school learning. We see very few kindergarten programs that have strong, researched-based symbolic play curricula (Westby, 1987; see Chapter 2). We see fewer programs that incorporate some of the early metalinguistic milestones described in Chapters 2 and 7. Language arts activities are frequently separate parts of the curriculum, and many are inappropriately sequenced. One thing we have become increasingly concerned about is the growing emphasis on reading programming *in kindergarten.* The reading programs we have observed nationally and in Canada at kindergarten levels tend to emphasize sound segmentation activities (decoding activities), which are quite sophisticated developmentally (see Chapters 4 and 7). Whereas some children might be ready to learn to read and to handle phonics in kindergarten, what happens to those who are not?

## OVERCOMING OBSTACLES TO CREATIVE AND INNOVATIVE LANGUAGE INTERVENTION

There are many challenges facing professionals working with language learning disabled students in schools. Questions such as, "What types of language intervention best meet the individual needs of children in our school systems, regardless of their labels or their educational categories?" and "How can we develop meaningful curricula that are most closely matched to students' language abilities?" remain central to the development of creative and innovative language intervention programs at school-age levels. Professionals are beginning to evaluate the usefulness of diagnostic and educational labels, the persistence of territoriality that exists across disciplines, and the appropriateness of different models of language intervention. We hope to move toward the goal of providing integrated programs for students with problems in our schools, but we have some obstacles to overcome along the way.

## Evaluating Diagnostic Labels

There are many disputes about labeling and service delivery in language, special education, and reading circles (Smith, Osborne, Crim, & Rhu, 1986). Professionals argue about who shall be called *language disabled* versus who shall be called *learning disabled* (Wallach & Liebergott, 1984). The notion that learning disability is largely a continuation of language disabilities is widely challenged and misunderstood (see Wallach & Butler, 1984). Such misunderstandings about language and learning disabilities connections show themselves in many ways. For example, speech-language pathologists may be excluded from LD assessment teams. Learning-disabled students may not receive the language support they need because their problems are perceived as being academic and reading related rather than being language related (*American Speech-Language and Hearing*, 1982). Special educators without backgrounds in language acquisition and language disorders may underestimate the single most critical component of a student's learning disability. Language arts classes, as mentioned earlier, may be inappropriate for LLD students because they are highly metalinguistic, frequently missequenced, and added to the curriculum as separate parts of the school day.

The endless amount of time spent trying to differentiate between *learning-* and *reading*-disabled populations also seems misguided and even unhealthy from both theoretical and practical vantage points. Many standardized tests fail psychometrically to differentiate between these two groups of children (Bloome & Theodorou, 1985; Christenson, Ysseldyke, & Algozzine, 1982; Mirkin & Potter, 1982; Otto, 1986). Moreover, "labels are often used to determine programming yet experts do not agree on the clearly definitive way to decide whether a poor reader should be labeled 'reading disabled' or 'learning disabled '" (Gaskins, 1982, p. 81). Ysseldyke and his colleagues (Epps, Ysseldyke, & McGue, 1984; Ysseldyke & Algozzine, 1983) go on to say that there is much variation nationally over who is declared "learning disabled" in spite of federal definitions. They add that it is difficult to discuss and conduct research on interventions that are successful with LD students because there is so much confusion over who is LD and who is not (see Otto, 1986, for an excellent summary).

Idrisano (1987) argues persuasively that "the team responsible for diagnosis, planning, and intervention for the learning-disabled student needs to include a professional with knowledge and competence in the student's area of major academic difficulty" (p. 2). She encourages professionals to use a direct approach to assessment and intervention based on careful observation of the curriculum and the contexts in which the student is having difficulty. Bashir (1987) supports Idrisano but asks us to be careful about the assumptions made regarding the "knowledge and competence" of team members based on their identification with a particular discipline. A speech-language pathologist, for example, might be quite capable of helping a student with story writing although his or her identification with the discipline might suggest otherwise, especially if traditional definitions of speech and language pathology are used by other team members.

## Breaking Down Territorial Boundaries

We label each other as well as the students in our schools. Statements such as: "Speech-language pathologists should work exclusively on auditory/oral language whereas LD specialists or reading teachers should work on visual/written language" reflect assumptions about the competence of professionals involved, split spoken and written systems arbitrarily, and divide educational services. Otto (1986) points out that we all need to become more aware of research from disciplines other than our own because we are teaching children not individual parts of children. He says that reading specialists and special educators often miss what each other have to say because they tend to focus on information from the teachers, journals, and books of their own discipline. We would venture to say that many speech-language clinicians might also miss some excellent articles in journals like *Reading Research Quarterly* and *The Reading Teacher* because they also tend to focus on information that is explicitly identified with their own discipline.

School programs that integrate language, reading, and academics for LLD students will evolve as preservice, inservice, and continuing education programs for regular and special educators change. An example of a preservice teacher education program that has taken positive action is the National College of Education. Undergraduate students in preparation as regular classroom teachers are encouraged to take coursework in the language bases of reading and writing taught by one of the authors of this text (Miller). In this course, students are exposed to the relationships and connections between oral and written language, including the oral-literate discourse continuum, metalinguistic development, and children's narrative development. Universities such as the University of South Florida, the University of Arizona, and Western Michigan University, among others, offer interdisciplinary training at both preservice and continuing education levels. The language-learning-reading disabilities connection is becoming more explicit as researchers apply innovative models to language intervention and cognition (Blank, 1986; Bloom & Lahey, 1978; Gardner, 1983; Sternberg, 1985; and van Kleeck, 1984b). For practitioners, there is much research and practical information available. It is a delightful challenge to begin applying this information to practice.

## Understanding Language Intervention Models

As practitioners working with students on a daily basis, we should be aware of the theoretical models that underpin the tests, programs, procedures, and biases we bring to our team meetings, clinics, and classrooms. Van Kleeck (1984b) discusses the strengths and weaknesses of various models of language. She points out that models relate to intervention and assessment in different ways. For example, medically oriented models which focus on the etiological and neurological correlates of language and learning disabilities may provide useful information from a theoretical point of view, but they have little to do with intervention. Further, medical model orientations, which encourage a "take the kid out for treatment" approach, may be inappropriate for educational settings. Van Kleeck goes on to say that many of the auditory-processing models, which focus on symptoms like auditory discrimination and auditory sequencing, reflect a discrete skills orientation. With a discrete skills approach, breakdowns in auditory processing and perception are frequently viewed as an underlying cause of a child's language and learning problems. Intervention might lead to working on these symptoms, i.e., working on auditory discrimination and auditory sequencing. Adherents to auditory-processing models believe that these skills represent prerequisites for higher level language functioning.

We often hear statements such as, "Jane has an auditory memory problem that is causing her language problem," or "Bill has a visual sequence problem that is causing his reading problem," or "John has an attention deficit disorder that is causing his classroom problems." These statements sound as if memory, language, and attention are unified entities or boxes in children's heads that reflect separate functions. The statements made about Jane, Bill, and John also make it sound as if one or two distinct symptoms could become the focus of intervention. Blank (1985) uses the example of color naming to make a point about symptoms, causes, and intervention. She reminds us that color-naming difficulties are quite pervasive in both language- and reading-disabled populations but goes on to say that color naming is certainly not the cause of a language or reading problem. Consequently, it would be erroneous to conclude that teaching color naming would help children communicate or read better. Reiterating the notion of relevance versus validity, Blank says that just because a behavior (or a symptom) exists does not mean we should focus assessment and intervention on it (see Goldstein, 1939, for an excellent discussion of pathology induced by assessment and remediation procedures; see also Blank and Marquis, 1987; and see Chapter 8).

Increasingly, models of language are emerging that integrate information-processing principles with descriptions of the social and non-social uses of language (see Chapters 2 and 5). These integrated models contain significantly more refined analyses of the contexts surrounding children and adolescents with language learning disabilities. Because this is a text about academic success and failure, the context of greatest concern to us is school. Traditional models of language and learning that encourage the splintering of skills, children, and professionals fail to consider the most critical factors in children's development by failing to address the contexts in which they must survive. Because all models of language and learning represent abstract and incomplete descriptions of complex behaviors, the greatest failure lies not within the models themselves, but within the professionals who interpret them literally.

## LOOKING AHEAD

We are still learning about language intervention. Blank (1987) said recently that we have to begin to collapse the number of language categories we assess and teach. She says that clinicians and educators have become overwhelmed by the amount of information they must incorporate into their assessments and IEPs. She points out that we keep adding categories to language intervention programs with each decade. She argues that we must stop and reevaluate the usefulness of such a strategy because we cannot possibly teach children everything they need to know. Following Blank's argument, we utilized a set of intervention principles outlined in Chapter 1 to integrate the information we presented in the different chapters. However, we are still struggling with decisions about what to teach and what not to teach children *at which points in time.*

Our thinking about language intervention is reflected in the intervention principles. We have begun to focus on four interacting and overlapping aspects of the principles: (1) helping children become active learners; (2) helping them become more aware of their own strengths and weaknesses across learning domains; (3) providing students with smoother transitions to literacy; and (4) keeping sight of the meaningfulness and relevance of the content we are attempting to teach. Bashir (1987) reminds us that much of what we teach should involve helping children understand the critical compared with the noncritical. Our intervention principles are designed to organize our own thinking so that we can teach children how to differentiate the critical from the noncritical. In the language domain, the process of differentiating critical from noncritical involves what Bashir calls linguistic economy (Bashir, 1987). Linguistic economy is comprehending and expressing what one needs to comprehend and express situationally, and we believe it is the core of being an active learner and effective communicator.

## POSTSCRIPT

Although we have a long way to go in our study of language intervention, we have come a long way. It is true that with each decade we accumulate more information which encourages us to readjust our models of language and learning (see Chapter 2). Language is a complicated business. The business of stimulating and teaching language is an overwhelming task. To pretend it is easy is to be naive. We hope we are beginning to outgrow our quest for the perfect test and program. The realities that exist in our schools and clinics and the tremendous weight of local, state, and federal mandates cannot be underestimated. Nevertheless, each of us can make a difference. Through our individual actions, we can make it better for the children and adolescents in our schools. Many of the reseachers and practitioners referenced in this text have begun to make changes in their own school districts, clinics, and universities. As Hoskins (1987a) reminds us, communication and language involve ongoing conversations of many different types. We have begun a conversation about language intervention in this text. As is the case with many conversations, this one invites the future. In preparation for a future conversation about language, we share the following anecdote from a speech-language colleague of ours:

> She was watching out her kitchen window as her six-year-old daughter and ten-year-old son raced each other to get inside the house first, it being a rule of the house that the first child inside got to talk first. Surprisingly, the six-year-old burst through the door first, and in breathless fashion, said, "Mom, Mom, why did the lady sell her bra?" Disappointed at being beaten in the race for the door, the ten year old said, "You'll mess it up! Let me tell it!" Undaunted, the six year old went on. "She sold her bra because she needed the money!" The ten year old doubled over in laughter, as the mother puzzled over the humor of the riddle for a few seconds. When the boy straightened up, he said, "No, no! She sold her bra because she was flat-busted!" The six year old was miffed because her brother insisted on retelling the ending by saying what she had just said.

We leave the conversation for now. To be continued . . .

# References

Ackerman, B. P. (1986). Referential and causal coherence in the story comprehension of children and adults. *Journal of Experimental Child Psychology, 41,* 336–366.

Allan, K. K. (1982). The development of young children's metalinguistic understanding of the word. *Journal of Educational Research, 76,* 89–93.

American Readers. (1983). Lexington MA: Health Publications.

American Speech-Language-Hearing Association Committee on Language Learning Disabilities. (1982). The role of the speech-language pathologist in learning disablilties. *ASHA, 8,* 937–944.

Applebee, A. N. (1978). *The child's concept of story: Ages two to seventeen.* Chicago, IL: University of Chicago Press.

Athey, I. (1977). Syntax, semantics, and reading. In J. Guthrie (Ed), *Cognition, curriculum, and comprehension* (pp. 71–98). Newark, DE: International Reading Association.

Backman, J. (1983). The role of psycholinguistic competence in the acquisition of reading: A look at early readers. *Reading Research Quarterly, 18,* 466–479.

Bartlett, F. (1958). *Thinking.* New York; Basic Books.

Bashir, A. (1986). *The continuum of language success and failure.* Reaction discussion presented at the Language Learning Disabilities Institute, Boston, MA: Emerson College.

Bashir, A. (1987). *Language and the curriculum.* Workshop presented at the Language Learning Disabilities Institute, Emerson College, Boston, MA, and San Diego, CA.

Bashir, A., Kuban, K., Kleinman, S., & Scavuzzo, S. (1983). Issues in language disorders: Considerations of cause, maintenance, and change. In J. Miller, D. Yoder, & R. Schieflebush (Eds.) *ASHA Report No. 12* (pp. 92–106). Rockville, MD: American Speech-Language-Hearing Association.

Bates E. (1976). *Language and context: The acquisition of pragmatics.* New York: Academic Press.

Bates, E. (1979). *The emergence of symbols: cognition and communication in infancy.* New York: Academic Press.

Baumann, J. (1986). Teaching third-grade students to comprehend anaphoric relationships: The application of a direct instruction model. *Reading*

Research Quarterly, 21, 70–90.

Bennett, W. J. (1986). *What works: Research about teaching and learning.* *Washington, DC: U.S. Department of Education.*

Berlin, L., Blank, M., & Rose, S. *(1982).* The language of instruction: The hidden complexities. In K. G. Butler & G. P. Wallach *(Eds.),* Language disorders and learning disabilities (pp. 47–58). Rockville, MD: Aspen Publications.

Bever, T. J. (1970). The cognitive basis of linguistic structures. In J. R. Hayes (Ed.), *Cognition and the development of language* (pp. 279–362). New York: Wiley.

Blachman, B. (1984). Language analysis skills and early reading acquisition. In G. P. Wallach & K. G. Butler (Eds.). *Language learning disabilities in school-age children* (pp. 271–287). Baltimore, MD: Williams & Wilkins.

Blanchowicz, C. (1978). Semantic constructivity in children's comprehension. *Reading Research Quarterly, 13,* 188–199.

Blanchowicz, C. (1986). Making connections: Alternatives to the vocabulary notebook. *Journal of Reading, 29,* 643–649.

Blank, M. (1985). *Instructional and classroom discourse.* Workshop presented at the Language Learning Disabilities Institute, Emerson College, Boston, MA.

Blank, M. (1986). *Natural language exchanges and coding techniques.* Workshop presented at the Language Learning Disabilities Institute, Emerson College, Boston, MA.

Blank, M. (1987). *Looking for LD in some of the right places.* Workshop presented at the Language Learning Disabilities Institute, Emerson College, Boston, MA.

Blank, M., & Marquis, A. (1987). *Teaching discourse Tucson, AZ: Communication Skill Builders.*

Blank, M., Rose, S., & Berlin, L. *(1978).* The language of learning: The preschool years. New York: Grune & Stratton.

Blank, M., & White, S. (1986). Questions: A power form of classroom exchange. *Topics in Language Disorders, 6,* 1–12.

Bloom, L., & Capatides, J. B. (1987). Sources of meaning in the acquisition of complex syntax: The sample case of causality. *Journal of Experimental Child Psychology, 43,* 112–128.

Bloom L., & Lahey, M. (1978). *Language development and language disorders* New York: Wiley.

Bloome, D., & Theodorou, E. (1985). Reading, writing, and learning in the classroom. *Peabody Journal of Education, 62,* 20–43.

Bohannon, J. N., Warren-Leubecker, A., & Hepler, N. (1984). Word order awareness and early reading. *Child Development, 55,* 1541–1548.

Bowey, J. A. (1986). Syntactic awareness in relation to reading skill and ongoing reading comprehension monitoring. *Journal of Experimental Child Psychology, 41,* 282–299.

Brannan, A. D., Bridge, C. A., & Winograd, P. N. (1986). The effects of structural variation on children's recall of basal reader stories. *Reading Research Quarterly, 21,* 91–104.

Bransford, J. D., Barclay, J. R., & Franks, J. J. (1972). Semantic memory: A constructive vs. interpretive approach. *Cognitive Psychology, 3,* 193–209.

Bransford, J. D., & Franks, J. J. (1971). The abstraction of linguistic ideas. *Cognitive Psychology, 2,* 331–350.

Bransford, J. D., & Johnson, M. (1973). Considerations of some problems in comprehension. In W. Chase (Ed.), *Visual information processing* (pp. 383–438). New York: Academic Press.

Brown, A. L., & DeLoache, J. S. (1978). Skills, plans, and self-regulation. In R. Siegler (Ed.), *Children's thinking: What develops?* Hillsdale, NJ: Erlbaum.

Brubaker, S. H. (1985). *Workbook for reasoning skills;* Detroit: Wayne State University Press.

Bruner, J. S. (1975). The ontogenesis of speech acts. *Journal of Child Language, 12,* 1–19.

Buday, E. S., Newhoff, M., & Perry, B. W. (1983). *Metalinguistic ability in normal and language-disordered children.* Paper presented at the American-Speech-Language-Hearing Association Convention, Cincinnati, OH.

Bush, W. J., & Giles, M. T. (1969). *Aids to psycholinguistic teaching.* Columbus, OH: Charles Merrill.

Camp, L., Winbury, N., & Zinna, D. (1981). Strategies for initial reading instruction. *Bulletin of the Orton Society, 31,* 175–188.

Carlson, J., Gruenewald, L., & Nyberg, B. (1982). Everyday math is a story problem: The language of the curriculum. In K. G. Butler & G. P. Wallach (Eds.), *Language disorders and learning disabilities* (pp. 59–69). Rockville, MD: Aspen Publications.

Carr, E., & Wixson, K. (1986). Guidelines for evaluating vocabulary instruction. *Journal of Reading, 29,* 588–595.

Chafe, W. (1970). *Meaning and the structure of language.* Chicago, IL: University of Chicago Press.

Chafe, W. (1982). Features distinguishing spoken and written language. In D. Tannen (Ed.), *Spoken and written language.* Norwood, NJ: Ablex.

Chomsky, N. (1966). *Aspects of the theory of syntax.* Cambridge, MA: MIT Press.

Christensen, S., Ysseldyke, J., & Algozzine, B. (1982). Instructional constraints and external pressures influencing referral decisions. *Psychology in the Schools, 19,* 341–345.

Clark, E. (1978). Awareness of language: Some evidence from what children say and do. In A. Sinclair, R. Jarvella, & W. Levelt (Eds.), *The child's conception of language.* New York: Springer-Verlag.

Collins, J., & Michaels, S. (1980). The importance of conversational discourse strategies in the acquisition of literacy. *Proceedings of the Sixth Annual Meeting of the Berkeley Linguistic Society,* Berkeley, CA.

Crais, E., & Chapman, R. (1987). Story recall and inferencing skills in language/learning disabled and nondisabled children. *Journal of Speech and Hearing Disorders, 52,* 50–55.

Early, M. (1974). The big hat. In *A magic afternoon* (pp. 62–64). Harcourt Brace Jovanovich.

Eder, D., & Felmlee, D. (1984). The development of attention norms in ability groups. In P. L. Peterson, L. C. Wilkinson, & M. Hallinan (Eds.), *The social context of instruction: Group organization and group process* (pp. 189–208). New York: Academic Press.

Elkonin, D. B. (1973). U.S.S.R. In J. Downing (Ed.), *Comparative reading.* New York: MacMillan.

Emerson, H. (1979). Children's comprehension of "because" in reversible and nonreversible sentences. *Journal of Child Language. 6,* 279–300.

Emerson, H. (1980). Children's judgments of correct and reversed sentences with "if." *Journal of Child Language, 7,* 127–155.

Epps, S., Ysseldyke, J., & McGue, M. (1984). I know one when I see one — differentiating LD and non-LD students. *Learning Disability Quarterly, 7,* 89–101.

Evertson, C., Weade, R., Green, L., & Crawford, J. (1985). *Effective classroom managment and instruction: An exploration of models.* Final Report NIE-G-83-0063. Washington, DC: National Institute of Education.

Ferreiro, E., Othenin-Gerard, H., Chipman, H., & Sinclair, H. (1976). How do children handle relative clauses? A study of developmental psycholinguistics. *Archives of Psycholinguistics, 172,* 229–266.

Flavell, J. H. (1976). Metacognitive aspects of problem solving. In L. B. Resnik (Ed.) *The nature of intelligence.* Hillsdale, NJ: Lawrence Erlbaum.

Flavell, J. H. (1977). *Cognitive development.* Englewood Cliffs, NJ: Prentice-Hall.

Flavell, J. H. (1981). Cognitive monitoring. In W. P. Dickson (Ed.) *Children's oral communication skills.* New York: Academic Press.

Fluck, M. J. (1979). Comprehension of relative clause sentences by children aged five to nine years. *Language and Speech, 21,* 190–201.

Fowler, P. C. (1986). Cognitive differentiation of learning disabled children on the WISC-R: A canonical model of achievement correlates. *Child Study Journal, 16,* 25–37.

Fox, B., & Routh, D. (1975). Analyzing spoken language into words, syllables, and phonemes: A developmental study. *Journal of Psycholinguistic Research, 4,* 331–342.

Fox, B., & Routh, D. (1984). Phonological analysis and synthesis as word attack skills. *Journal of Educational Psychology, 76,* 1059–1064.

Franklin, M. (1979). Metalinguistic functioning in development. In N. Smith & M. Franklin (Eds.), *Symbolic functioning in childhood.* Hillsdale, NJ: Lawrence Erlbaum Associates.

Fujiki, M., Brinton, B., & Dunton, S. (1987). A grammatical judgment screening test for young elementary school-aged children. *Language, Speech, Hearing Services in Schools, 18,* 131–143.

Gardner, H. (1974). Metaphors and modalities: How children project polar adjectives onto diverse domains. *Child Development, 45,* 84–91.

Gardner, H. (1983). *Frames of mind.* New York: Basic Books.

Gardner, H. (1985). *The mind's new science: A history of the cognitive revolution.* New York: Basic Books.

Garvey, C. (1977). Contingent queries and their relations in discourse. In M.

Lewis & L. A. Rosenblum (Eds.), *Interaction, conversation, and the development of language.* New York: Wiley-Interscience.

Garvey, C. (1982). Communication and the development of social role play. In D. L. Forbes & M. T. Greenberg (Eds.), *New directions for child development: Children's planning strategies.* San Francisco: Jossey-Bass.

Gaskins, I. (1982). Let's end the reading disabilities/learning disabilities debate. *Journal of Learning Disabilities, 15,* 81–83.

German, D. J. (1986). *Test of word finding.* Allen, TX: DLM.

German, D. J. (1987). Spontaneous language profiles in children with word finding problems. *Language, Speech, Hearing Services in Schools, 18,* 217–230.

Glenn, C. G., & Stein, N. L. (1980). *Syntactic structures and real world themes in stories generated by children* (technical report). Urbana, IL: University of Illinois, Center for the Study of Reading.

Goldstein, K. (1939). *The organism.* New York: American Book.

Goodman, K. (1970). Behind the eye: What happens in reading. In K. Goodman & O. Niles (Eds.), *Reading: Process and program.* Urbana, IL: National Council of Teachers of English.

Gregg, N. (1986). Cohesion: Inter and intra sentence errors. *Journal of Learning Disabilities, 19,* 338–351.

Guilford, J. P., & Hoepfner, R. (1971). *The analysis of intelligence.* New York: McGraw-Hill.

Hakes, D. (1982). The development of metalinguistic ability: What develops? In S. Kuczaj (Ed.), *Language development: Language, thought, and culture* (vol. 2). Hillsdale, NJ: Erlbaum.

Halliday, M. A. K., & Hasan, R. (1976). *Cohesion in English.* London: Longman.

Hansen, J., & Pearson, P. D. (1983). An instructional study: Improving the inferential comprehension of good and poor fourth-graders. *Journal of Educational Psychology, 75,* 821–829.

Heath, S. B. (1986). Taking a cross-cultural look at narratives. *Topics in Language Disorders, 7,* 84–95.

Hedberg, N. L., & Stoel-Gammon, C. (1986). Narrative analysis: Clinical procedures. *Topics in Language Disorders, 7,* 58–69.

Heller, M. F. (1986). How do you know what you know? Metacognitive modeling in the content areas. *Journal of Reading, 29,* 415–422.

Hirsch, E. D., Jr. (1987). *Cultural literacy: What every American needs to know.* Boston: Houghton Mifflin.

Hoskins, B. (1987a). *An integrated approach to language intervention: Pulling the pieces together.* Workshop presented at the Language Learning Disabilities Institute, Emerson College, San Diego, CA.

Hoskins, B. (1987b). Personal communication.

Idrisano, R. (1987). Testimony to the Interageny Committee on Learning Disabilities of the National Institutes of Health. *Reading Today, 4,* 2.

Israel, L. (1984). Word knowledge and word retrieval: Phonological and semantic strategies. In G. P. Wallach & K. G. Butler (Eds.), *Language learning disabilities in school-age children* (pp. 230–250). Baltimore, MD: Williams & Wilkins.

Johnson, D. D., & von Hoff Johnson, B. (1986). Highlighting vocabulary in inferential comprehension. *Journal of Reading, 29,* 622–625.

Johnson, J., & Smith, L. B. (1981). Children's inferential abilities in the context of reading to understand. *Child Development, 52,* 1216–1223.

Johnson-Laird, P. N. (1983). *Mental models: Toward a cognitive science of language, inference, and consciousness.* Cambridge, MA: Harvard University Press.

Juel, C. (1983). The development and use of mediated word identification. *Reading Research Quarterly, 28,* 306–327.

Kail, R., Hale, C., Leonard, L., & Nippold, M. (1984). Lexical storage and retrieval in language-impaired children. *Applied Psycholinguistics, 5,* 37–49.

Kail, R., & Leonard, L. (1986). Word-finding abilities in language-impaired children. *ASHA Monographs, 25.*

Kamhi, A. (1987). Metalinguistic abilities in language impaired children. *Topics in Language Disorders, 7,* 1–12.

Kamhi, A., & Koenig, L. (1985). Metalinguistic awareness in normal and language-disordered children. *Language, Speech, Hearing Services in Schools, 16,* 199–210.

Kamhi, A., Lee, R. F., & Nelson, L. K. (1985). Word, syllable, and sound awareness in language disordered children. *Journal of Speech and Hearing Disorders, 50,* 207–212.

Kaplan, E. (1975). Personal communication.

Karmiloff-Smith, A. (1979). Language development after five. In P. Fletcher & M. Garman (Eds.), *Language acquisition* (pp. 307–323). New York: Cambridge University Press.

Karnes, M. B. (1968). *Activities for developing psychiolinguistic skills with preschool culturally disadvantaged children.* Washington, DC: Council for Exceptional Children.

Karnes, M. B. (1972). *Goal program: language development,* Springfield, MA: Milton Bradley.

Keller-Cohen, D. (1987). Context and strategy in acquiring temporal connectives. *Journal of Psycholinguistic Research, 16,* 165–183.

Kemper, S., & Edwards, L. C. (1986). Children's expression of causality and their construction of narratives. *Topics in Language Disorders, 7,* 11–20.

Kirk, S. A., & Kirk, W. D. (1976). *Psycholinguistic learning disabilities: diagnosis and remediation.* Urbana, IL: University of Illinois Press.

Klecan-Aker, J. S. (1985). Syntactic abilities in normal and language deficient middle school children. *Topics in Language Disorders, 5,* 46–54.

Klein-Konigsberg, E. (1984). Semantic integration and language learning disabilities: From research to assessment and intervention. In G. P. Wallach & K. G. Butler (Eds.), *Language learning disabilities in school-age children* (pp. 251–270). Baltimore, MD: Williams & Wilkins.

Lee, R., & Kamhi, A. (1985). *Verbal metaphor performance in learning disabled children.* Paper presented at the American Speech-Language-Hearing Association Convention, Washington, DC.

Lee-Schachter, A. D. (1985). *Story retelling in good and poor readers.* Qualifying paper for the Ontario Institute for Studies in Education Ph.D. Program, Toronto, Canada.

Lee-Schachter, A. D. (1987). Personal communication.

Leonard, L. (1986). *Word finding abilities of language disabled children.* Workshop presented at the Language Learning Disabilities Institute, Emerson College, San Diego, CA.

Leonard, L., Nippold, M., Karl, R., & Hale, (1983). Picture naming in language-impaired children. *Journal of Speech and Hearing Research, 26,* 609–615.

Liben, L., & Posnansky, C. (1977). Inferences of inference: The effects of age, transitive ability, memory load, and lexical factors. *Child Development, 48,* 1490–1497.

Liberman, I., & Shankweiler, D. (1979). Speech, the alphabet, and teaching reading. In L. Resnik & P. Weaver (Eds.) *Theory and practice of early reading* (vol. 2). Hillsdale, NJ: Lawrence Erlbaum Associates.

Liberman, I., Shankweiler, D., Camp, L. Blachman, B., & Werfelman, M. (1980). Steps toward literacy: A linguistic approach. In P. J. Levinson & C. Sloan (Eds.), *Auditory processing and language.* New York: Grune & Stratton.

Liles, B. Z. (1985). Cohesion in the narratives of normal and language disordered children. *Journal of Speech and Hearing Research, 28,* 123–133.

Liles, B. Z. (1987). Episode organization and cohesive conjunctions in narratives of children with and without language disorder. *Journal of Speech and Hearing Research, 30,* 185–196.

Liles, B. Z., & Shulman M.D. (1981). Linguistic intuitions and comprehension of meaning as demonstrated by linguistically normal and linguistically deviant children. *AVISO: A Journal of Special Education,* 1–19.

Liles, B. Z., Shulman M. D., & Bartlett, S. (1977). Judgments of grammaticality by normal and language-disordered children. *Journal of Speech and Hearing Disorders, 42,* 199–209.

Lindamood, C. H., & Lindamood, P. C. (1969). *Auditory discrimination in depth.* Boston, MA: Teaching Resources.

Lindamood, C. H., & Lindamood, P. C. (1971). *Auditory conceptualization test.* Austin, Texas: DLM/Teaching Resources.

Lomax, R. G., & McGee, L. (1987). Young children's concepts about print and reading: Toward a model of word reading acquisition. *Reading Research Quarterly, 22,* 237–256.

Lorch, R. F., Lorch, E. P, & Morgan, A. M. (1987). Task effects and individual differences in on-line processing of the topic structure of a text. *Discourse Processes, 10,* 63–80.

Maxwell, S., & Wallach, G. P. (1984). The language-LD connection: Symptoms of language disability change over time. In G. P. Wallach & K. G. Butler (Eds.), *Language learning disabilities in school-age children* (pp. 15–33). Baltimore, MD: Williams & Wilkins.

McGee, L., Charlesworth, R., Cheeck, M., & Cheeck, E. (1982). Metalinguistic knowledge: A look at beginning reading. *Childhood Education, 10,* 123–127.

Mentis, M., & Prutting, C. (1987). Cohesion in the discourse of normal and head-injured adults. *Journal of Speech and Hearing Research, 30*, 88–98.

Menyuk, P. (1983). Language development and reading. In T. M. Gallagher & C. A. Prutting (Eds.), *Pragmatic assessment and intervention issues in language.* San Diego, CA: College-Hill Press.

Michaels, S., & Collins, J. (1984). Oral discourse styles: Classroom Interaction and acquisition of literacy. In D. Tannen (Ed.), *Coherence in spoken and written discourse.* Norwood, NJ: Ablex.

Miller, G. E., & Pressley, M. (1987). Partial picture effects on children's memory for sentences containing implicit information. *Journal of Experimental Child Psychology, 43*, 300–310.

Miller. L. (1978). Pragmatics and early childhood language disorders: Communicative interactions in a half-hour sample. *Journal of Speech and Hearing Disorders, 43*, 419–436.

Miller, L. (1984). Problem solving, hypothesis testing, and language disorders. In G. P. Wallach & K. G. Butler (Eds.), *Language learning disabilities in school-age children,* Baltimore, MD: Williams & Wilkins.

Miller, L. (1986). *Language disabilities, organizational strategies, and classroom learning.* Workshop presented at the Language Learning Disabilities Institutes, Emerson College, San Diego, CA.

Mirkin, P., & Potter, M. (1982). *A survey of program planning and implementation practices of LD teachers.* Research Report No. 80. Minneapolis, MN: University of Minnesota, Institute for Research on Learning Disabilities.

Morris, W. (1969). *The American Heritage dictionary of the English language.* New York: American Heritage.

Moskow, S. P. (1980). *Basal stories — Are they even minimal narratives?* Unpublished manuscript. Lexington, KY: University of Kentucky.

Murphy, S. (1986). Children's comprehension of deictic categories in oral and written language. *Reading Research Quarterly, 21*, 118–131.

Naisbitt, J., & Aburdene, P. (1985). *Re-inventing the corporation.* New York: Warner Books.

Nelson, L. K., Kamhi, A. G., & Apel, K. (1987). Cognitive strengths and weaknesses in language-impaired children: One more look. *Journal of Speech and Hearing Disorders, 52*, 36–43.

Nelson, N. (1984). Beyond information processing: The language of teachers and textbooks. In G. P. Wallach & K. G. Butler (Eds.), *Language learning disabilities in school-age children* (pp. 154–178). Baltimore, MD: Williams & Wilkins.

Nelson, N. W. (1987). *Lecture notes from: Language of instruction: Children and school success.* Evanston, IL: Language and Learning Institute.

Nelson, N. W. (in press). *Planning individualized speech and language intervention programs* (2nd ed.). Tucson, AZ: Communication Skill Builders.

Newcomer, P. L., & Hammill, D. D. (1976). *Psycholinguistics in the schools.* Columbus, OH: Charles Merrill.

Nippold, M. A. (1985). Comprehension of figurative language in youth. *Topics in Language Disorders, 5,* 1–20.

Nippold, M., & Fey, M. (1983). Metaphoric understanding in preadolescents having a history of language acquisition difficulties. *Language, Speech, and Hearing Services in Schools, 14,* 171–181.

Nippold, M., Leonard, L., & Kail, R. (1984). Syntactics and conceptual factors in children's understanding of metaphors. *Journal of Speech and Hearing Research, 27,* 197–205.

Olson, D. R. (1977). From utterance to text: The bias of language in speech and writing. *Harvard Educational Review, 47,* 257–281.

Olson, D. R. (1982). The language of schooling. *Topics in Language Disorders, 2,* 1–12.

Otto, W. (1986). Ysseldyke and Algozzine — Those two guys are friends of mine. *Journal of Reading, 29,* 572–575.

Paris, S. G., & Carter, A. (1973). Semantic and constructive aspects of sentence memory in children. *Development Psychology, 9,* 109–113.

Paris, S. G., & Lindauer, B. K. (1976). The role of inference in children's comprehension and memory for sentences. *Cognitive Psychology, 8,* 217–227.

Paris, S. G., Lindauer, B., & Cox, G. (1977). The development of inferential comprehension. *Child Development, 48,* 1728–1733.

Pearson, P. D. (1984). Guided reading: A response to Isabel Beck. In R. C. Anderson, J. Osborne, & R. J. Tierny (Eds.), *Learning to read in American schools: Basal readers and content texts.* Hillsdale, NJ: Erlbaum.

Pearson, P. D., & Spiro, R. J. (1982). Toward a theory of reading comprehension instruction. In K. Butler & G. P. Wallach (Eds.), *Language disorders and learning disabilities* (pp. 71–88). Rockville, MD: Aspen Publications.

Peshkin, A. (1978). *Growing up American: Schooling and the survival of the community.* Chicago, IL: University of Chicago Press.

Piaget, J. (1926). *The language and thought of the child* (translated by M. Gabain). London: Routledge and Kegan Paul Ltd.

Piaget, J. (1954). *The construction of reality in the child* (translated by M. Cook). New York: Basic Books.

Piccolo, A. (1987). Expository text structure: Teaching and learning strategies. *The Reading Teacher, 5,* 838–847.

Postman, N. (1985). *Amusing ourselves to death.* New York: Viking Penguin.

Prawat, R., & Jones, H. (1977). Constructive memory of normal and learning disabled children. *Psycholinguistic Reports, 41,* 474.

Rees, N. S. (1973). Auditory processing factors in language disorders: The view from Procrustes' bed. *Journal of Speech and Hearing Disorders 38,* 304–315.

Reynolds, R. E., & Ortony, A. (1980). Some issues in the measurement of children's comprehension of metaphoric language. *Child Development, 51,* 1110–1119.

Ripich, D., & Spinelli, F. (1985). *School discourse strategies.* San Diego, CA: College-Hill Press.

Roller, C. M., & Schreiner, R. (1985). The effects of narrative and expository organizational instruction on sixth-grade children's comprehension of expository and narrative prose. *Reading Psychology, 6,* 27–42.

Rosner, J. (1975). *Helping children overcome learning disabilities.* New York: Walker and Company.

Roth, F. P. (1987). *Discourse abilities of learning disabled students: Patterns and intervention strategies.* Workshop presented at the Language Learning Disabilities Institute. Emerson College, Boston, MA.

Roth, S., & Perfetti, C. (1982). A framework for reading, language comprehension, and language disability. In K. Butler & G. P. Wallach (Eds.), *Language disorders and learning disabilities* (pp. 15–28). Rockville, MD: Aspen Publications.

Rubin, H. (1986). *Linguistic awareness in relation to reading and spelling abilities.* Workshop presented at the Language Learning Disabilities Institute, Emerson College, San Diego, CA.

Rubin, H., & Liberman, I. (1983). Exploring the oral and written language errors made by language disbled children. *Annals of Dyslexia, 33,* 11–20.

Saxe, G. (1981). Number symbols and number operations: Their development and interrelation. *Topics in Language Disorders, 2,* 67–75.

Scannell-Miller, M. (1982). A comparison of the development and use of inference: A mnemonic strategy for the disabled and normal-achieving students. *Dissertation Abstracts International, 43,* 12.

Schmidt, C. R., & Paris, S. G. (1983). Children's use of successive clues to generate and monitor inferences. *Child Development, 54,* 742–759.

Schmidt, C. R., Schmidt, S. R., & Tomalis, S. M. (1984). Children's constructive processing and monitoring of stories containing anomalous information. *Child Development, 55,* 2056–2071.

Schwartz, R., Leonard, L., & Folger, M. K. (1980). Early phonological behavior in normal-speaking and language disordered children: Evidence for a synergistic view of linguistic disorders. *Journal of Speech and Hearing Disorders, 45,* 357–377.

Sheldon, A. (1974). The role of parallel function in the acquisition of relative clauses in English. *Journal of Verbal Learning and Verbal Behavior, 13,* 272–281.

Shugarman, S. L., & Hurst, J. B. (1986). Purposeful paraphrasing: Promoting a nontrival pursuit for meaning. *Journal of Reading, 29,* 396–399.

Silliman, E. R. (1984). Interactional competencies in the instructional context: The role of teaching discourse in learning. In G. P. Wallach & K. G. Butler, *Language learning disabilities in school-age children.* Baltimore, MD: Williams & Wilkins.

Silliman, E. (1986). Forrword. *Topics in Language Disorders, 6,* iv.

Silliman, E. (1985). *Are we really helping school-age language disabled students in school?* Paper presented at the American Speech-Language-Hearing Association Convention, Washington, DC.

Silliman, E. (in press). Individual differences in the classroom performance of language impaired children. *Seminars in Speech and Language.*

Smith, C. L., & Tager-Flusberg, H. (1982). Metalinguistic awareness and language development. *Journal of Experimental Psychology, 34,* 449–468.

Smith, J., & Elkins, J. (1985). The use of cohesion by underachieving readers. *Reading Psychology, 6,* 13–25.

Smith, R. W., Osborne, L. T., Crim, D., & Rhu, A. H. (1986). Labeling theory as applied to learning disabilities: Survey findings and policy suggestions. *Journal of Learning Disabilities, 19,* 195–202.

Snow, C. E. (1977). The development of conversation between mothers and babies. *Journal of Child Language, 4,* 1–22.

Snyder, L. (1982). Have we prepared the language disordered child for school? In K. G. Butler & G. P. Wallach (Eds.), *Language disorders and learning disabilities* (pp. 29–46). Rockville, MD: Aspen Publications.

Spache, G. D. (1981). *Diagnostic reading scales.* Monterey, CA: McGraw-Hill.

Spreen, O., & Haaf, R. G. (1986). Empirically derived LD subtypes: A replication attempt and longitudinal patterns over fifteen years. *Journal of Learning Disabilities, 19,* 170–180.

Stahl, S. A. (1986). Three principles of effective vocabulary instruction. *Journal of Reading, 29,* 662–668.

Stein, N. L., & Glenn, C. G. (1979). An analysis of story comprehension in elementary school children. In R. O . Freedle (Ed.), *Advances in discourse processing (vol. 2). New directions.* Norwood, NJ: Ablex.

Stephens, M. I. & Montgomery, A. A. (1985). A critique of recent relevant standardized tests. *Topics in Language Disorders, 5,* 21–45.

Sternberg, R. J. (1985). *Beyond IQ.* Cambridge, MA: Cambridge University Press.

Sternberg, R. J., & Baron, J. B. (1987). *Teaching thinking skills: Theory and practice.* New York: W. H. Freeman.

Stoel-Gammon, C., & Hedberg, N. L. (1984). *A longitudinal study of cohesion in the narratives of young children.* Third International Congress for the Study of Child Language, Austin, TX.

Sundbye, N. (1987). Text explicitness and inferential questions: Effects on story understanding and recall. *Reading Research Quarterly, 22,* 82–97.

Sutton-Smith, B. (1986). The development of fictional narrative performances. *Topics in Language Disorders, 7,* 1–10.

Taylor, M. B., & Williams, J. P. (1983). Comprehension of learning disabled readers: Task and text variables. *Journal of Educational Psychology, 75,* 743–751.

Thelen, J. N. (1986). Vocabulary instruction and meaningful learning. *Journal of Reading, 29,* 603–609.

Thomas, L. (1975). *The lives of a cell.* New York: Bantam Books.

Trelease, J. (1985). *The read-aloud handbook.* New York: Penguin Books.

Tunmer, W. E., & Grieve, R. (1984). Syntactic awareness in children. In W. E. Tunmer, C. Pratt, & M. L. Hermann (Eds.), *Metalinguistic awareness in children: Theory, research, and implications* (pp. 12–35). New York: Springer-Verlag.

Van Dongen, R., & Westby, C. E. (1986). Building the narrative mode of thought through children's literature. *Topics in Language Disorders, 7,* 70–83.

van Kleeck, A. (1984a). Metalinguistic skills: Cutting across spoken and written language and problem solving abilities. In G. P. Wallach & K. G. Butler

(Eds.), *Language learning disabilities in school-age children* (pp. 128–153). Baltimore, MD: Williams & Wilkins.

van Kleeck, A. (1984b). Assessment and intervention: Does "meta" matter? In G. P. Wallach & K. G. Butler (Eds.), *Language learning disabilities in school-age children* (pp. 179–188). Baltimore, MD: Williams & Wilkins.

van Kleeck, A., & Schuele, C. M. (1987). Precursors to literacy: normal development. *Topics in Language Disorders, 7,* 13–31.

Vellutino, F. (1979). *Dyslexia: Theory and research.* Cambridge, MA: MIT Press.

Wallach, G. P. (1984). Later language learning: Syntatic structures and strategies. In G. P. Wallach & K. G. Butler (Eds.), *Language learning disabilities in school-age children* (pp. 82–102). Baltimore, MD: William & Wilkins.

Wallach, G. P. (1985). What do we really mean by verbal language proficiency? Higher level language language learning and school performance. *Peabody Journal of Education, 62,* 44–69.

Wallach, G. P. (in preparation). Processing complex sentences: The clinical and educational implications of learning disability subgroups.

Wallach, G. P., & Butler, K. G. (1984). *Language learning disabilities in school-age children.* Baltimore, MD: Williams & Wilkins.

Wallach, G. P., & Lee, A. D. (1982). So you want to know what to do with language-disabled children above the age of six. In K. G. Butler & G. P. Wallach (Eds.), *Language disorders and learning disabilities* (pp. 99–113). Rockville, MD: Aspen

Wallach, G. P., & Lee, A. D. (1983). *Bostron: A language program for school-age children.* Unpublished manuscript, Boston, MA, Emerson College, and Toronto, Canada, Scarborough Board of Education.

Wallach, G. P., & Lee-Schachter (1984). *Language activities for learning disabled students.* Emerson College, Boston, MA, and Toronto, Canada, The Scarbrough Board of Education.

Wallach, G. P., & Liebergott, J. W. (1984). Who shall be called "learning disabled": Some new directions. In G. P. Wallach & K. G. Butler (Eds.), *Language learning disabilities in school-age children.* Baltimore, MD: Williams & Wilkins.

Wallach, G. P., & Turner, J. (1985). *Meta-tations panel: Judgments and corrections of ungrammatical time sentences.* Paper presented at the American Speech-Language-Hearing Association Convention, Washington, DC.

Warren-Leubecker, A. (1987). Competence and performance factors in word order awareness and early reading. *Journal of Experimental Child Psychology, 43,* 62–80.

Weade, R., & Green, J. L. (1985). Talking to learn: Social and academic requirements for classroom participation. *Peabody Journal of Education, 62,* 6–19.

Weiner, P. (1985). The value of follow-up studies. *Topics in Language Disorders, 5,* 78–92.

Wepman, J. (1958). *Test of auditory discrimination.* Beverly Hills, CA: Learning Research Associates.

West, J. E. (1983). Aphasia: Cognitive considerations. *Topics in Language Disorders, 3,* 49–66.

Westby, C. (1984). Development of narrative language abilities. In G. P. Wallach & K. G. Butler (Eds.), *Language learning disabilities in school-age children* (pp. 103–127). Baltimore, MD: Williams & Wilkins.

Westby, C. E. (1985). Learning to talk — Talking to learn: Oral-literate language differences. In C. S. Simon (Ed.), *Communication skills and classroom success: Therapy methodologies for language-learning disabled students.* San Diego, CA: College-Hill Press.

Westby, C. (1987). *Narrative language: Components, oral-literate connections, developmental milestones.* Workshop presented at the Language Learning Disabilities Institute, Emerson College, San Diego, CA.

Wiig, E., & Semel, E. (1980a). *Language assessment and intervention for the learning disabled.* Columbus, OH: Charles Merrill.

Wiig, E. H., & Semel, E. M. (1980b). *Language disabilities in children and adolescents.* Columbus, OH: Charles E. Merrill.

Wilkinson, L. C., & Milosky, L. M. (1987). School-age children's metapragmatic knowledge of requests and responses in the classroom. *Topics in Language Disorders, 7,* 61–70.

Winner, E., Engel, M., & Gardner, H. (1980). Misunderstanding metaphor: What's the problem? *Journal of Experimental Child Psychology, 30,* 22–32.

Winner, E., Rosensteil, A., & Gardner, H. (1976). The development of metaphoric understanding. *Developmental Psychology, 12,* 289–297.

Wong, B. (1980). Activating the inactive learner: Use of questions/prompts to enhance comprehension and retention of implied information in learning disabled children. *Learning Disability Quarterly, 3,* 29–37.

Yoshinago-Itano, C., & Downey, D. M. (1986). A hearing-impaired child's acquisition of schemata: Something's missing. *Topics in Language Disorders, 7,* 45–57.

Ysseldyke, J., & Algozzine, B. (1983). Where to begin in diagnosing reading problems. *Topics in Learning and Learning Disabilities, 2,* 60–69.

Zhurova, L. (1973). The development of analysis of words into their sounds by preschool children. In C. A. Ferguson & D. I. Slobin (Eds.), *Studies of child language development.* New York: Holt, Rinehart, & Winston.

Zivian, M. T., & Samuels, M. (1986). Performance on a word-likeness task by normal readers and reading disabled children. *Reading Research Quarterly, 21,* 150–170.

Zucchermaglio, C., Pontecordo, C., Tonucci, F., & Blanchowicz, C. (1986). Literacy and linguistic awareness: A study of Italian first-grade students. *Reading Psychology, 7,* 11–25.

# A P P E N D I X   A

## Puzzle Picture Answer

# A P P E N D I X   B

## Expository Text Organizer

**1.** Write down the title of the book or article at the top of a sheet of paper.

**2.** On the same sheet of paper, copy down the chapter headings (or major article headings). Anytime you find a word you don't know, copy it down on a separate sheet of paper. What do you think this book or article is about after writing down the chapter headings or article headings? Write down in one sentence what you think it is about.

**3.** Copy down the major boldface headings of the chapter or section. What do you think this section or chapter is about? Write in two or three sentences what you think it is about.

**4.** Follow the instructions in step 3 for each of the other chapters or sections.

**5.** Choose a section of interest to you from the chapter or article. Have your teacher help you if you are undecided. Copy down the major heading of the section on a piece of paper. Find the paragraph that best describes what this section is about. Find the sentence in that paragraph that best describes what this section is about. Copy the sentence on your paper. Now do the same thing for each paragraph in this section. Reread what you have just written. Does it tell you what the section is about? Write down what you think the section is about.

**6.** Follow the instructions from step 5 for the next section of the chapter or article. Continue until you have completed the chapter or article. Now reread the entire summary. Does it tell you what the chapter or article is about? Write down in several sentences what it is about.

# I N D E X

## Author

# I N D E X

## Subject